PAUL SCOFIELD

An Actor for All Seasons

Le Théâtre en Grande-Bretagne

French Theatre Today

Different Circumstances

Dialogue Between Friends

The Pursuit of Perfection: A Life of Magic Teyte

Ralph Richardson: An Actor's Life

*Darlings of the Gods: One Year in the Life of
   Lawrence Olivier and Vivien Leigh*

Olivier in Celebration (editor)

Sean O'Casey: A Life

The Mahabharata

Darlings of the Gods

William Shakespeare: A Life

*Campion's Ghost: The Sacred and Profane Memories
   of John Donne, Poet*

Alec Guinness: Master of Disguise

The Secret Woman: A Life of Peggy Ashcroft

William Shakespeare: A Popular Life

PAUL SCOFIELD

An Actor for All Seasons

GARRY O'CONNOR

APPLAUSE
THEATRE & CINEMA BOOKS

Paul Scofield
An Actor for All Seasons
by Garry O'Connor

Copyright © 2002 by Garry O'Connor

All rights reserved

First published in Great Britain by Sidgwick&Jackson, an imprint of Pan Macmillan, 2002. This edition published by Applause Theatre & Cinema Books.

Cover photo: Photofest

Library of Congress Cataloguing-in-Publication Data
Library of Congress Card Number: 2001094684

British Library Cataloguing-in-Publication Data
A catalogue record for this book is available from the British Library

ISBN: 1-55783-499-7

APPLAUSE BOOKS
151 West 46th Street
New York, NY 10036
Phone: 212-575-9265
Fax: 646-562-5852
email: info@applausepub.com

COMBINED BOOK SERVICES LTD.
Units I/K, Paddock Wood Distribution Centre
Paddock Wood, Tonbridge, Kent TN 12 6UU
Phone: (44) 01892 837171
Fax: (44) 01892 837272
United Kingdom

SALES & DISTRIBUTION:
HAL LEONARD CORP.
7777 West Bluemound Road
P. O. Box 13819
Milwaukee, WI 53213
Phone: 1-414-774-3630
Fax: 1-414-774-3259
email: halinfo@halleonard.com
internet: www.halleonard.com

In Memory of
FRANCIS HASKELL
1928 – 2000

"Great actors are now a species infinitely more endangered than white rhinos and far more important to the health and happiness of the human race. I am referring to `live' actors, of course — not their manufactured images on screens large and small. In our age where most performers have been reduced to forms of puppetry — neutered by naturalism, made into miniaturists by television, robbed of their voices by film editors — the Authentic Great Actor has virtually disappeared from the earth. Much as I enjoy them, film performances don't finally count in this regard: they can be too easily faked. The stage and only the stage can offer proof of whether a man or woman can act greatly."

— **Peter Shaffer**

"The things that call attention to themselves are never interesting for long, which is why our attention span grows shorter by the years."

— **Jonathan Sacks**

CONTENTS

1

You Would Pluck the Heart
Out of My Mystery?

One of the first questions I ask Paul is, "What was that defining moment that made you an actor?"

> I was not a good pupil at school and seemed to lack concentration; but at thirteen years old I joined the school dramatic society and for my first role I played Juliet. Odd that I should immediately be trusted with so difficult a part, but, thinking back, I may have been noticed when reading an extract from Joseph Conrad's *Youth*, my own choice, to the English class. Suddenly pitched into Shakespeare I seemed to be at last on my feet, there was something I could do.
>
> That knowledge, or rather instinct, gave me a new sense of security, and thereafter I knew what I could and must do. Confidence is not the word, rather an understanding of limitations, and of the possibility of enjoyment in work.

On his 53rd birthday, just before he opened in London as Prospero in *The Tempest*, he went further, revealing how Shakespeare saved him from an unhappy childhood: "I was a dunce at school. But at the age of twelve I went to Varndean School at Brighton where I discovered Shakespeare. They did one of his plays every year, and I lived just for that."

Jean Anouilh is the author of the play *Ring Round the Moon* (the French title is *L'Invitation au château*), in which Paul appeared in 1950 for almost — two years, his longest ever run at the Globe Theatre in Shaftesbury Avenue.

Anouilh shared something in common with Paul. Little is known about him, and he said of himself, "I have no biography, and I am happy with it so." After listing his date of birth and one or two factual details, such as when he started writing for the theatre, he concluded "The rest is my life, and . . . I shall keep the details to myself."

For two years Paul played Anouilh's twins, Hugo and Frederick, who differ greatly in character. He goes off as one, and immediately comes back as the other. "I was sometimes *almost* simultaneously on stage as Hugo and Frederick — same clothes, same make-up . . . an almost schizophrenic experience."

"Brilliant," Anouilh's English translator, Christopher Fry, called it, "though I wonder whether brilliant is exactly the word because the difference between the two young men was conveyed so subtly and yet so unmistakably — it was clear at each entrance which we were meeting, and yet each was the natural man." Much later, when Paul played Martin Chuzzlewit on television, the rich, elderly head of his family, he also acted the part of Martin's evil brother Anthony, although here in separate scenes and different costumes. This was in a fine but somewhat underrated BBC adaptation of Dickens's sprawling masterpiece. Janus-faced, the actor shows two sides of the mask, comedy and tragedy, good and evil, in the Chuzzlewit brothers, remaining distinctively apart — himself.

Since Chuzzlewit we have had Paul's towering performance as the eponymous broken giant of Ibsen's *John Gabriel Borkman*, in 1996, at the Royal National Theatre. The obsessive character progresses, he says, from "a man frozen and trapped by the past, who recaptured for a moment his knowledge of passionate human love . . . until brain and body simply cracked under the force of his avid desire to dominate his own small kingdom. A long and hellish journey."

Yet above and beyond the parts he has played, Scofield is unusual, so much more than the description often found in newspaper cuttings: "The greatest actor in the world."

"He sometimes seems like the Unassertive Angel, sent here below to give us all, here in this country today, lessons in integrity." This was written in 1975, but seems to apply with greater force in 2001, his eightieth year. He has played so much, so well, yet beyond all this he demonstrates lasting human qualities. The need for self-knowledge. The satisfaction of personal independence. The limits, or stupidity, of being insensitive to other people. He is the very opposite of exploitative. He listens. He maintains the values of freelanceship. As a result, he and his talent have stayed independent and flexible.

But he also has his foibles, his weaknesses. Some believe he has not pushed his talent as far as he could, others would like to know more about his private side, his temptations, and the shortcomings, of one kind or another, he shares by virtue of his ordinary humanity. Yet he remains and is to remain a private man. He prefers to keep the shadow side, the mysterious side of himself which is God or the Devil — or both — or neither — to himself.

Of himself and his family he tells me, "We have a closeness and a pattern I am reluctant to try to define."

So here are limits, right from the start. This will not be an intimate biography, perhaps something more, but at least different, charting if possible the progress of an actor's soul. Maybe that is too ambitious. I hope it will tell you all you need to know about Scofield, his professional milieu, how he works, what he is like, and why, as Irving Wardle once wrote, of all English leading actors he is "the most difficult to define."

As Frith Banbury, the veteran director, said to me, talking about Paul, "You can only get so far — and you will get no further — you come up against a wall — that's what makes him such a fascinating character."

If the occasional brick or stone has been taken out of this wall, I have left this to Scofield himself to do. I make no attempt to tear it down, or hoist myself up to peer over. Maybe, after all, the wall does not really exist. Maybe it is an illusion — in the eye of the beholder.

2

Obligation to the Few

We meet for the first time on the last day of November 1999 in the Osteria Basilico, near the Portobello Road, Notting Hill. We have corresponded for some months before, with Scofield, as might be expected, intent on putting me off my stated aim of writing his life, although he repeatedly expresses this in a kind and gracious way. Frankly, I have dithered as to whether I should go ahead, and he wishes to know my decision if he is to cooperate. When at last I say my intention is to proceed he writes suggesting we should meet sometime, specifically not at his home, but somewhere in London.

I am full of trepidation and self-doubt. But I am clear in several respects. As a well-known actor and film star bluntly expressed it — reluctantly confessing to yielding to the pressure from the film companies' publicity department to give interviews — "No dirt!" (the "r" distinctively and Scottishly rolled), "You've a difficult job here!" The emphasis may be different but the message was the same when Hunter Davis wrote of Scofield in 1967, "He has all the virtues which everyone wants to meet but few want to read about. Baddies make great reading."

I choose the Osteria because the food has quality without being grand, or designer food, decoratively insubstantial. It has a quiet downstairs room that encourages warmth and contact. Because, also, the tables are not crammed one on top of the other, customers can enjoy space around each other.

Paul is here before me — "I sat here. We can move if you like." He gestures easily, frequently, and, I notice, often from the elbow. The hands, delicate slicing movements used for emphasis, well shaped, long fingered, perfectly manicured. I notice he chooses the table I would have chosen, which is not pushed right into a corner. A table halfway down the room, opposite the stairs, a table from which you can observe, but also be at ease. A table for four so you can unload clothes, hats, other impedimenta on the unused chairs.

Paul is not far off eighty years old — he was born on 21 January 1922. His appearance is that of a marvellously well-preserved, middle-aged man. His figure, clothed in the tweeds of a Sussex country-dweller, is lithe, flexible, virile, not compact and solid. He is large boned. He is tall, but not that tall, but his height naturally gives him a commanding presence. The hair, now mainly white and grey, adds height to the appearance. Here is a man who moves, who gestures, who appears at once amazed, at ease with himself and with others.

The face is fascinating, riveting; the nose has a straightness, a distinctiveness that is not common to many actors. The eyes, which are dark brown, are well set. There is a softness, a sensitivity, even a sensuality, well preserved with age. When he acts, the face, which is well defined, distinctive, never stays in the same key, and the eyes can quickly become veiled. Yet for the most part the face is reasonable, appraising, one that inspires trust and confidence.

Here at once I sense also a man of power. Of inner power. The power of Paul, everyone who knows him, has worked with him, or seen him, is quite exceptional and referred to frequently. There is a massive potential here, either creative or destructive. Yet the impression is that he reins it in. He gives the feeling that he does not know what he is capable of. The manner is modest, friendly, restrained and assured. He could be your reassuring country solicitor, the senior partner in the firm giving you advice on making your will, except that the features are a little too large, the eyes too knowing, the mouth too expansive and exotic. The voice, too, hints of a glottal, even adenoidal, complexity, but well trained and, like the dogs of war in Mark Antony's speech over the murdered Caesar, held back on a strong leash.

I have never spoken to Paul on the telephone. Those who have say he disguises that extraordinary vocal range he can deploy: "When you telephone his home and he answers, not sure who is calling, he has a rather good line in sub-cockney that is usefully unrecognisable. When he is being interviewed his voice somehow takes on the tones of the consulting room: even, slow, careful, considering, it seems to regard everything, including himself, with deliberating, professional calm. It is soft, slightly feminine, innocent of endearments or theatrical slang (one could never imagine him calling anyone "duckie" as [Laurence] Olivier does. Occasionally it drawls a little, but it is almost entirely uninflected, inanimate, which is unusual in actors."

I have decided not to attempt to interview him as such, I avoid the "consulting room" manner, but try to enjoy the lunch as best I may in the hope it will be a satisfactory encounter, so that we may begin as friends. It could even enable me to proceed with some degree of cooperation from him. We talk of dogs, for as a dog lover Paul has acquired a Border terrier that he has named Fingal and has been six months training him. Christmas, he says, will not be spent with his son Martin, who lectures in nineteenth-century English literature at Kent University, because Paul is anxious that Fingal should be well house-trained and fears that he is not and might not get on with his son's dog.

A few family details emerge incidentally in the course of lunch. His mother, whose maiden name was Wild, died two or three years ago at the age of a hundred. Latterly his older brother lived with her: he never married and was until retirement head of a Department of Brighton Council. He had a sister, now also deceased, who was ill as an adolescent and who never recovered. She lived all her life with her mother and father. Illness unspecified. His father, formerly the headmaster of the local village school, died twenty years ago. Later I learn from a friend of his that Paul, in looks, is something of the cuckoo in the nest — "in his family" but "too beautiful" to be a cuckoo. "His mother did at one stage bear some resemblance to Marlene Dietrich."

There is one tiny confession: of an addiction to chocolate. He declines a pudding largely of this substance, but with regret. "I am a purist," he tells me. "I just like it neat, without trimmings, and dark. As dark as possible . . . "

The film director Michael Winner, with whom Paul had two professional engagements, told me of Paul's presence at one of Winner's own dinners, in his London W8 bourgeois palace: "I had a cook that did an incredible hot chocolate sponge with whipped cream and hot chocolate sauce. Paul loved it."

At the end of lunch, as he leaves to meet his wife Joy in the West End to do some shopping, I am put in mind of Shakespeare's sonnet:

> They that have power to hurt and will do none,
> That do not do the thing they most do show,
> Who, moving others, are themselves as stone,
> Unmoved, cold, and to temptation slow;
> They rightly do inherit heaven's graces,
> And husband nature's riches from expense.

The sonnet is ambiguous, however. Shakespeare praised his subject, suggesting a kind of unusual self-control, but ends by exhorting the subject to spend himself: "Lilies that fester smell far worse than weeds."

Can Paul really be such a complete and integrated person, I ask myself? A superior man (not in any elitist or condescending sense) as is described by Aristotle or in Eastern philosophy: "The dedicated man embodies an enduring meaning in his way, and thereby the world is formed," we find in the *I Ching*, known in English as *The Book of Changes*.

Yet Paul, on the superficial first impression of a convivial and amiable lunch, is not only one, in the words of the sonnet, of those who are "the lords and owners of their faces" but patently enjoys unambitious activities besides acting. The many parts he has played might well be interpreted as "the thing they most do show." So how will he behave as the subject of a book?

At our meeting he is at pains to indicate he is not a nervous actor. In our exchange of letters prior to the meeting he has pointed out that in my book about Alec Guinness I have misquoted him on the terror of performance, suggesting that, like Guinness, he lived sometimes on the edge and experienced desperate feelings. I quote Scofield as saying:

> What is the worst sensation you can have in your life — worse than pain, worse than cancer or bereavement? . . . It's sitting in front of your dressing-room mirror with perhaps flu coming on, or a bad headache, looking at yourself in the glass and then suddenly realising, "I can't do it, I can't do it, I can't do it."

He corrects this statement, which is second-hand, relayed to me by Angela Fox, a neighbour and wife of his former agent Robin Fox.

> It is not that one is nervous. One is more nervous about the trains, catching them, or are they running on time? But as soon as one is in the theatre, sitting in front of the mirror, putting on make-up and preparing to get into the role the nerves vanish. One is calm, and sure of oneself — anxious butterflies at the work ahead in the morning, but nothing lasting.

As time goes by I am even more aware of how, in this respect, I had got him wrong.

He adds, "I must confess I didn't read your book through — just the bits indexed at the back — the publisher misspelt my name." And so they had. As Schofield.

We part, agreeing I should send him some questions to answer. I continue sending him questions over the next months which he answers with painstaking clarity and modesty, always thanking me — when it is I who should be thanking him — and applying deliberate and professional care over his answers.

3

Sunshine and Summer

I begin with a short dream. It is not my dream, but is told by an actress, one of Paul's colleagues. Well known and highly attractive, aged twenty-three at the time, she came to audition for an exacting director three times for a role in a production with Paul. She had seen the play with Joan Plowright and Laurence Olivier in the two roles. But the severe director told her, "You're not ugly enough."

She is only fourteen. The director then telephones her, saying, "You can play it. I'll send a carriage for you." The carriage arrives, drawn by a finely caparisoned horse. She bends down, goes under the horse, releases it from the shafts. "I'll pull it," she says and does so, like a pit pony, all the way to the theatre. Arriving there she is so happy she is singing, which the director hears. "You ought to be a singer," he says. "I want to be an actress," she answers.

She enters the stage area, but Plowright and Olivier are playing their great scene. She breaks down in floods of tears. "How can I play when Joan Plowright is here?"

"You can play it *when* she stops," says the director.

Acting is a hierarchical profession. Where does Scofield's magnetic authority come from? Paul confesses a need for faith "by instinct, or by natural feeling." Peter Hall, who like most of those I talk to about Scofield considers him to be among the very few, greatest actors of the 20th century, speaks of him, "conducting a dialogue with some strange private god." Hall admits to having found this, on occasions, disconcerting.

Paul says his upbringing was divided. His mother came from a

Catholic family and he was born and baptised a Roman Catholic.

His father, Harry Scofield, came from Worcestershire. He was head-master of their local village church school at Hurstpierpoint in West Sussex, and Paul was born on the 21st January 1922. It was not an espe-cially significant year. He attended his father's school with his brother John and his sister Mary. His mother was a Catholic, but his father was a Protestant, so that "some days we were little Protestants and, on others, we were all devout little Catholics." Had the dramatics of the Roman Catholic services at all ignited his interest in the theatre? "You know, they just might have; certainly there was no theatre in our blood. I don't like the way the Church dominates the people in, say, Spain or Mexico but, certainly, they have something within the Mass: a marvellous atmos-phere." Paul saw very little theatre during his childhood and schooldays. His experience was all in the cinema.

Paul does not seem to have been unduly affected by the fact that his father was a local figure of authority, nor does his father appear to have exerted any influence over him other than benign. "I always called my father Sir at school, then Dad as soon as I got home. I never for an instant thought of him as my father in the day, but it was difficult because you were inclined to forfeit the trust of your peers. And if you did achieve anything — in my case very rarely — it was thought to be favouritism." There is no distinguishable guilt or ambivalence, such as Graham Greene would seem to have imbibed or absorbed (or self-generated) from a father who was a headmaster (in Greene's case of Berkhamstead School), no identification with, or terror from, bullies or malefactors. There is no Russian roulette in Paul's past, no identification or involvement with the deceptions of governments, spies, sexual reprobates, marital or other betrayals, criminality or adolescent delinquency. Yet no one has given greater performances of two archetypal Greene characters.

In the aftermath of First World War decimation, universal flu, and financial deprivation, the society of West Sussex must have suited Paul's temperament, for it was here to which he returned as soon as possible to live, and has done happily ever since he settled in the village of Balcombe.

Paul has never had, at any time in his life, a need to follow the inclination of many creative people, namely to become an exile in some form or other. ("Exile" can in a wider sense be extended to include forms of behaviour, such as embracing an extreme political leaning, or sexual lifestyle outside the norm — or even drugs and drink.)

He has also never felt a need to assume any of the mantles of fame or celebrity, or to reinvent himself continually — or even just once or twice to adapt to changing fashion or social attitudes. He has remained the man, or child, he was from eleven to fourteen, with whom he would appear even now familiar and at ease.

His childhood, like any childhood, had its periods of isolation and difficulty, yet early on, unusually early on, did he identify his talent, and his own enjoyment of it. He stayed for his summer holidays with his maternal grandparents, when he went to church and practised as a Catholic. Back at Hurstpierpoint he was "to all intents and purposes a Protestant. A lack of direction in spiritual matters is still with me," he confesses.

The photograph of him as Juliet, framed in plaits, shows an uninhibited and mischievous girl ("uncontrollably" so, writes the critic J. C. Trewin, although how this can be seen in a still shot eludes me). Simon Callow says of the same photo, "He seems like a changeling. He looks extraterrestrial — with, in contrast, a beautiful sensuality of mouth evident."

> I wore blue in the first act and pale gold at the end. And a blond wig — that was a bit embarrassing, actually. But the play was a kind of turning point in my life, because thenceforward there was nothing else I wanted to do.

He is thirteen, a pupil at Varndean. Soon after, in the following year, he plays Rosalind, then in 1938, aged sixteen, he plays Prince Hal in *Henry IV, Part II.*

Everyone, himself included, believed that because his talent was so manifest at such an early age, he would go on the stage. At thirteen he appears during the summer waving a cudgel as one of twenty-five extras in Sir John Martin Harvey's production of *The Only Way* at the Theatre Royal, Brighton.

With manifest talent, he early creates a cocoon around himself; he learns how, even while being present in a situation, to absent himself. He senses his own potential and protects it — and finds, in time, others to protect it.

Donald Sinden lived nearby in Ditchling and though he was the same age as Paul they did not know each other, although their parents did. He recalls his father, a chemist, meeting with Scofield senior, a distinguished looking man, to talk about their progeny. Sinden saw *The Only Way* and after it Charles Smith gave him the hat that Martin Harvey wore as Sidney Carton. Scofield kept his cudgel as a memento.

Dirk Bogarde was another near childhood neighbour. His father was the editor of the *Times* Arts page: all three actors were born and brought up near one another and shared an uncommon degree of articulacy as well as acting talent. I suggest to Sinden that it might be the exoticism of Brighton, for there is something very flamboyantly theatrical, even camp, not only in the architecture of this prince, as well as showgirl, of seaside resorts. Sinden replies it could also have been the extra sunshine enjoyed by the inhabitants.

Whatever it was it contrasted with the rural peace of the Sussex countryside, something always supremely valued by Paul.

The Man on the Hill is a Channel 4 film made in 1985 about the nineteenth-century romantic visionary Richard Jeffries. Visually it is undistinguished, with scenes of nature and one or two crowds and faces, but mainly grass, butterflies, streams, oaks — at one point, it seems, they film a great spread of oak, actually growing over months. The music is excellent. What lifts it on to a higher, even sublime, plane is the words of the writer, and the extraordinarily moving delivery of these words by Paul. You feel that in Jeffries' visionary response to the natural world, there is more than an echo in Scofield — it is something with which he identifies deeply.

Jeffries lived only 40 years and died of tuberculosis, in an awful state — his doctor apparently wrote, "a marked case of hysteria in men." His closeness to finding an "inscape," a visionary or religious meaning, the innate God, call it what you will, in the natural world, came over as similar to that expressed in the poems of Gerard Manley Hopkins — their illness and sensitivity must have been in many ways similar too.

Paul catches beautifully, in soft, lyrical voice, the inner harmony and aspiration of this deeply tormented man. I am moved by the film and I play it through twice. "I think I heard the rain come down," he begins, "there are too many memories . . . " He looks at oaks, "they are never the same, nothing in nature ever remains the same. The words are the same but the sentiment is different."

Jeffries tried to be a novelist but did not succeed, writing instead *The Story of My Heart*, an autobiographical account of his engagement with the natural world . . . His account is of a surface changed beyond all recognition: "I would live my own life . . . of the sun I was conscious, of the sun's presence . . . pleasantly, and of the sensuous enjoyment of the beautiful green earth — all these elements of nature poured out their love on me. . . . The inner meaning of the sun translated into some growth that I might be higher in myself."

As for the future, he would like to see the sunshine and the summer becoming interwoven into man's existence, and he foresaw surely what is now happening, that future generations may be idle nine-tenths of their time. "They shall not work for their bread, but for their souls."

Through his mellow, and gently loving tones, one senses that Scofield completely identifies with Jeffries. There is no barrier, no thought resistance, nothing of that "bend flow" that Laban the theorist of movement and drama identified — he simply gives himself to inhabiting the flow of these very rich but simple sentiments. They *are* Paul.

Did Paul (does he still?) show traces of Sussex in his voice? Sinden claims that when Scofield played Mercutio in the 1946 Stratford production of *Romeo and Juliet* both he (as Paris) and Paul had Sussex accents. This could be heard in Mercutio's line, "I have it, and soundly too," which comes over as "sounderly" — with a lengthening of the "ou" sound.

4

Virtue and Fallibility

But not just words. He brings the skies and seas with him through the stage door. And real people neither good nor bad. He belonged to a schoolmaster's family sharply critical of other people. "I grew up with that influence, people watching people, imitating foibles and mannerisms, often quite malicious, and funny within the family circle." Paradoxically, it is his sharp eye for human fallibility that has made him unique as a performer of virtuous characters.

In 1939, when he was seventeen, Paul left school and went off to Croydon Repertory Theatre to start training as a professional actor: he did not stay long, although Croydon was near to home and it must have been convenient. War was declared in September, when he was only four months off the call-up age of eighteen. Here fate, providence, or, as Shakespeare commonly terms it, "heaven," the "heavens" or "the gods," strongly intervened. When he arrived for a medical he was rejected as medically unfit. The reason for this: "They found I had crossed toes: I was unable to wear boots. I was deeply ashamed."

He confessed this in an interview. It set him apart from the majority of young men of his generation, but it confirmed his destiny to become an actor. Unlike many others in his profession, who have at one time or another dreamed of, or been forced into, doing something else, the concentration entirely on acting during his late teen years and early twenties gave him a sound and secure grounding. As Christopher Fry noted in a letter to me, "The remarkable thing — one of the remarkable things — about Paul is how early he seemed to have reached a quiet mastery of his skills."

The air-raid sirens wailed. The Croydon school closed down. Paul now began to study in the centre of London at the London Mask Theatre, which was run by John Fernald who, with Michel Saint-Denis and George Devine, became a significant influence on post-war theatre. The first line Scofield spoke on the London stage was "Yes, sir" as the Third Clerk in John Drinkwater's *Abraham Lincoln*. This line he repeated in the same play as the First Soldier. He also had walk-on roles in Eugene O'Neill's *Desire Under the Elms* and *Cornelius* by J.B. Priestley.

While he grew adept backstage at helping with scenery he was now thoroughly caught up with the rather mixed society of actors at this time: the aged, the conscientious objectors, and the medically unfit — this applies, of course, only to then. Westminster by the autumn of 1940, when the "phony war" ended, and the Blitz proper began, was now, as the prime target for ceaseless Luftwaffe raids, probably one of the most dangerous places outside a battlefield in Europe.

Two of the teachers at the school, Eileen Thorndike and Herbert Scott, who taught voice, evacuated a number of the students to North Devon and, calling themselves the Thorndike-Scott Student Theatre, ran a highly successful repertory season from early January in that very dark and dismal year of 1941.

Eileen Thorndike was theatrical royalty. She was herself no mean player. Her elder sister was Sybil Thorndike, the great classical actress and star of the Old Vic who created and acted many famous roles, among them that of Saint Joan in the play by Bernard Shaw. Her brother-in-law was Sybil's husband, Lewis Casson, who equally, as actor-manager and director, had a formidable reputation. The marriage of this pair lasted sixty years. Paul is today well on the way to emulating this span with his own marriage to Joy Parker.

On first sight it might appear that Scofield was very much out in the sticks in a semi-amateur company in the Devon market town haven of Bideford. But this was far from the case. It was not actually that far from the ravages of war. Plymouth was virtually razed to the ground in April 1941, Exeter in May, and many air raid victims were local to North

Devon, their bodies being brought back for burial in nearby Appledore, or Bideford itself. When the Thorndike-Scott company was performing *Berkeley Square* by J.L. Balderston a twin-engined Heinkel III bomber crashed on nearby Lundy Island and burst into flames. Its five Nazi aircrew escaped the wreckage, and were rounded up by islanders.

The repertory theatre in Bideford was a new building called the Garden Theatre, and Scofield became the prime attraction of that season. He was only nineteen years old, and while the company began with a mosaic of Shakespeare extracts, in which Paul played for the first time Lear, Macbeth and Petruchio (this last he has never played again, although he did intend much later to play him at Stratford), Paul quickly graduated to major leads.

These began with the saturnine but smooth talking murderer in Emlyn Williams's *Night Must Fall*, described by "Candidus," the local critic, as a thrilling performance full of suspense and terror. Candidus could not have been more accurate in his assessment of the nineteen-year-old actor:

A Brilliant Study

Paul Scofield gave us yet another amazing performance. He played Dan very quietly, with a most nauseating charm and a combined simplicity and cunning that was quite horrible. Every movement, every inflection, was in keeping, the silence of the audience when he was on the stage alone, saying nothing, is a tribute to the strength and intensity of his acting. One would hesitate to put any limit to what this actor is going to be able to do as he grows older. If he can keep the enthusiasm and capacity for hard work which he obviously has now, he will be a great actor before many years have passed, and we in Bideford will feel very proud to have seen and followed his early work.

It creates the impression that Scofield the actor has been born fully armed and equipped, rather like Pallas Athene, the Greek goddess known as Minerva to the Romans, the goddess of wisdom.

In February they played Noël Coward's *Hay Fever*, with the company's teamwork highly commended, and especially appreciated was their contact with the audience. Bettina Carrol and Phoebe Noël-Smith alternated the role of Judith Bliss. Scofield's Richard was praised for its solid worthiness. With their adventurous choice of plays the company's next success was *Berkeley Square*, with dramatic contrasts between the eighteenth and twentieth centuries; Paul, although not playing the leading role of Peter Standish (admirably acted by Seth Holt), made a powerful impression as Tom, "a grand piece of work, his sense of the period was unerring, and the crude vitality of his playing exactly what was required."

During the run of *Berkeley Square* Paul broke his ankle but played on using crutches. The company lived in a large rented house in Instow. Eileen Thorndike's daughter Sybil had a crush on him:

> He was my first love — I was thirteen at the time and just adored him! He was a rather shy, spotty young man who was nevertheless a bit of a scamp! He did naughty things like climbing into locked rooms by the window!
>
> There was an incident on the beach when Paul gallantly fought some youths who were annoying some of the girls. He was being badly treated and I was very worried — but one of the girls took the spectacles off one of the attackers and threw them into the sand — they stopped then — as glasses were expenses and hard to get!

Their most serious offering so far, in April 1941, was the innocently named *Ladies in Retirement* which in the previous spring had run in London. It seems, from the records, of anonymous authorship.

The play is a study of Leonora Fiske, a calculating spinster, and how her love for her two half-mad sisters drives her to murder. While noting that this was the company's best production so far — and as with previous plays they changed the cast to give everyone a chance to act major roles — Candidus had now run out of praise for Paul, contenting himself that (as Albert Feather) he gives "the excellent performance we now expect from him."

Goodness, How Sad! by Robert Morley featured Paul on the poster as "the Film Star," and was another hit. This was followed by Coward's triple bill *Tonight at 8:30*, which showed Scofield as a jack of all trades, and *The Importance of Being Earnest* in which he plays "a most satisfying John Worthing, who got every ounce of comedy possible out of the glorious announcement of his brother's death."

The work was dedicated, true "rep." It had a lighter side —

What promises to be one of the most spectacular variety shows seen in Bideford for a long time is to be staged at the Garden Theatre, Bideford, on 6 May, in connection with War Weapons Week. The theatre has been generously placed at the disposal of the cause by Mr W.D. Hackney and contributors to the programme include the famous Coco and Co. (late of *Westward Ho!*), international artistes and orchestra, the promising Thorndike-Scott Theatre students, and Marcelle, "Man of Mystery," an artiste of wide repute who is serving locally in HM Forces. The show will be bubbling over with fun and music. The Student Theatre will present various excerpts and one-act plays, including one by Ronald Jeans whose son is a member of the company.

So we now have the lightly coloured-in picture of a formidable apprenticeship. For Paul, in his twentieth year — early on in life — found complete fulfilment:

I enjoy the loss of myself, of inhabiting a writer's human creation, of discovering more and more about people. The quality of listening in an audience, which fluctuates, sometimes by divided attention, a diversity of focus, a distraction, difficult to locate, when complete clarity is needed to draw them into the narrative, to will them to listen. And at other times, blissful and rare, they are silent and rapt — the silence of concentration.

Comedy I love, to make an audience laugh is a special happiness for an actor, a confirmation of mutual understanding. The great tragic roles are another matter, there are few spaces where, as in comedy, you may wait and catch breath until the laughter has gone. In a tragedy there are no such moments of rest, the mountain has to be climbed, step by step, without respite, until the story is told.

This may be hugely satisfying or hugely frustrating, dependent on the sense of having, or not having, fulfilled what you hoped to do. And in answer to your questions both emotionally and physically you use yourself, but wouldn't wish it to be otherwise. The best moments are often the intangible moments, perhaps a silence at the end of a play, when lights fade, you are alone with an audience, and gradually disappearing from them, and the silence tells you that something has been found for them in what we, the actors, have given.

After this season Eileen Thorndike, who by this time, according to their family biographer, Diana Devlin, had "run out of money and sanity," moved her company to Cambridge. Paul played Noah in Andre Obey's eponymous play. The Casson/Thorndikes were a close-knit family group, and Paul gained from his early association with them. They were joined by Patricia Chester-Master, who married Lewis's son John. Devlin writes about Patricia and the grand Knightsbridge wedding, and how the family she got to know was more eccentric than it realised.

To the Cassons' complete unselfconsciousness, promoting individuality to the point of oddity, had been added the flamboyance and theatricalism of the Thorndikes. The relationship between Sybil and Lewis had shown the children that "love" could tolerate any amount of argument and independent activity so long as it was part of a search for what was truthful, good and fulfilling. This search all six carried out with fierce intensity.

A Casson was rarely idle. At 74 Oakley Street Paul would have found an "artistic monastery": Lewis working on his elaborate line-learning system which involved filling up whole notebooks with a nearly illegible scrawl; Sybil keeping up her music by running through a few Bach fugues; John mysteriously manipulating billiard balls to improve his conjuring skills; Christopher practising ballet steps; Mary singing; Ann working on poetry.

At mealtimes all converged in the basement dining room where everyone argued loudly for it was taken for granted that everyone had their own opinion. Music, theatre, religion, ethics and politics were the chief topics, the last three burning most brightly. All was conducted fortissimo, with beautiful delivery and a gamut of expression from screams of laughter to shouts of anger. The extraordinary thing was that after it all, there were no feelings of discord, resentment or animosity.

Paul was deeply influenced. The Cassons were so different. As he says, with characteristic understatement:

> Earlier turning points must include my training. As a student of the London Mask Theatre School, and though much of this sort of training is an interesting game, I was lucky in being taught by Eileen Thorndike, sister of Dame Sybil. Eileen was herself a distinguished actress and brought with her, to our classes and in our acquaintanceship, a glimpse of the history and traditions of acting, traditions of delivery and behaviour, a modesty, and the driving power exemplified by her sister. Through her I came to know the Casson/Thorndike family, most of whom were actors, who demonstrated in their lives both the serious and the humorous aspects of theatre.

When Patricia had integrated herself as a Casson/Thorndike family member, much later, Lewis sent her to close down Eileen's company. She reported to Lewis. At the end of it he said, "Were any of them any good?"

"Not really," Patricia answered, "except for one quite brilliant young man who played Noah. I think his name was Paul Scofield."

Lewis sent for him and offered him a job with his company touring South Wales (this would have been the Old Vic tour of *Medea* and *Candida*). Paul joined them and immediately got mumps. Sybil Mitchell reports that he arrived already having them: she recalls that her mother did not even let him in the front door of the family home because of the children. Through this meeting Paul got his first West End job with Lewis in John Steinbeck's *The Moon Is Down*. Years later, when Patricia was in London on a visit from Australia, she went with Sybil to see Paul in *A Dead Secret*. Afterwards they went round to see him; Paul walked straight across the room to Patricia, flung his arms round her and said to the others, "Ladies and gentlemen, this is the lady who discovered me!" ("Not true I'm afraid, though I'm sure I greeted her warmly" — this was Paul's comment in my typescript on 10 August 2000.) He felt he owed his discovery mainly to Eileen Thorndike.

The part he had already begun to play was that of the Messenger in *Medea*, which Thorndike and Casson were due to take on a round of the Welsh mining village halls. Mumps is a depressing illness. Wales was not exactly an uplifting place in early 1942. John Trewin wrote in his 1956 monograph on Scofield that Paul had already, before contracting mumps, played the aged Vincentio in Robert Atkins's touring production for ENSA of *The Taming of the Shrew*, and that later he was promoted to Tranio. With swollen neck Paul now was despatched to the Betws-y-coed military hospital in the Welsh hills, quarantined and on his own. On the way there they stopped at Bronygarth.

"He came in a car down to the Casson house and I was only allowed to see him through the window — in case I caught it!" Sybil Mitchell tells me. "He looked so pathetic."

Scofield picks up the thread: "After which, seriously out of work, I met Robert Thornley in Miriam Warner's lift having just been turned down by her [theatrical agency]. Robert T., in the lift, said, 'Do you want a job?'"

Robert Thornley was rehearsing a tour of *Jeannie* (a play by Aimee MacDonald) which had just had a successful run in the West End with Barbara Mullen. In *Jeannie* Paul played a hotel receptionist, and later in the tour several other parts as well. Robert Thornley followed this tour with one of *Young Woodley* in which he offered Paul the part of Ainger, the head prefect — originally played by Jack Hawkins; in this production

Woodley was played by the brilliant Geoffrey Hibbert (who later played in the film *Love on the Dole*). This tour played for a week at the Birmingham Repertory Theatre ("Sir Barry Jackson's, not the present horror"), which was then occupied temporarily by Basil C. Langton and his TRT (Travelling Repertory Theatre).

This was in June 1942. Ainger, the school prefect, is "nearing nineteen, good-looking, and athletic" in John Van Druten's *Young Woodley*, which was directed by Kathleen O'Regan. One line he says, to the hero, played by Geoffrey Hibbert, is "Look here, kid, for the thousandth time, what's the trouble?"

Basil Langton saw a performance of *Young Woodley* and offered Paul the part of Horatio in his forthcoming production of *Hamlet*, as well as that of Stephen Undershaft in *Major Barbara*. Prior to these productions he sent Paul on a tour of munition factory hostels, playing Algernon in *The Importance of Being Earnest.*

"Returning to the Rep," Paul continues, "we did *Major B.* and *Hamlet*. Margaretta Scott played Barbara. After which, Basil left Birmingham with his company, including me and Joy [Parker] who had played Ophelia. And we toured munition factory hostels for CEMA [Council for the Encouragement of Music and the Arts] with *Arms and the Man* in which I played Sergius Saranoff and Joy played Louka — Basil was Bluntschli and Yvonne Mitchell was Raina."

One touring company led to another. A mass of different names, different parts and different experiences. The Travelling Repertory, which leased the Station Street Rep Theatre and played in the parks, as well as all over the country, was to employ Paul continuously over the next two years, until he placed his foot firmly on the next rung of the professional ladder.

Ben Greet, Nigel Playfair, Annie E. Horniman, Donald Wolfit, William Poel, to take a few names at random. There are so many lost and forgotten figures who in the last century helped to raise English acting to its peak in the last fifty years, when it has enjoyed unbroken ascendancy. To this list should now be added the obscure name of Basil C. Langton, who began the CEMA touring company TRT.

Langton trained with the illustrious Old Vic School before the war with Michel Saint-Denis, George Devine and Glen Byam Shaw.

"Basil C. Langton," Paul calls him, (the C. was because there was another actor called Basil Langton, later David Langton of *Upstairs Downstairs*). "We never found out what the C. represented. Yes, Canadian — darkly brooding, very talented — used Shostakovich's Fifth Symphony for his music in *Hamlet* — original ideas — his own performance as Hamlet traditionally romantic." Basil was then married to an ex-ballet dancer called Louise Soelberg, who was American. From Basil Paul gained the opportunity to work again in the classics and assimilate fresh ways of looking at work in the theatre. Paul did not feel that Basil gained anything from him, although Langton taught him much. He had, Paul says, played Hamlet at Stratford in 1940, and he gave Paul the chance to play his first memorable Shakespeare role. He remains a shadowy figure, hard to distinguish as more than a name on tour from city to city in war-torn Britain with Birmingham as a base, but, impressionable as Paul is in these two years (two years are a long time in the life of a twenty-year-old) he conferred on Paul some part of an identity that has remained. This is that of the strolling player, the vagabond, the outsider even; however well Paul may later have become integrated into rural Sussex society and the main, establishment theatres, the heart of the strolling player, the rambler who was also a pathfinder, keeps its integrity.

He has remained the man who walks alone. His refusal to embrace the mateyness of "official" theatre stems from a conviction that it can stifle talent: "Too much respectability can take the edge away . . . It's important to keep a certain distance and not to lose altogether the gypsy feeling that acting had in the past."

5

Interlude: Scofield's Tear

"A dog?" he asks me at our lunchtime meeting when I disclose we have just acquired a black Labrador puppy. His eyes light up. "How amazing!" He asks me what animals I have. The dog. A rabbit. A hamster. Three cats. Children? I bring the subject back to himself and his work, and mention the *Hamlet* which, in those far-off days when traditional culture had value, is played in two parts, on consecutive nights. The first part ended at the conclusion of the play scene: this was then repeated as prologue to the second part, then they went through to the end. "What a good memory you have," he says, playfully, "How clever!" I detect no irony, nor disparagement.

One of Scofield's most moving performances is as Vanya in the Royal Court production which runs for six weeks in 1979. During one performance Scofield really cries. This is when Vanya is supposed to cry. He comes up to various members of the cast after the call at the end of the show. Pointing with a finger of his left hand to his left eye, "Look," he says, with an expression of humorous surprise, "I've got a tear. Look, that's a real tear." And so it is, a distinct pearl of moisture on his cheek beside his eye.

The feeling of emotion has often been confused with the simulation of emotion. This question as to what the actor feels and what he pretends to feel has caused controversy not only through history but today, with just about everyone in society acting a role, with politicians continually acting out their convictions on television, pretending feelings they do not necessarily have, hiding their true selves; it is perhaps a relevant question.

Denis Diderot, French man of letters, encyclopedist, minor playwright and acting theoretician, wrote a thesis called *Paradox as the Actor*, based on observations of David Garrick, in which he demanded "tears from the brain." He saw Garrick, on a visit to Paris in 1765, entertain friends in a drawing room by "letting his face run through the whole gamut of emotions without feeling anything himself." Constant Coquelin, great comedian of the Comedie Française argued in his influential *Art of the Actor* (1880), "one can be a great actor only on the condition of being able to express at will feelings one does not experience, will never experience, and is not capable of experiencing."

Against this view has been ranged — and continues to be ranged — a whole series of arguments from theorists and practitioners, led chiefly by Constantin Stanislavsky, claiming that the actor cannot be convincing unless he stimulates emotions and feels them himself while playing a part. William Archer, the critic, was preparing a questionnaire for actors on the very subject of whether they felt emotion when acting, and asked a leading French dramatic critic for help: the reply was that he was wasting his time as, first, few actors had the intelligence, and, second, none the sincerity, to answer his questions aright!

Even so, Archer began his catechism: "in moving situations, do tears come into your eyes?" But tears are so easy to fake, even in ordinary members of the public, as anyone watching television news today can see for themselves. The playwright A.W. Pinero stated that with a week's practice anyone can learn to produce tears at will. A director, Alfred Emmet, once rehearsing an actress in an emotional scene, saw that, as she sat on the bed, she was twisting her legs round one another in a kind of knot. "Oh," she told him, "I find I can cry better if I do that."

Paul claims his emotions are not real, but make-believe, ("I think they *are* real but they are not mine," he added to my typescript) and I suspect he would incline more towards Constant than to Constantin. This question is a complex one. What could be more contrived, more stereotyped, for example, than the false, generalised emotions of most television soaps? Yet to many viewers they are real, and they identify the character's feelings wholly with the real-life emotions of the actor.

What is incontrovertible is that during this two years of constant touring, when the TRT experienced all kinds of living and playing circumstances, keeping alive a hard-pressed and undermanned theatre in the provinces, Paul built up a bank of remembered emotional experiences on which he would be able to draw when faced with an analogous situation in some role or another. But as these experiences are largely unconscious, or he is himself largely unconscious of them, and as he works almost wholly on intuition and instinct, these will remain unprobed.

Hamlet plays in Birmingham: one critic wrote ten years later, "Midland people think still of Scofield's Horatio, faithfulness incarnate, a man fit, as not all Horatios are, to be held in Hamlet's heart of hearts."

6

Joy

In the same production was an Ophelia "of gentle, bewildered pathos: no reeling, writhing or fainting in coils" (I am not sure what is meant by this, its Alice in Wonderland allusiveness apart). Anyway, unpretentious and straightforward in her feelings, this Ophelia was played by Joy Parker.

Joy is a London-born actress. When Paul first met her, she had enrolled as a student at the Birmingham Repertory Company and lived in the Birmingham suburbs with another student. She had bus journeys through bomb-devastated areas but that was the closest she got to danger. They fell in love and, although one cannot but believe there must have been some dramas attendant upon this very early attachment, both choose to remain silent. They married only nine months after the opening of *Hamlet* in October 1942.

Whether they were naturally and instinctively suited to one another, similar in outlook and attitude, or found in one another complimentary qualities to their own, is beside the point. This is a love that will in time seem to have turned upside down the various dicta of poets, playwrights and philosophers, such as D.H. Lawrence's "Two fierce and opposing currents meet in the narrows of perfect love . . . when once they are consummated in marriage it becomes inevitably a perfect hell of storms and furies." Theirs is, by all accounts, a lasting love, if not perfect (as perhaps no marriage can be) at least a very good one.

There is no doubt that Paul at this time was, as love object (if we reverse the usual sexual orientation for a moment), a great catch with commendable and even almost gilt-edged prospects. In the years when most men of his age were away at war here he was, distinctively handsome, although craggily lined, and available for marriage.

From the very beginning he was, as Sally Beauman the novelist described him later at the age of forty-eight, "flamboyantly handsome . . . the perfect matinee idol profile of high cheekbones, deep-set eyes, jutting nose and chin."

Did his mother and father approve of his early marriage?

Joy and I simply decided to be married, we were both of age and were determined. Any doubts from our families were overruled and they were the usual ones — too young, etcetera. We had a week out at the end of *The Moon Is Down* tour, married during that week, and went straight into the Whitehall Theatre.

Social attitudes to the theatre and the marriage of an actor to an actress were in consideration of the good sense of the pair involved, waived on this occasion. It was at the start, and remains, a rare union.

Paul and Joy married just before Paul opened in John Steinbeck's *The Moon Is Down*, presented by Basil C. Langton at the Westminster Theatre. A patriotic piece, with much of Steinbeck's poignant realism, it depicts a Nazi-occupied country whose spirit still survives, despite bloodshed and oppression. There is a clear but not explicit parallel with Norway, and King Haakon attended a performance. Paul played the part of a young miner sentenced to death, and made an auspicious start to his London career. He found himself acting at last with Lewis Casson, whose role was Major Orden. Joy was an understudy, but the play enjoyed only a limited season.

Paul then worked at the Q Theatre, Kew Bridge, which championed experimental theatre. Theodore Komisarjevsky, Peggy Ashcroft's husband at that time, directed her here in *Fraulein Elsa*, a morbidly experimental piece. Paul's play was St. John Ervine's *The First Mrs. Fraser*. Edward Stirling, the director, sacked him after one day's rehearsal, without any explanation. "I was either wrong for the part, or not good enough." The Q then engaged him to act in Priestley's *Dangerous Corner*, which played one week in Kettering, then "I hasten to add, terminated."

Both he and Joy returned to TRT parts in the autumn. Neither of them worried about the war or the future — they knew no other life. "Wartime? Remember how young Joy and I both were. We had no retrospective adulthood to compare our lives in peacetime with the climate of war. That was how things were, we accepted conditions without question. We certainly didn't feel deprived."

He played Donald, the egotistical author in Gertrude Tonkonogy's *Three-Cornered Moon*, then in early 1944 the Stranger in *The Cricket on the Hearth*, adapted from Dickens, Oliver Farrant, Priestley's donnish but decisive character in *I Have Been Here Before*. He also played Tybalt in *Romeo and Juliet* when they visited Bristol.

On tour they performed in munition hostels to mixed audiences of workers and serving forces on leave, as well as old and retired people. I would love to know how the audiences in Birmingham respond to half a *Hamlet*. Do they patiently return for Part Two?

Munition hostels were contemporary custom-built buildings — long and one-storey, with many, many tiny sleeping cubicles: there were several dotted about in Lancashire, Stafford, Crewe, etcetera. They each had a concert hall in which we performed, sometimes, for the night shifts, at ten in the morning. There were canteens, so we ate, slept, performed and passed on to the next venue. We would do perhaps six performances in each.

"The audiences, at the morning shows, still in their overalls and compulsory headscarves [because of the danger of hair being caught in machinery]. Good audiences — sometimes derisive.

Shaw's *Arms and the Man* was a very popular wartime play, and in this Paul had been cast as Sergius Saranoff, the humourless buffoon, a role Olivier hated but then learned to love in the revived Old Vic seasons at the end of the war.

7

Interlude: Baddie Number One

I sometimes see Paul as a Casanova reversed — in fact, he would make a wonderful Casanova, poring even now over his sexual conquests and recapturing them a second time as he writes them down.

Casanova has an undying zest for conquest, he falls in love with all those women who tempt him, he positively relishes the seductions, the deceptions, he enjoys every moment. His appreciation of the different quality of a beautiful woman's sensual or affective side borders on worship: he is a complete professional. As a lover he is dedicated.

Paul's dedication is to acting. He is as dispassionate as Casanova, but the involvement is as complete. "Watch him in love, playing a role," says Felicity Kendal. "He is totally and utterly in love. He has perfect concentration to centre his character so quickly and so firmly." Like Casanova, he is focused on the role. "When he was Othello, I Desdemona, I was sure he was in love with me. He wants me to take my clothes off. But it's not Paul, it's the character. It's a technique. You're there to point that character and not to take that character into you. You go out to it."

Paul is to acting what Casanova is to sexual conquest. His total dedication, says Felicity, "bleeds out into the rest of the company." I asked her whether Paul became the part he played. "He doesn't become it — except on stage." The perfect answer, because it is accurate. Most actors are so imprecise. "Tonight . . . I *was* the character," Macready records in his diary, "*Ce soir, le dieu n'est pas venu*," sighs Mounet-Sully. These are woolly, subjective assessments.

The truth is, if one feels emotion it is real. With Paul, says Felicity,

"The reality of the moment and the concentration is total."

It is dreaming to order. The desire or will of the character (Stanislavsky's "objective") and the action aimed at achieving it are accessible to the will of the actor, who can consciously identify with it.

As Eugene Vakhtangov, the dynamic leader of the Moscow Art Theatre during his short life, says, "The fundamental thing which an actor must learn is to wish, to wish by order, to wish whatever is given to the character."

This is what Casanova does in his self-styled role of seducer. And Paul no less as an actor: both similarly practise a labour of love with total dedication.

But is Paul's profession of total dedication real, or is it, in itself, a performance?

Similarly, did Casanova really want to seduce and fornicate with all the women he met or claimed he desired, or was he acting his profession of seducer? What lies behind such total dedication?

8

The Temple

Joy and Paul's first child, a son, named Martin, was born in 1944. Paul was twenty-two.

They began a quiet family life that has continued so. During these early years Joy and Paul resembled one another, and might have been brother and sister. They were from the start totally self-sufficient as a unit. "They don't need any of the rest of us," says John Harrison, oldest of their friends. "Finding one another so young they've had all the hassle taken out of that side of their life. To their friends it is always Paul and Joy together — even their handwriting is similar. They have changed less than anyone I know. They love sitting round the Aga. They don't even have central heating."

Their placid ordinariness, even so, makes some people suspect that it has been deliberately shaped as a kind of earthing device for Paul's talent of electric extraordinariness.

For now this talent was about to send its charge across the footlights, introducing wildness and danger to the greyish if mellifluous proprieties of the postwar scene. As Peter Hall says to me, "To me he was the first postwar actor who grasped a very modern idea, and stripped his character of their glamour and sentimentality. There was a lack of crowd pleasing: he revealed the character, warts and all." Others repeat this view.

Paul had already acted the Stranger in Barry Jackson's adaptation of *The Cricket and the Hearth* and had therefore met Jackson; he had served his apprenticeship, and now he was to be granted his colours, a first season at what is then by far and above the best theatre in England. Jackson's Birmingham Repertory.

Jackson had for a long time been a legendary figure, the pioneer, between the two world wars, of serious drama. He nurtured a formidable array of talent, both in writing and acting. Donald Sinden called him, "The nearest the British have come to producing a Diaghilev."

Yet he was the mildest of men. A cautious Midlander with private means, derived from Maypole Dairies, although he had with his own money put on many of Bernard Shaw's plays in London, he viewed "the great city with suspicion and dislike," and now had withdrawn "to the security of his grimy but dependable Birmingham base."

Why was it so successful in training three generations of classical actors? John Harrison, who joined Jackson's company at the same time as Paul, answers, "The building . . . which Trewin called a brown cigar box. A long, narrow auditorium . . . because of its steep rake you presented yourself night after night to a wall of faces. You weren't projecting yourself into or across a void. You found yourself invited, forced even, to interact with the audience. It was intimate, 450 seats, but not pint-sized." Continuity of work was another factor. "Modern actors waste much nervous energy justifying their talents afresh with every fresh engagement. We knew each other."

John Moody directed seven of the plays in which Paul appeared during that long Birmingham season; the legendary H.K. Ayliff directed two, and a 20-year-old newcomer, Peter Brook, the final three. Sharp, deft, crisp, sensitive, admirable, are the epithets generally applied by the critics to John Moody's direction of these plays, but for Harrison the reality was different. "The man was a wimp. He once said to me vaguely, 'I don't know, John . . . it's something about the way you stand' . . . He made the poor actor so self-conscious he could hardly go on stage." His productions were "limp-wristed" in the extreme, in glaring contrast to those of Brook and Ayliff.

Eileen Beldon, a distinguished and long-serving member of the Birmingham Company — she won glowing plaudits for her Juno in O'Casey's *Juno and the Paycock* in which Paul played the sober, wooing role of Jerry Devine — describes what it felt like acting in that unique blend of intimacy and austerity. "To encounter a wall of pink faces instead of the usual inhospitable void on a first night was very off-putting until one got used to it." The beast. The audience.

John Harrison, also exempt Grade 3, but with a heart murmur, became friendly with Paul at this time and has remained his closest male friend. He recalls walking in Lightwoods Park and talking, as young men do, about the future, like asking him what his ambition was — "To be a good actor, he answered. He has stuck with that."

On stage Harrison was struck at once with Paul's stillness. I am driven often to describe the turning world of Paul's life in order to define him as the "still point," which he so often is, of the life around him.

The productions held plenty of glamour and prestige, and most received at least four reviews: the doyen of reviewers was T.C. Kemp who, as "Candidus," had been in Bideford, and now became Paul's testifier. As the Prince in James Lavers' *Circle of Chalk*, Paul "assumes a dignity and grace worthy of the Son of Heaven"; as Reginald in Shaw's *Getting Married*, an "angular assumption of years" (while Joy was praised for her "crisp exposition" of Edith's radical views); as Toad in *Toad of Toad Hall*, "inflates himself to bombastic proportions"; as Valentine in a translation of Molière's *Le Malade Imaginaire* (*The Hypochondriac*), "a light romantic touch, an effective compound of whimsical humour and courtly grace"; as Young Marlow in *She Stoops to Conquer*, "brought out [the] dual personality with excellent distinction."

Only the *Gazette* took a contrary line to *The Seagull*, describing with jaundiced eye how "The eyes of these parasitic, hyper-sensitive decadents were turned inwards . . . it cannot be pretended that these introverts make for a hilarious evening." For Paul this was the most satisfying of Moody's productions; he played Konstantin with a surprising maturity, according to the unnamed critic of the *Mail*, "almost unbearably [epitomising] youth in despair because its reticences are so finely observed" (16 May 1945).

Ayliff, who directed Paul in *The Winter's Tale* and *The Empress Maud*, by Andrew Leigh, which is set in the reign of King Stephen, had a more distinctive directorial manner and power. "Jackson was the enabler, but Ayliff was the maker, the craftsman," says Harrison, "their theatre was a temple and we were its priests and acolytes." Ayliff was very tall, thin, and bald as an egg, with a deep, sepulchral voice. He never praised. Careful and unobtrusive in his quality Ayliff plotted the actors' moves beforehand and had an excellent eye for detail, especially with the advanced lighting board Birmingham possessed, and for furniture. He could be awesome:

Paul remembers him as having "A terrifying warning signal for the unwary and inept — he sat at rehearsals with legs crossed at the knee and when displeased would swing the upper leg and foot like a pendulum of doom. We all recognized the signal and trembled."

Harrison admiringly notes his example: "I remember every single blessed word he said to me, as if they were tablets from the mountain. What counted most was . . . a caring seriousness, dignifying what we were about as if nothing else mattered . . . He wasn't interested in self-display . . . You trusted his instinct and went along with it unswervingly."

Paul played the Clown in Ayliff's outstanding production of *The Winter's Tale* which displays, according to the notice, "prodigious efforts of backstage artifice in this sixth year of war."

Trewin, who as a London reviewer would visit Birmingham, recalled Scofield as broadly bucolic, "from Warwickshire's rural heart . . . one had never more resented the guile of Autolycus . . . all were happy when he announced that he and his father had been gentlemen born any time these four hours . . . The Scofield crackle was here the crackling of clean straw."

Donald Wolfit returned from seeing the production to tell Ronald Harwood, his dresser, "There's this remarkable actor in *The Winter's Tale.*"

In *The Empress Maud*, the other production of Ayliff's "master hand," was Eileen Beldon, whom on stage Paul admired and studied much: she gave a brilliant performance, while Paul as William d'Albine "temporized entertainingly, secure in neutrality."

Eileen Beldon taught Paul a lifelong lesson (especially as Arkadina in *The Seagull*): "How to sustain intensity without being boring. She was astonishing. I used that in *Hamlet* and *Lear*. Above all she taught me how to go too far. A revelation. You don't understand the boundaries of possibility until you see them."

What astonishes me about this statement is that Paul has the confidence to go so far, knowing he can overreach his "natural reach" and yet never lose himself, never become carried away, so as to lose his sense of his own identity.

But now Peter Brook appeared on the Birmingham scene. Paul's career was ready to be launched into a higher orbit. This is supreme good fortune, but also the reward for six years of unremitting hard work. Paul says:

I have worked with Peter since I was twenty-two and he several years younger, and more than with any other director. It was impossible to imagine that he could be mature enough to do so. Hitherto I had been directed by men twice or three times my age. But by the end of the first week I was eating my words. There was authority, there was insight and inventiveness, at that time rare in my experience.

He was disconcertingly confident and apparently without doubts or misgivings as to the outcome of our work. I felt he had no preoccupation with success, the productions would be as they would be, liked or disliked, simply a culmination of ideas and work.

9

Peter and Paul

"The productions would be as they would be, liked or disliked, simply a culmination of ideas and work." A telling sentence. Brook came into Paul's life because, unlike Paul, he was determined to start at the top. His father's pharmaceutical business in London was burned to the ground by Hitler's fire bombs. Left behind while his father and mother evacuated to the country, Brook directed fairly tawdry productions of Jean Cocteau's *The Infernal Machine*, and, for an ENSA tour, *Pygmalion*. William Armstrong, an elderly West End director, had seen the latter and wrote recommending him to Birmingham.

A letter arrived one morning from Barry Jackson inviting Brook to direct *Man and Superman*, for a fee of £25. Jackson and Ayliff had fallen out over Ayliff's expectation of a greater say in play and cast, and Ayliff had left. "A pall of gloom hung over the building. It was like the fall of an angel."

Jackson, who chain-smoked through a cigarette holder, struck Brook as a tall, ageless figure with clear blue eyes. He greeted the gnome-like figure.

Brook himself, Kenneth Tynan wrote, "is a small sausage-shaped man: he looks edible, and one gets the notion that if one bit into him he would taste like fondant cream or preserved ginger . . . His miniature hands are limp, and flutteringly expressive: the rest of him stands quiet, dapper, casual and smug . . . His voice is flat and high-pitched, like a kazoo. One feels he has never travelled anywhere on foot or on buses, but is wrapped up in silk and carried."

John Harrison observed him for the first time as, "Short, shuffly, a cross between a penguin and a teddy bear, with a small squeaky voice and a beatific smile borrowed from a canvas cherub." Teddy bear or sausage-shaped? Squeaky or smug?

No one recorded what Jackson thought of Brook.

"In that small office," writes Brook, "he quickly lost his reserve as he told me with boyish excitement of the new young actor for whom he wanted to stage the Shaw play. A moment later the door opened. 'Ah, here he is!' said Sir Barry. 'This is Paul Scofield.'"

As we shook hands, I looked into a face that unaccountably in a young man was streaked and mottled like an old rock, and I was instantly aware that something very deep lay hidden behind his ageless appearance. Paul was courteous, distant, but as we began to work an instant understanding arose between us, needing very few words, and I realised that beneath the gentle modesty of his behaviour lay the absolute assurance of a born artist. This was the start of a partnership that lasted many years.

Retrospectively, as we regard Paul from the vantage point of his Lear, his Salieri, his Sir Thomas More and his Borkman, or the mammoth performances on television as Martin Chuzzlewit and his brother (and likewise Brook from his exotic *Mahabharata* and *L'Homme Qui*), John Tanner in Shaw's *Man and Superman* does seem an unlikely first meeting point for these two complex talents.

The actors found Brook a "natural": "You just knew you had to play well for him," says Harrison. He insisted on intense white light for the Granadan heat. Unheard of, "there was usually a preponderance of Strand Electrics No. 36. Surprise pink gels in the footlights because its soft violet hue was supposedly flattering to the actor."

Auburn beard, advanced doctrines, gift of the gab, author of the *The Revolutionist's Handbook*, Paul, under Brook's discerning eye, imitated or rather incarnated the young Shaw. Uncut except for the Don Juan section in Granada, and running well over four hours, the production held audiences rapt. Brook encouraged Paul to break down and analyse the structure of the thought in long speeches. It was arduous work for the 24-year-old actor, but he felt more than equal to it.

There was a charge of underplaying from some quarters, but this early exposure to complexity of thought — Shaw packed enough material into one play for a dozen plays written at the end of the twentieth century (*Man and Superman* was written at its very beginning) — undoubtedly gave Paul a confidence in dealing with heavy intellectual mouthpieces he was never to lose, although he was not especially enamoured of them.

The voice, now becoming distinctively Paul's ("his voice grated and exploded uncontrollably" writes Brook), irritated some, but none doubt the extraordinary revelatory power it carried. T.C. Kemp commented:

> Paul Scofield's John Tanner is the best thing this excellent young actor has done. Although it suffered more than most parts from the prevailing quietism, it bristled with intelligence. Mr. Scofield showed us the man thinking. We always perceived the argument evolving just a point or two in advance of the spoken word. The actor admitted us to the intimacies of the character's progress.

The last sentence is especially perceptive of why Scofield became the great actor he is: "The actor admitted us to the intimacies of the character's progress." As such it was prophetic, and showed at once what was to become Paul's striking difference from the main thrust of the ego-bound acting of many other famous actors. He is already the servant of the part, and not the other way round. At this early age he is never self-serving. Harrison attests to me that, even then, "I've always found it simple acting with him — I am aware of a bond between him and the audience, and he knows them better than he knows you. He doesn't exclude you, but it's an extra something you are not part of."

Next, with Brook's directorial discernment intricately drawing entertainment and inventive unity from the sprawling, bewildering diversity of *King John*, Scofield as the Bastard whipped the ferocious message of "Commodity, commodity" ("Expediency, expediency" in this production) with all the zest of a manic clown. One critic wondered about this Bastard, so "undeniably attractive, spirited and glib of tongue" — "Is he a Feste who has been given the wrong turning?"

The role haunted Trewin: "The performance in *King John* lingered with me; the extraordinary personal magnetism, the loping stride, eyes in which one could trace the growing thought, vocal gusts that almost startled the speaker."

Here, in *King John*, appropriately directed by Brook, and recorded by Paul's first apostle Trewin, was the epiphany of The Scofield Voice:

> The voice we heard in the "Commodity" speech (Peter Brook, a decision almost unnoticed, had altered the word to "Expediency") has become one of the most idiosyncratic on the stage. Today the voice, as taut or as huskily caressing as of old, has strengthened to odd splendour: to a mountain voice, rifted, chasmed, that can glitter on the peak and fall, sombre, in the sudden crevasse. It has what a poet called long ago, "The random music of the turning world."

Joy was now much involved in raising Martin and was living with her parents in Esher, so Paul moved in with Harrison. "We walked on the Clent Hills on a Sunday. Paul striding always a few yards ahead. We brewed Ovaltine nightcaps on an ancient gas ring back at 321 after the show, giggling into the night so uproariously that we brought down the wrath of our landlady Doris in her nightgown with her hair unpinned. We were both writing poetry which we showed each other. His was rather good."

The third play on which Scofield and Brook worked together was Ibsen's *The Lady from the Sea* in William Archer's stilted translation. Kemp astutely observes of Brook that "he tacitly proffers an intelligent reason for everything he does: but I do not agree that his reasons are always the right ones." The production apparently was slow and underplayed "Ennui and Sea Spray." Brook was probably not at his best with Ibsen and, as Dr. Wangel, Paul (though looking dangerously like Dr.

Crippen) "communicates a certain tender pathos . . . he conceals the qualities that must have been there to attract — and keep — the lady from the sea."

When Ellida makes her final choice between her husband and the stranger, Brook experimented with "one of the longest pauses in the history of the theatre." He had it "meticulously stop-watched" in the wings — it seemed aeons until broken by the steamer's whistle in the harbour. "This was not something that Peter was then prepared to let the actor control, with the audience. It was ordained. He was testing his strength."

With fitting symmetry Paul's attachment to the Birmingham Repertory Theatre was brought to a resounding finale with the Christmas Show of 1946: *1066 and All That*, adapted as a musical and peppered with topical anachronisms. Special mention for Paul: "his truculent crusader and his fire-eating old diehard, Colonel Bygadsby — both of which are brilliant little sketches in primary colours."

All the company annually had to double and treble and quadruple and sing and dance their way twice daily through this "Comic-strip History of England."

We were forever charging up and down stairs to and from the dressing rooms changing costumes and wigs and make-ups . . . Paul and I and an actor called Bill Ross were three medieval saints — in long white robes and tonsures that balanced wobbly haloes — hymning the barbarian Celts:

> ALL: Three saints
> From Rome
> Came over the hill,
> If they hadn't
> Left Rome
> They'd be there still.
> They all
> Left home
> To escape their wives:

> PAUL: St. Patrick . . .
>
> ME: St. Pancras . . .
>
> BILL: And of course St. Ives.

During *1066 and All That*, in a ghoulish touch, Harrison's father died in bed in Hastings — away from home. John had to leave the cast in a hurry to identify his father's body. Paul gallantly offered to take on Harrison's parts as well as his own: "For a brief spell it became *1066 and all Scofield.*"

10

Theatrical Lordlings

Brook, who sojourned in the Queen's Hotel where Sir Barry kept a permanent suite and thereafter dined virtually every night with him and his lifelong partner Scott Sunderland ("They were an old married couple, two very conventional British gentlemen in tweeds, liked and respected by the waiters who would accept the yearly tip of £1, to be shared among them all."), had been summoned to accompany Jackson to Stratford-upon-Avon.

Rumour was rife. Who will be leaving with Sir Barry? Paul, if no one else, it was decided. "He and Joy had dined at the Queens . . . Paul didn't let on much. Actors are superstitiously cagey until the contract is signed. But on the stairs *Henry V* was whispered."

Scott, Sir Barry's lover and an "unstoppable source of information, much of it doubtful," told them he won't be going. But Paul, he said, is being very difficult. Won't go unless Joy is in the Company too. Scott was scathing, even bitchy: "Shouldn't have saddled himself with a wife. Great mistake." ("Naughty Scott — I made no request for Joy to be in the company," wrote Paul on my typescript.)

The importance of the Stratford Memorial Theatre, which became the Royal Shakespeare Company, dates from the time of the Barry Jackson transfer to run it. It had been until then a parochial backwater, and when he and Brook visited it and pottered around the red-brick building, which to Brook appeared charmless, Jackson outlined his vision: "This place could be as important as Salzburg." Brook felt at first condescending to the "quiet, elderly figure."

Jackson's plan was to transform it. "To begin with," he said to Brook, "there shouldn't be one producer desperately rushing five productions on to the stage in the first five days, which is why the present system is so bad. There should be a different producer and a different designer for each play, and they should open every four weeks so that each work can be properly rehearsed. As a result, instead of just lasting three weeks, the season should stretch through to the end of the summer . . . " and so he went on, until in a few quiet phrases, so Brook related, he had drawn the outline of what was to become the Stratford revolution that one day would put Warwickshire far ahead of Middle Europe, when "an ignored museum piece rose into a powerhouse of the British stage."

Brook's debut at Stratford was the third production of the season — he was scathing as well as jealous of *The Tempest*, the first production, overdressed in lace and velvet, until he saw the text drowning "like the great realistic galleon of the opening scene." "Nothing in the theatre," Brook wrote, "has any meaning out of its context in performance." He might well have been learning this lesson for Scofield as well as for himself.

He based his own production of *Love's Labour's Lost* on Watteau's painting. It was a crucial, shaping moment in his life. He was well aware of this. He agonized all night before the first rehearsal, wondering how to "block" the movements of the actors with forty pieces of cardboard and a model of the set. Next day, when he started to move the actors according to his preset plan, he knew it would not work.

> They were not remotely like any cardboard figures, these large human beings thrusting themselves forward . . . We had only done the first stage of my movement, lettered A on my chart, but already everyone was wrongly placed and movement B could not follow. My heart sank.

After a moment of panic, in which he reflected on whether he should re-drill the actors, he gave in to the impulse to open himself to the pattern of the actors; movement that was unfolding in front of him. "Rich energy, full of personal variations, shaped by individual enthusiasms and laziness, promising such different rhythms, opening so many unexpected possibilities . . . I think, looking back, that my whole future work hung in the balance. I stopped and walked away from my book, in among the actors. I have never looked at a written plan since." This, of course, was the method that suited Paul.

The reviews were excellent. Suria Magito, a ballerina who was living with the legendary French director Michel Saint-Denis, invited Brook to dinner with the maestro. After dinner Saint-Denis sat back, pulled on his pipe and told Brook it was a great mistake to imitate famous paintings, as theatre is theatre in its own right and the theatre art should not refer to anything outside itself.

"I can see you in rehearsal," he admonished Brook, "making your compositions and placing the actors with a book of Watteau in your hand." Brook reacted with concealed fury, and only later could he see the truth of Saint-Denis's criticism.

But it had not been like that. Sinden recalls finding it anarchically funny to watch the 21-year-old Brook, his body stiff with nerves, trying to demonstrate to 15-year-old David O'Brien, a "natural," how to move as Moth. Brook's sinews tightened and creaked, and O'Brien studiously copied his spastic-like mannerisms. "No, no," cried Brook, "not like that!"

"We lordlings," wrote Harrison, "lounged and languished in pale silks and satins in a park in eighteenth-century Navarre . . . Against this he placed judicious and witty anachronisms . . . The pedant Holofernes and his friends were viewed at dinner through the eye of a monstrous telescope . . . Not since Komisarjevsky's prewar productions had such *lesemajeste* been perpetrated against the bard."

Brook's awakening perceptions worked wonders with Paul, who played Don Armado in *Love's Labour's Lost*. to Donald Sinden, also at Stratford for the first time, Paul was "astonishing," and gave a haunting melancholy to lines such as, "Rust, rapier! be still drum! for your manager is in love; yea, he loveth." Philip Hope-Wallace found him "faintly reminiscent of an over-bred and beautiful old borzoi," an astonishing feat for a 25-year-old. Trewin wrote that he, while "curiously, meditative-ly detached from the rest of the play, managed to humanise a part that had been deemed almost unactable . . . generations of grandees spoke in his voice."

Another early Brookian eccentricity was that of taking away Don Armado's last line in the play — "You that way, we this way" — and giv-ing it to the Princess. Even with these liberties *Love's Labour's Lost* became the most sensational production of that season, "the definitive revival of its generation," with Scofield's haunting performance reverberating down the years. Most recently it is mentioned in a trenchant study, *The Lost Summer*, by Frith Banbury: "Scofield's Armado looking like Don Quixote." *Love's Labour's Lost* was revived the following year.

With future consequences for Paul, the teddy bear was now filled with dynamite.

Nugent Monck, the director of *Cymbeline*, the previous production, was 69, nearly three and a half times Brook's age, and described to me by Peter Hall as "a crazy old man who ran the Maddermarket Theatre for Shakespeare." Harrison believes "his unexpected translation to the big world had blown his mind." Clearly here was his pay-off, and in the next season he would direct Paul in the title role of *Pericles*. Sinden played Arviragus, and he recalls Nugent, a small, bald man who looked like Picasso, piping at him in his highly articulated tones, from the back of the empty stalls, "Donald — you have a *beautiful* voice — (enough pause for the compliment to sink in) "but it's like having a Bechstein when you're only going to vamp on it." Nugent, like Brook, despised boredom and kept up the pace: "The audience may be bewildered but they won't be bored."

The costumes, which came out of the Stratford wardrobe, had not even seen better days. Paul as Cloten attacked the dresser over his: "Oh, it's terrible." (Paul queried this on typescript: "Dear old man — couldn't *attack* him.") His dresser agreed: "It didn't look no better on Balliol Holloway."

My favourite Nugent remark is in retaliation to Sinden, even then a master of anecdote, expatiating on the qualities of a juvenile lead: "An old friend of mine, Charles Smith, said that to be a good juvenile you must make half the audience want to mother you, and the other half want to go to bed with you." Nugent cut in, "If of course that fails, Donald, you can always try acting!"

No one could have acted a more complete, "miraculously brainless" Cloten than Paul in Nugent's production. Eric Keown said he "asked for decapitation and got it!"

But Paul could not help but smile when Valerie Taylor as Imogen, lapsed when reading from her letter; instead of saying, "Thy mistress, Pisario, hath play'd the strumpet in my bed," actually said, "Thy mistress, Pisario, hath play'd the *trumpet* in my bed." ("I was lying dead on the floor." — Paul.)

11

What Is Amiss?

During this season Joy was acting alongside Paul: she played Miranda in *The Tempest*, the first play of the season, and now Celia in *As You Like It* (Paul played Oliver de Boys, which made Oliver's attachment to Celia even more credible than usual). She was also as Katharine, one of the "intensely beautiful Watteau figures" in *Love's Labour's Lost*. She finds time, while looking after Martin, to write a children's book, *The Story of Benjamin Scarecrow*, published by Heinemann, which she illustrates herself with intricately detailed drawings. It is dedicated to Paul, and in the book we meet, briefly, a young actor. "A young man came walking through the field this afternoon . . . He stopped and spoke to me . . . He was tall and his hair shone like new pennies in the sun. He walked with long strides, he was happy — and he sang and talked to himself."

Paul's shot at *Henry V* misfired, or rather lacked the evangelical muse of fire. It seemed, young as he was, he was not yet ready for the heroic part around which the play is built. Maybe it was just a poor production, by Dorothy Green. Atmosphere, wrote Trewin, "laboriously summoned, melted at once. No wonder Scofield could not find the note."

He did, however, look for the note and improve, as if graduation to youthful spontaneity would be a slow process. Sinden was his understudy and complained, "He never was off!"

Joy and Paul lived in the centre of Stratford. Joy, possibly the more sociable of the pair, enjoyed it while Paul "loved it and was not ungregarious." The landlady of their flat, in a crumbling Elizabethan palazzo, 18 High Street, was Mrs. Denne Gilkes, widow of Professor Martin Gilkes.

We fell under her spell. She was a dynamic woman with a most pronounced and earthy sense of humour. She took music lessons in her music room in this house, and also coached members of the theatre . . . her appearance was very sanely eccentric, dressing as she did almost entirely in home-woven capes and skirts and hats purchased from a shop, just along the road, called The Web. A striking figure rosy and grey-fringed and sturdy, she had behind her a career as a contralto — creating such roles as "The Seal Woman" and closely associated with the composer Granville Bantock. She smoked incessantly, sometimes a pipe.

So they moved in with their one-year-old son Martin and remained there for two happy years.

The ability to make goodness interesting was possibly manifest for the first time in Paul's Malcolm, Duncan's avenging son, which revealed another side of Paul's acting self, his conviction in self-doubt and personal uncertainty. The scene when he accuses himself of many vices to Macduff was outstanding.

Sinden recalls how Paul suffered a setback during the performance. They were at the point when the king has been murdered — members of the household are told the terrible news as they arrive. "His two sons Malcolm and Donalbain appear and Donalbain asks, 'What is amiss?' to be told, 'You are and do not know't' (hitherto his sex had never been in doubt!). Macduff then tells them, 'Your noble father's murdered,' to which Malcolm [Paul] replies in a line so apparently offhand that it is fraught with danger, 'O, by whom?'"

Paul was talking and smoking a cigarette in Donald's dressing room when he missed his call.

We suddenly heard shouts (this was before the installation of a tannoy system) and the sound of running feet: I opened my door and saw an approaching stage manager shouting, "Paul! Paul! You're off!" [i.e., in other words, "when you should be on!"]. Paul went out of the room like a rocket, leapt down the stairs, arrived breathless on the stage and was informed, "Your noble father's murdered," Only when he tried to say, "O . . . " did he realise he had a cigarette in his mouth. He removed it, threw it to the floor, ground it with his foot, and continued, "By whom?" Later it was pointed out that he had also failed to put on his wig [which, it seems, was a long blonde one].

There was little pressure, those days, towards typecasting (and few casting directors, who can be a huge impediment to the nurturing of talent and versatility). In the final play of the 1946 season, Paul played the dissolute, callous, impudent Lucio, in *Measure for Measure*, in which he could give full rein to a complexity of vicious and voluptuous frivolity. Lucio has to marry the woman he has wronged: "marrying a punk," declares Lucio, is "pressing to death, whipping, and hanging." For this production Jackson imported an American scholar, Frank McMullan from Yale, to direct. They sometimes needed an interpreter: "I want a couple of you in the corner pitchin' a woo."

Paul recalls that there was a line in which Lucio said of the Duke, speaking to the disguised Duke, "His urine is congealed ice."

Sir Barry approached me just before the first night, asking me to cut that line, it clearly shocked him. I pondered long, and decided to forget his injunction, and kept the line in. No repercussions.

So the Stratford Festival of 1946 came to an end with Paul at its inspiring core: the impact and influence on future theatre and film people was inestimable . . . on the young director Tony Richardson for one:

In the summer of 1946 a group of us, Doreen included, went up to Stratford for a week. We lived in a boarding house, all in the same room, eating nothing but seeing eight separate plays in the same week, including Peter Brook's first big production, *Love's Labour's Lost*, and Paul Scofield's Stratford debut, demonstrating his versatility as a performer. And somehow, because of what we'd done, we felt not intimidated but stimulated and spurred on.

12

Stir Fry

Christopher Fry, wrote Richard Findlater in 1952, "has brought back to the English drama wit, rhetoric, humour, gaiety and colour. He has reinstated comedy as a high theatrical form, and reconciled it with tragedy."

Fry began writing early radio playlets for BBC religious broadcasting. Unfortunately, he never really developed a strength of depth and structure in his plays to measure up to the verbal fireworks, the wit and rhetoric that were his forte. Paul appeared next in Fry's *A Phoenix Too Frequent*, a title almost as memorable as his best known *The Lady's Not for Burning*, which was adapted by Ronald Millar, Mrs. Thatcher's speechwriter and also a playwright of this era, into "The Lady's Not for Turning."

Paul played the Roman N.C.O. Tegeus-Chromis. Fry's verse at this time demonstrated his exuberant "intensification as a defect of precise imagination" (Raymond Williams), and his characters are similarly undifferentiated, although productive of considerable zestful enjoyment.

Even so, audiences relished the paradoxical dexterity, judging by the glowing reviews for this production by Noël Willman, in the intimate Arts Theatre, London, for a short run, where Paul gained confidence that he could mesmerize with the brilliant surface quality. Willman was to join the Stratford Company the following season. He was, comments Paul, "highly intelligent, amusing and very clever. Both sociable and remote, not encouraging as a director but you knew he wouldn't have cast you if he hadn't thought you were OK."

Harold Hobson, now the new critic for the *Sunday Times* since James

Agate retired, noticed Paul's way of ending a phrase on a rising note in a suddenly detached and meditative tone. Fry's message ultimately is one of hope and determination: Tegeus-Chromis, who has lost his body, convinces the beautiful widow Dinamene, played by Hermione Hannen, not to follow her husband in sacrificial suicide. Fry says, "I remember feeling how very safe I felt the part to be in the young man's hands."

There is no gossip in the papers about Scofield, his wife, or his child, at this time, and it may be said that he laid down what has become a life-long practice. At once, and for ever after, Scofield's private life is private. There are no conditions: privacy is not negotiable.

One night, after drinking hours when Harrison was unwinding with a pint in the Rose and Crown in Sheep Street under the indulgent eye of the local bobby, Paul and Joy turned up with something very serious to tell him. They marched Harrison round Stratford to sober him up. Finally, over coffee in the kitchen they tell him their important news: Paul has been offered a seven-year contract with Universal Pictures in Hollywood.

He says no.

About this time Paul was offered other parts: one, for example, was Captain Hawtree in T.W. Robertson's *Caste*, which was subsequently played by Frith Banbury (with monocle and moustache) before he turned to directing. In the next season, showing how Paul's progress was now unstoppable, his range astonishing (although Jackson did not repeat the mistake of casting him as the juvenile leads), he played Mercutio, Mephistopheles in Marlowe's *Doctor Faustus*, Sir Andrew Aguecheek and Pericles, as well as the roles of Lucio and Don Armado from the previous season. As Mephistopheles he spoke the verse quietly, "For where we are is hell, seeming to know eternity and its torment."

But he was not at all tempted by fame and the trappings of a growing reputation as the finest young actor in England. He modestly approached Val Gielgud, brother of John and head of BBC radio drama, from where they now live at Joy's mother's house, 249 Avondale Avenue, Esher (not even on headed notepaper): "Would you consider me for possible broadcasts in the Drama Department? I was in the recent Stratford festival season, playing Henry V, Don Armado in *Love's Labour's*, Lucio in *Measure for Measure* and Malcolm in *Macbeth*. My only broadcasting experience was in last Sunday's Northern Regional Children's Hour Programme, in which I played Bassanio in *The Merchant*."

In December 1946 they recorded *Love's Labour's Lost* and we find him again writing modestly to the producer, . . . "May I correct an error in the spelling of my name — there is no 'H' in it."

Brook's production of *Romeo and Juliet* was to some a complete mess. According to Harrison he hardly bothered to rehearse Paul, cast as Mercutio, spending all his time with the lovers. This was now Paul's third immersion in the text of this play: he had already played Juliet and Tybalt. Brook employed Sinden, "Er, Paris . . . Young Guards Officer I think." That is all Brook ever told him.

On the first day of rehearsal they shivered, for outside there was three feet of snow in Stratford High Street. Brook's first words, "I want you all to remember this is a scorching hot day in Verona," stirred scornful laughter. Harrison (Benvolio) and Paul went off to work in the circle bar on their own. Now, with the great thaw, they arrived at the stage door in punts. Harrison was called by Peter to watch Juliet (Daphne Slater). He noted Brook had deliberately thrown away her "naturally fluttering youth . . . her porcelain fragility." She "lurched downstage and gobbed it ('Spread thy close curtain, love-performing night,' etc.) at the audience like a randy old hag on the verge of menopause." Harrison spoke his mind and Brook was offended. We were both, Harrison thinks today, "in thrall to sex-in-the-head and would dearly have liked his Romeo and Juliet to make it to sex-in-the-bed, off-stage as well as on."

Brook grew high-handed, his measure of the dictatorial increased: capriciously, he often changed his mind. He managed the crowd scenes through a loudhailer, like a midget Joseph von Sternberg. Nancy Burman, the production manager, soothed everyone and quelled mutiny. A great deal, comments Harrison, was left to chance inspiration at the dress rehearsal.

"Hot, violent, unromantic — and much criticised," was how Brook described it. Jackson took adverse criticism of his directors in his stride, but what angered him was that Brook and his designer had spent far too much money. The ultimate insult came when most of the set and design, as Brook hysterically kept calling "Cut!," was left lying in the wings. "We came to an empty orange arena," admitted Brook, "a few sticks — and the wings were full of elaborate and expensive discarded units. We were proud of ourselves, but the management was furious."

Brook was not invited back. "I had transgressed against a vital aspect of Sir Barry's values." Harrison records that the veteran actor Walter Hudd's Papa Capulet face was ashen with horror, but he still retained his gentle dignity and supported the new young genius with a touching loyalty that brushed off on the rest of them.

With this *Romeo and Juliet* (Romeo is played by Laurence Payne) Brook began his obsession with the empty space. This was not only centrally important to Brook as a director, but once again crucially important to Paul's development. Brook called it, after the event, "a play of wide spaces in which all scenery and decoration easily become an irrelevance, in which one tree on a bare stage can suggest the loneliness of a place of exile; one wall, as in Giotto, an entire house. The atmosphere is described in a single line, 'these hot days is the mad blood stirring,' and its treatment must be to capture the violent passion of two children lost among the warring fury of the southern houses."

The critics wildly dissented, but people flocked to see it. On the first night there was a storm within and without (thunder and lightning). "Wrongly cast, worse directed and nonsensically enscened," wrote Ivor Brown in the *Observer*, "hordes of Chu Chin Chow must have swarmed west and occupied Verona": Kenneth Tynan, still an Oxford student, rhapsodized over the young tragedy played out "under a throbbing vault of misty indigo . . . I can imagine no better Juliet." Paul's Mercutio — "not the noisy bragger who usually usually capsizes the play . . . but a rapt goblin, ruddy and likeable." Peter Ustinov said of the Queen Mab speech that Scofield spoke it as "a vague elusive nocturne . . . It was a man who didn't like to be referred to as a poet, talking in his sleep."

He is not dreaming when his steel flashes upon the Capulets. "Quite the most memorable Mercutio I have seen," says Donald Sinden. Harrison captures the essence of the magic of Paul's bond with his audience. When he speaks the Queen Mab speech, lying on his back surrounded by smashed figures, Harrison reports that it was "so quiet I couldn't hear it on stage. Everyone in the audience heard it."

Joy was by no means trailing behind Paul:

Richard II was followed by *The Merchant of Venice* in which I [Sinden] was to play Lorenzo opposite Joy Parker, Paul Scofield's enchanting wife. Joy had been in the company the previous year and as well as Jessica was now playing an interesting range of parts — the Queen in *Richard II*, Katharine in *Love's Labour's Lost* and she had taken over Ariel from David O'Brien. Lorenzo was the best part I had had at Stratford; he and Jessica have some of the most beautiful lines in the play.

The wife is in Venice. Paul moves to Illyria to play Sir Andrew Aguecheek, a wistful, pliant knight "made of pink blancmange," with Walter Hudd as Malvolio in Hudd's production. This *Twelfth Night*, together with *Romeo and Juliet*, and *Richard II*, were presented in the autumn at His Majesty's, the first London season ever of the Stratford Memorial Theatre. It was to be thirteen years before the newly named Royal Shakespeare Company started their seasons at the Aldwych — with Scofield's Lear their most distinguished triumph.

Paul also played Pericles at the end of this Stratford season. Nugent Monck directed in complete submission to the fear of boredom, cutting the peripatetic text down to a hundred minutes (including the interval). He cut the Antiochus and Pericles arrival in Tarsus, and began with Pericles' shipwrecked arrival in Pentapolis. Paul was impressive as the maturing Prince in his many reversals of fortune, but there is now some criticism of that voice: of its danger of becoming mannered, of its harshness, of its unconventional and unpredictable flights. He was, not sur-

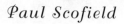

prisingly, tired, but he had captured Stratford, and next year he was to attempt the greatest role of all for any actor under thirty.

13

That Earth That Kept the World in Awe

Years later Brook asked John Harrison why he wanted to be a director: "Why, when you're a good actor?" From this, Harrison felt that Brook, throughout his career, always aspired to be the actor, always pursued his "desire to get closer and closer to living in the actual moment of performance." To which actor did Brook, in his mimetic desire, reach out most? To Paul, it would seem.

"After a few years," Brook wrote, "Sir Barry in turn was pushed out by a group of governors, above all, I was told, because although he knew every stagehand and cleaning lady and would stop daily to enquire about their ailments, when he met a governor, he could never remember his name."

The true reason for Jackson's departure was because the ex-military Chairman of the Governors, Colonel Sir Fordham Flower, descendant of the Flowers who had donated the site and most of the money for the building of the theatre, could neither appreciate Jackson's long-established method of benign dictatorship, nor realise the acute sensitivity behind it.

Harrison believes Jackson was elbowed out by "Major Anthony Quayle, recently returned from a distinguished war . . . The two military gentlemen were determined to be rid of this turbulent aesthete."

Fordham Flower admired his subsequent directors, Anthony Quayle, Glen Byam Shaw, and Peter Hall, but he never warmed to Jackson.

Only Scofield was retained for a third season, although Jackson remained nominally in charge. Even Paul was discomfited by Quayle. He felt that "Tony and I were not made for each other. Our compatibility was tenuous, his manner to me always cool. Perhaps, having just returned from a very active war, he felt I had too easy a time, as a civilian. I understand that. He was jovial always, with a quite natural underlying unease. Natural because his workload at Stratford in 1948 was very heavy. Both directing and acting and moving towards the artistic directorship in 1949."

But anyway, Paul was now down to play Hamlet in the 1948 season. Paul is speaking out in 1994, forty-six years on, yet that earlier moment recaptures its immediacy:

> I do recognise that I haven't done enough theatre recently and I do have a need to communicate with people. But I wouldn't want to say that I ought to do more because it's required of me by the public, because that's not the truth. The public doesn't mind, really.
>
> One of the greatest strengths of the theatre is that it is ephemeral. It does exist only in what you remember and you can't check up on it afterwards and think, "That's not as good as I remember." If any performance I've ever given stays in someone's mind that's so much more exciting than being able to put it on the video and play it again. It's not that I don't want to take risks — the opposite is true, in fact. But the more you know about acting, the more you are aware of the pitfalls and the more nerve-racking it becomes. When I was young, I wasn't nervous at all. Even doing *Hamlet*, I just had a go.

In 1948, now that Joy was no longer a member of the Stratford Company, Paul moved out of Stratford to digs in the village of Luddington. He overlooked the village green. Joy was often there with Martin, but she was working too, staying mostly in Esher, in Priestley's *Home Is Tomorrow*, with Lesley Banks and Irene Worth.

"There were so few of us," Harrison observes to me of the acting profession at this time and in contrast to today.

Television was in its infancy. Most of the public did not have a set.

Without any visual record I have formed the impression, from having read widely about it, that Paul's *Hamlet* was not so much an interpretation that reflected his own personal style, ego, and technique — a strong interpretation in so far as he "saw" the role as such and such — but something both more simple yet at the same time more complex and profound.

It was an unusual penetration, of which I am sure he was largely unconscious, to the essence, or mystery, at the centre of what Brook calls "the secret play." Many claimed at the time that Paul was the "Hamlet of his generation" — Paul played the role seven years later in 1955 in Brook's equally famous production at the Phoenix Theatre. This opened in Birmingham, ran in London at the Phoenix Theatre, then travelled to Russia where it drew adulatory crowds at the Moscow Art Theatre: (they were the first British actors to make such a visit since the 1917 Revolution). Is to call him "the Hamlet of his generation" an understatement?

Or was he as close to Shakespeare's Hamlet as we shall ever get? "Imagine that Hamlet really existed," once said Brook. "Imagine that someone followed him secretly wherever he went so that the words he spoke were really his own." Let me now try to follow the mystery of Paul as Hamlet and see if we can edge closer to his secret.

Paul liked working with Michael Benthall the director:

He blinked a lot; was somehow both nervous and assured — a charming man whose work was perhaps traditional, but deeply imaginative and with a strong feeling for design. His production of *Hamlet*, which was set in the Victorian era, was, from a design point of view, based on Winterhalter — the settings were Gothic-inspired and the costumes voluminously magnificent (the women's, I mean — the men were more severely dressed — as in that period). I alternated Hamlet with Robert Helpmann, with whom I shared a dressing room, which meant that when we played *Hamlet* we had it to ourselves.

In other plays, *Merchant of Venice*, *King John* etcetera, we both inhabited it; Bobby was one of the funniest men I have known, and our preparations for these plays were enlivened by his caustic observations, his imitations of actors, and his infectious ribaldry. His great experience as a dancer and actor in no way caused him to treat me with patronage — he was kind and very frank and honest.

Not very much to go on here. Turning to the professionals, Trewin, as the most diligent and perceptive Hamlet-watcher of the twentieth century — the eighty-five Hamlets he records in his classic account range from 1908 to 1987 — concluded, "I have not met a performance less externalized from Scofield's, able to communicate suffering without emotional pitch and toss; he had that within which passeth show."

Brook commented on Paul's acting (and it was true even then of the Hamlet of 1948 as opposed to the more mature second shot), "Its absolutely personal structure of rhythms, its own instinctive meanings: to rehearse apart he lets his whole nature — a milliard of supersensitive scanners — pass to and fro across the words. In performance the same process makes everything he has apparently fixed come back each night the same and absolutely different."

I am watching Paul on the afternoon of April 23, 1948, together with the earliest Scofield-watcher who observed our quarry:

Leaning over the Tramway Bridge and staring, perhaps longingly, into the Avon: a tall, spare, high-cheekboned figure, the forehead deep-lined under dark, curling hair, a face strangely Elizabethan as if it looked out from a miniature by Isaac Oliver. He was playing Hamlet at night: with this only a few hours off, any actor might have felt unnerved. As it was, the performance had no trace of strain, even if the young Elizabethan was here an early Victorian (of the year 1848) in black frock coat and narrow, strapped trousers.

A few hours later Paul became "most dreadfully attended" by the thronging phantoms of his brain. Harold Hobson a few days later said he had "never seen a Hamlet more shot with the pale agony of irresolution." Trewin reported: "He appears to be younger than we are told he is: young to be burdened with so terrible a duty. At core he is a sensitive boy longing for affection: his father dead, his mother disloyal, Ophelia lost — 'Forty thousand brothers could not, with all their quantity of love, make up my sum.' Prompted to his revenge by heaven and hell, he finds himself now, like Lear, bound upon a wheel of fire."

Trewin forgot the frockcoat, the strapped trousers: "He is simply the timeless Hamlet . . . None could forget Scofield's pathos, the face folded in grief, at 'When you are desirous to be blessed, I'll blessing beg of you.' We have known too many correct, almost formal Hamlets, aloof from Elsinore. Scofield was ever a prisoner within its bounds: the world held many confines, wards, and dungeons, Denmark being one of the worst."

A.V. Cookman continued the image of the frail Hamlet as "a spiritual fugitive who seeks not so desperately the fulfilment of his earthly mission as some steadfast refuge for the hard-driven imagination. Only in death the refuge is found. It is the distinction of Mr. Scofield's playing that makes us free of this imagination, and its inner distractions have for us such intense dramatic reality that the melodramatic bustle of the court appears unreal, like the shadows outside Plato's cavern."

And yet the mystery remains. "The emotions," as Paul says, "are real, but they aren't mine." Whose, then, are they, where do they come from? It would seem that some have the power to summon up characters, as Owen Glendower claims he can summon up ghosts from the deep.

Siriol Hugh Jones, similarly probing, called Paul's Hamlet complex but not complicated. She observed how the great ratiocinative speeches sprang naturally from emotion, and she remarked, as critics have done so often, on Scofield's "almost motionless nervous excitement, peculiar to himself." Motionless — is this the key word? Philip Hope-Wallace caught Paul's "lenitive cadence and curious moth-like fragility." W.A. Darlington, in a review for *The New York Times*, said that what he really looked forward to was the Hamlet that Scofield would give us in five years' time.

There were complaints about too rapid diction. One review, full of praise but desperately pompous, from an Oxford undergraduate, called Paul "a wandering plant, in sapless perambulation."

Ronald Harwood significantly remembers Scofield once telling him that on the couplet, "The play's the thing/Wherein I'll catch the conscience of the king," Helpmann, with a perfect throw, unerringly pierced the stage floor with his dagger where it stuck quivering in the wood. Scofield, following suit, could never get it right. It slithered, bounced, skidded, but never went in clean. Does this never getting it right take us a little nearer to the heart of the Scofield mystery?

That was the centre of this Stratford season.

14

I Have That Within

Every watcher and listener has a private, an intimate, Hamlet. The question remains, "Was Paul *merely* the greatest Hamlet of his generation, or was he the timeless Hamlet, the true Hamlet for all generations?" Modernist, post-structuralist advocates of the new historicism or other "isms" would deride such a question. Our age has endless jostling "isms," competing heartlessly: the worst and most influental are "relativism," guaranteeing poor quality in art, morals and just about everything else, and its close partner "reductionism," debunking everything, cutting everything down to size, reducing the dimensions of whatever is unknown and mysterious. Perhaps the "ism" managers are at the level of Paul's "derisive" audiences in munition factory canteens. But here comes a new voice, a new theatrical hot gospeller.

As he proved seven years ago at Stratford, no living actor is better equipped for Hamlet than Paul Scofield. On him the right sadness sits, and also the right spleen; his gait is a prowl over quicksands; and he can freeze a word with an irony at once mournful and deadly. He plays Hamlet as a man whose skill in smelling falseness extends to himself, thereby breeding self-disgust. He spots the flaw in every stone, which makes him either a born jeweller or a born critic. He sees through Gertrude, Claudius, Rosencrantz, Guildenstern, Polonius, and Ophelia: what remains but to see through himself? And this Mr. Scofield does superbly, with a might bawl of "O vengeance!" followed by a rueful stare at his own outflung arms and a decline into moans of derisive laughter. His eulogy of Horatio is not only a hymn to the only honest man in Denmark, it is the tribute enviously paid by complexity to simplicity.

Kenneth Tynan, who paradoxically became Paul's most keen advocate while he was literary manager of the National Theatre, from 1963 to 1973, reviews the later performance of *Hamlet*. I say paradoxically, because no two men could have had a lifestyle and philosophy more opposite to one another in every way. Tynan lights upon the most distinctive trait Paul possesses. Not only with Hamlet does Paul see through and into every character he plays. Yet he is not Hamlet, never becomes Hamlet, whose mental confusion does not enable him to draw the line or see the limit — or when he does, when his self-perception is at last complete and whole, it is too late to avoid the necessary tragedy. He is Scofield the actor, servant of his writer.

Many other actors have failed for personal reasons: become too neurologically identified, or simply remained far too detached, outside, removed, merely show. Alec Guinness is one of the former. The latter are legion, including Olivier. Paul showed the ideal balance, which of course is what makes him the great actor he is, between becoming the role he plays and finding it, impersonating it, or entering it from outside. The truth he demonstrates is that he acts the author's intentions, he never tries to be the person. The dictum of Vakhtangov, which I have quoted earlier, is supremely apt. Paul has learnt to wish, to wish by order, to wish whatever is given to Hamlet.

What more perfect typecasting could there have been opposite Paul than the as yet unknown Claire Bloom as Ophelia. She had just narrowly missed being cast as Ophelia in Olivier's film of *Hamlet* — the part went to Jean Simmons and not to Vivien Leigh (to the latter's chagrin). Claire Bloom stated about herself in this Ophelia period: "I was always ill at ease in the company of men. The sexual feelings that I undoubtedly had were repressed in me. I was able to act out these hidden desires only in crushes on my leading men, which, in the charmed atmosphere of our work together, were almost as real to me as the real thing. I felt absolutely complete, and considered myself to be the luckiest of young women to lead such an enchanted life."

Offstage too, in the green room, she was Ophelia. Yet she also adored going back to supper after the show and hearing all the theatrical gossip: who was sleeping with whom, who was going to be asked back next season.

As the finest young actor in England, Paul Scofield was the subject of much speculation. Extremely reclusive, a countryman from Sussex, his onstage glamour and offstage reticence were a source of great frustration to the young and pretty actresses in the company. Since Scofield was happily married and had a young son, no one wanted seriously to interfere with his marriage; only perhaps to be flirted with and taken some notice of. But Scofield never so much as glanced at any of them. "I could never make up my mind which of my two Hamlets I found the more devastating: the openly homosexual, charismatic Helpmann, or the charming, shy young man from Sussex." Claire, however, soon went for the more vain and available Richard Burton.

For Paul his Ophelia was, "Sixteen years old I think — so very young and necessarily inexperienced, she looked lovely, she acted with a daunting assurance which belied entirely her inexperience of almost timid reticence. She was a very good Ophelia."

Why Paul is so "lovely," says Harrison, is that "he finds the good. 'Get thee to a nunnery,' so often delivered with rage or scorn, he says so gently. You have visions of quiet and prayer. A future for Ophelia."

It sounds in this triumphant season that Paul acted only Hamlet. This was far from the case. He had already, sandwiched between the two Stratford seasons, played Young Fashion in Vanbrugh's *The Relapse* at The Lyric, Hammersmith, an introduction to Anthony Quayle's direction. He acted Philip, King of France, with Robert Helpmann as a "baleful" King John "in full chrome make-up." He meditated on the tear falling on grief-torn Constance's hair — Shakespeare's worst-ever lines:

> Even to that drop ten thousand wiry friends
> Do glue themselves in sociable grief;

Like true, inseparable, faithful loves,
Sticking together in calamity.

He was Bassanio in *The Merchant of Venice*; Troilus in *Troilus and Cressida*; a very bitter Roderigo indeed in *Othello*, a peevish gull, flapping and wailing about the Cypriot shore; and the Clown in *The Winter's Tale*. Dame Laura Knight painted his staring eyes, his wild hair as she watched him from the wings, Barry Jackson chose this as his official gift to mark his departure.

An unbelievably full season, but as if this was not enough Paul recorded for radio *The Bronze Horse* and *The Merchant of Venice*, and defaulted only on the part of Satan in *Paradise Lost*: "The producer regretfully came to the conclusion that Mr. Scofield is not suitable for the part . . . I presume he will have to be paid." Apparently, the producer wanted the indigent Dylan Thomas as Satan, to give him a helping hand. In the event, Thomas was "very good, if a little pontifical."

Not suitable as Satan? Next year it would be Paul's turn as Tamburlaine.

15

At Large in Asia

The "putsch" of Quayle, Benthall and Fordham Flower had sacked most of the Company that came to Stratford from Birmingham with Jackson. Among them was John Harrison who had played in *The Tempest* of the first season as Ferdinand, opposite Joy Parker as Miranda. Later, in the second season, this *Tempest* was revived again, with Daphne Slater now cast as Miranda, while Joy played Ariel which, according to Harrison, she did very balletically, "all blue and silver and Kurt Jooss."

In May 1948 John Harrison married Daphne Slater in the Georgian church of St. Anne on Kew Green. She had played Juliet in the Brook production: too untutored and prattling a subject for the stratagems of fate, according to those who mocked the de-romanticised Verona, but to Tynan excitable and impetuous, communicating this "compulsive ardour."

Daphne was embarked on a successful film career, but Harrison, except for some radio work, was now unemployed. Brook, who had also left Stratford, was directing *Boris Godunov* at Covent Garden. Joy was in the new J.B. Priestley play *Home Is Tomorrow* at the Picadilly Theatre, playing the "native girl."

Paul was best man at Harrison's wedding, and the two friends strolled beforehand in Kew Gardens to "allay their nerves and are nearly late for the ceremony," during which, Harrison confessed, he felt ill at ease. But after an "odyssey" of ambiguous sexual orientation, which included a fascination with the actor playing Moth in *Love's Labour's Lost*, he was ready for radical change. Of Joy "Best friends' wives are quite untouchable," he declared, "and a bit of a mystery in fact . . . in those unregenerate times

. . . she was my friend's wife. Like his pipe or his bicycle." He admired her acting unreservedly. Fifty years later he discovered a scratchy 78-rpm recording of *The Tempest*, still finding her "alive and spring-like across the years, with a total unaffected freshness."

Paul was provided with a huge challenge for his first starring role in the West End, which opened in March 1950, after a pre-London tour, at the St. James's Theatre. This was Terrence Rattigan's *Adventure Story* in which Paul's role as Alexander the Great ran to some 6,000 words.

Alexander lies on his deathbed in Babylon and retraces his "conquering might" as the world's commander, wondering where it has all gone wrong. The play is ambitious, Rattigan's attempt to write at once a classic along Shakespearian lines and a contemporary serious play. Alexander lives the sequence of conquests that began when he was twenty, and ended when he was thirty-two, with his death. Like Shakespeare, Rattigan went to Plutarch for his source material and, like Plutarch, who only sketched in the military campaign, Rattigan explored the characters in the story, and the dramatic detail. "The fact is," wrote Plutarch, "you often learn nothing by the study of campaigns of what kinds of men the leaders were. On the other hand you can sometimes learn more from an occasional remark."

Rattigan employs everyday speech and English middle-class attitudes in *Adventure Story* and, although the play is well thought out, its focus is inconclusive. It lacked, said Rattigan later — acknowledging it did not work ("I wasn't ready") — "the language of the poet and the perception of the philosopher." Alexander is hard to believe in, although there lurk dark autobiographical threads in Rattigan's treatment. These are Alexander's close friendship with Hephaeston, reflecting a homosexual attachment to Kenneth Morgan, a young actor, and Alexander's affection for the Persian Queen — Rattigan's own mother love, and so on. Although unwieldy and, some thought (including Harrison), dull, *Adventure Story* was an important experiment for both playwright and actor. For Rattigan it prefigured the epic succinctness of *Ross*, even of *The Deep Blue Sea*.

Richard Burton was cast as Hephaeston, but he was sacked during rehearsals by Peter Glenville, the director. This was the closest Burton and Paul ever came to acting together.

For Paul it was a mammoth trial of strength. Mainly the theme is that of the man who can master the world but not himself. The idioms and battles belong more to 1939-45 than to the fourth century B.C. Paul proved himself equal, in an impressive display of his range from Hitlerian displays of monomaniacal rage, atrocity, to philosophic detachment, gentleness, tender and violent passion, weeping self-pity and gnawing self-doubt. He does everything, someone remarks, but bite the new Persian carpets.

Cecil Wilson, the *Daily Mail* critic, wrote of Paul: "What he lacked in technical finish he made up for with the magic, magnetic quality of an embryo Olivier."

"One saw the Prince of Denmark at large in Asia," wrote Harold Hobson, still in the early stages of a new critic's love affair with an actor. "All this fine actor's performances have something of the other world about them. Invariably he looks as if he had been reading *The Turn of the Screw* and seen ghosts at midnight. Invariably his sonatas have spooks in them."

Joy joined Paul again on stage as Roxana, the barbarian chief's daughter: she and Paul acted with affecting beauty in a macabre wooing scene. In one closed fist Alexander holds the wedding ring, in the other a knife to kill her if she refuses. Silently, she chooses the ring. "Yes," he tells her, "I think you'll make a good wife, Roxana. You also, I see, have the quality of luck."

Peter Bull, the exotic and highly articulate actor who was very much part of the H.M. Tennent world, in which Paul increasingly became a central figure, summed up *Adventure Story* when it closed in the summer heatwave of 1949 and Paul, Joy and Martin have left for a holiday: "I didn't care for it at all and thought Paul badly produced [by Peter Glenville]. I so wanted him to have the full success on his first big show but I hope next time he'll pull it off."

Brook wrote to Harrison on tour in Australia his response to Paul in *Adventure Story*.

When I saw it on the first night, he gave a quite wonderful performance. Unfortunately, although the evening seems a triumph, he hasn't quite made the total success and hasn't really *arrived* in London. The reasons seem to be (1) that the play isn't good and isn't drawing the town, and (2) that apparently Paul's performance is very variable. So you meet people who think Paul wonderful, and people who are disappointed — and the answer is just that they've been on different nights! I've got a play I want to do with a lovely part for him — we're going to decide about it in the next few days.

On his return from Devon Paul rehearsed the role of Constantin in *The Seagull,* which opened in October at the Lyric Theatre, Hammersmith, before transferring to the St. James's Theatre. This is the first time Harrison, returning from Australia, saw his name in such large letters. The billing was as large as Mai Zetterling, who played Nina: but he was accused of being flat, stiff, dull — because he is so still on stage. Once again that rapt, secret quality of stillness. "I went backstage to see him, really quite shy, because I'd seen little to nothing of him in the year in which he had become that distanced heavenly object, a 'star.' Almost the first thing he said as I tentatively poked my head round the dressing room door was, 'Look, nothing's changed. One's friends are one's friends, and I feel no more at home in London than you do.'"

During the run of *The Seagull* Paul acted with Peggy Ashcroft in the balcony scene from *Romeo and Juliet* in a London Coliseum charity performance. He was never to act in *Romeo* again, and similarly never with Ashcroft, except in a radio production of *Macbeth,* although much later he was cast opposite her in *The Taming of the Shrew:* were there shades of some incompatibility here? One might wonder he withdrew instinctively from the predatory toils of a lady who often fell in love with her leading man. But Paul comments curtly on my typescript, "Don't think I'd have been afraid of any 'sexual spell.' I withdraw."

16

Binkie-Land

On VE Day in 1945, H.M. Tennent Ltd, a commercial theatrical production company, and Tennent Plays, a non-profit-making company that ploughed back its profits to ensure good runs, had twelve plays running in the West End. Hugh "Binkie" Beaumont, the man who controlled the empire, assistant to Tennent and boyfriend of the original Harry Tennent who began the enterprise in 1936 and died in 1941, told his biographer, "The war has been the making of me . . . And to think I owe it all to Hitler."

Beaumont simulated a background of illegitimacy and dire poverty, but he was simply a Cardiff solicitor's son who took his stepfather's name after his widowed mother remarried (Beaumont sounded better than Morgan). As London's most powerful manager he had many detractors and enemies, but alliances and an astute business sense, plus a shared, often homosexual-inclined outlook, with supporters such as the economist Maynard Keynes, Chairman of the Arts Council, ensured that his skilful judgement and his broadly sound taste dominated any of his rivals. His critics claimed he operated a casting couch for favourites and fellow homosexuals, but at a Critics Circle lunch Frith Banbury, the most eminent Tennent director, was able to count through rapidly on his fingers to me the gay actors in Binkie's many productions to show this was definitely not the case. Standards were high, and many non-commercial plays and classic revivals had respectable, often lengthy runs. Today these would only manage a short spell at the Royal Court, Hampstead Theatre Club, or the Barbican Pit.

Beaumont went to the very first production by Brook of *The Infernal*

Machine at the Chanticleer Theatre in Kensington. Now he was return-ing to employ Brook for Paul's next production. Brook sees him as a sub-tly concealed dictator, but not entirely after power. He also wants the the-atre to be a place of style and beauty, so Brook feels they share the same ideal.

> He knew his world and he knew his people, and he could play on this keyboard with exquisite finesse. He was gentle, charming, and seemed to be totally self-effacing. He never made the managerial error of stealing the limelight from his performers, his name never appeared on the bills, he gave no interviews, he was rarely pho-tographed, and in his quest for absolute power he could never be caught opposing anything head-on. He was a perfect listener.

Beaumont could be purring, conciliatory on the telephone (but with a chilling expression on his face), talk tirelessly and knowledgeably on all subjects, but above all he had a shameless trick that never failed:

> When an actress, writer, or designer categorically refused to accept an idea that Binkie with his unerring instinct knew to be vital to the success of the show — such as rewriting a scene or changing a dress or a hairstyle — he would say, pointing to the obstinate adversary, "My friend here has just made the most brilliant sugges-tion." The person in question would look surprised and flattered in anticipation. Then, quite unabashed, Binkie would put his own thoughts into the other person's mouth, and the poor victim, con-fused but beaming, would generally end by acknowledging owner-ship of the idea and accepting the congratulations of the rest of the cast.

Paul, in late 1949, was at the beginning of ten years of working with Beaumont. He at once found he had "Respect for actors, was courteous and fair — would always *listen* with gravity to the actor's point of view. Sadly he is remembered by some as a monopolist in the theatre, whereas he was simply an astute chooser of talent, particularly of directors, who put him in touch with the best in contemporary and classical drama and which he then mounted with exemplary taste and skill."

Described as a charade with music, *L'Invitation au Chateau* is one of Jean Anouilh's *pièces roses*, his more cheerful pieces, though even in this the darker vein is sometimes visible, as Brook discovered:

> Binkie would work on seven or eight productions at the same time, but he always gave the impression that the one you were concerned with was the only one that mattered. "We," he would say to each group — "they" being the others — and so we all felt loved. When we did *Ring Round the Moon*, he persuaded me to take out Anouilh's sharp reference to real life when the melancholy banker reveals he is Jewish. "Why Jewish? Not very nice!" said Binkie, rumoured to be part Jewish himself, as he cut the words from the script, thus eliminating anything as ugly as real life. Perhaps "niceness" was the value that was most appreciated by the West End theatre of the day.

Paul met Anouilh. He found him very small, "with an enquiring, mouse-like quality of great charm and quietness." Christopher Fry had made the adaptation, and it had the perfect title. Add to this Oliver Messel's designs, and a cast that included Margaret Rutherford, Claire Bloom, and Cecil Trouncer, and you had the recipe for a long run on Shaftesbury Avenue.

The characters consist of the Twins (alike as peas in a pod, sharing an equally large fortune: Frederick, modest and sweet natured, Hugo, attractive and ruthless), both played by Paul; a Crumbling Butler, a Secretive Secretary, a Faded Companion, a Dyspeptic Millionaire (who tears up pound notes in an attempt to beggar himself to the level of the poor and aspiring), a Lepidopterist, a Ballet Dancer, a Teacher of the Pianoforte, a General, and an Aunt (Margaret Rutherford, "trumpeting like an imperious dragon-fly from her wheel-chair").

It was Paul's first West End production after *Adventure Story* and *The Seagull*, but also Brook's: the latter knew Paul was already recognised as the most extraordinary young actor of his time, although his movements were "awkward" and his voice "grated and exploded uncontrollably." Brook goes against the rules of typecasting by asking him to play these elegant Edwardian twins who have first a hint of existentialist philosophy in the moral difference exhibited between them. Brook worries there is insufficient grace in Paul's movements for this stylish comedy and asks Paul to take lessons from a ballet teacher. Paul looks at him strangely and then shakes his head: "I can't do it that way. You must explain to me what impression of elegance you want me to give. Then I'll act it."

Brook, notes Paul, then proceeded to do this day by day, in rehearsals. Although his characteristic movements do not change, by a mysterious alchemy of the imagination they end by expressing the "essence of the refinement that the part required." And it is never in doubt which brother is holding the stage. Anouilh expressed himself in awe at this elegant pyrotechnic display.

Harold Hobson called attention to the scene in the third act in which the young dancer Isabelle upbraids Hugo, as she thought, not realising that it is twin Frederick. During all this long speech Scofield

"stood absolutely motionless. His head was half-bowed, and his left arm hung at his side, the fingers loose and parted. They did not move by a fraction of an inch, until at the end of Isabelle's tirade. Mr Scofield raised his head, and one saw from the sad, concerned look on his face that he was not Hugo but Frederick . . . There was something extremely touching in the still and mute acceptance of undeserved reproach."

Attention is brought again to the mysterious and magical quality of Paul's stillness. Such a quality can never be registered on film or on television.

17

Warm-ups? Whatever For?

My first long run and still my longest. I learned a lot from that — how to combat the boredom of repetition, how to attempt to maintain always freshness and spontaneity. I learned that this could be achieved by an awareness of the different qualities of each audience, an awareness that they were hearing the words of Anouilh/Fry for the first time, and that I must speak them as if for the first time. It was good and happy experience.

Deservedly, too, Paul was earning good money now, £75 a week, the official top Tennent salary, as well as a percentage of the box office gross. This enabled him to begin buying the substantial Edwardian house known as The Gables set in its own delightful shrubbery and garden, a few minutes' walk from the post office in Balcombe.

He was now also a well-established radio actor, having followed Alexander the Great with his thunderous *Tamburlaine* (fee 30 guineas), *Chopin, Robert Browning, Axel, Eurydice, The Hawk and the Handsaw, The Homeless One of Europe* and ten episodes of *Portrait of a Lady*. There was still little television, and England had a culture, and a public broadcasting service, of which it could be proud. Paul loved radio drama, and no actor has ever been better at it. Asked to read a story for the Light Programme called "Local Yokel" in a strong Warwickshire accent, he wrote back to the producer, "It sounds delicious. It's just the sort of thing I love doing, and as you say is the perfect antidote to *Ring Round the Moon*. Yours, Paul (*il local yokelo Paolo*)."

He was beginning to be asked — a process that is to intensify — what parts he would like to play. "But what?" is his typical and gently self-effacing response. "I never can suggest parts for myself — a major failing."

By this time John Harrison sought to leave acting for directing.

> I sat in his dressing-room at the Globe one day sharing ice-cream between performances of *Ring Round the Moon* which was a colossal hit.
>
> "How can I help?" he asked.
>
> "Play in something on a Sunday?"
>
> He didn't hesitate.
>
> "What shall we do?"
>
> "Pericles."
>
> "Pericles, Prince of Tyre had been a pet project of mine for years."

Paul and Harrison went halves on all expenses. They booked the severely functional Rudolf Steiner Hall in Baker Street for two Sunday performances. Rehearsals lasted three weeks, mornings only in a church hall near the Marylebone Public Library, because Paul needed his energy for Hugo and Frederick.

All our friends were pressed into service. Peter Bull doubled the Pandar with Antiochus. Donald Sinden played a fisherman and press-ganged his brother Leon. Beatrix Lehmann was gloriously wicked as the Bawd. Daphne Slater doubled Thaisa and Marina, mother and daughter. Paul asked me to find a part for his *Ring Round the Moon* understudy, David Phethean, who made a sensitive Lysimachus. Boult was played by a friend we had made in Australia, Peter O'Shaughnessy, over in what Aussies still called "Home" to seek his fortune. Audrey Fildes, a colleague of Paul's in Ring . . . suggested her friend John Lindsay who brought a wondrous mesmerism to that very Alternative practitioner Cerimon.

And so on. The cast was rounded off androgynously by Mary Morris as a seductive, cross-dressed Gower/Chorus wearing a nakedly transparent gauze (a critic later said she was dressed like one of the naughty ladies in an Erich von Stroheim film).

"A lot of people don't know how to use rehearsal time," Harrison tells me. "In the 1940s and 1950s you didn't talk about the play. You never discussed it. It's not that Paul can't talk about it, he just felt it was an immense waste of time. As for warm-ups, Wendy Hiller once said to me, in her best Lady Bracknell voice, 'Warm-ups? Whatever for? I *arrive* warmed up.'"

Pericles, played without an interval, was an unqualified success. Both performances sold out, and the co-producers made a profit of £67. 71*s*. 3-1/2*d.* They threw a lavish party for their unpaid cast, and Harrison was launched on his distinguished directing career — later to include Paul in *The Tempest*, and Paul's first ever television play, *Henry IV* by Luigi Pirandello.

Henry IV was one of the few plays Paul ever suggested he would like to do on the radio: on the first occasion, to Val Gielgud, in August 1952, Gielgud rejected it as "perhaps a bit lofty." Other Paul suggestions define his taste — *Diary of a Scoundrel*, *The Idiot*, *Peer Gynt* — to which he added lightly, "I am well aware that none of these are strictly Light Programme!"

18

Interlude: The Rivals

(Baddie Number Two)

Scofield is now a star. He has, in Brook's word, "arrived." He is clearly identified and identifiable as the kind of actor he is. He is never to change yet he is to change all the time, because one of the mysteries of his acting is that he is never quite the same. Sören Kirekegaard, in his study *Crisis in the Life of an Actress*, wrote:

> There is one resistance against the power of the years, and that is perfectibility, which unfolds itself through the years; and there is another resistance to the power of the years, and that is potentiation, which precisely becomes manifest through the years. Both phenomena are essentially exceptions, and both have it in common that they become more exceptional with every year. Just because they are dialectically complex, their existence will also remain dialectical year after year. Each year will make the attempt to prove its thesis concerning the power of the year, but perfectibility and potentiation will triumphantly refute the year's thesis. This provides absolute tranquillity in the spectator, for . . . perfectibility and potentiation are absolutely dependable.

This passage may seem complicated. In this account, its meaning will, or so I hope, become clearer. It is the key to Scofield's consistency and longevity. It is part, but by no means the whole, of his secret.

Paul is compared to Laurence Olivier. Already in his twenties, he is identified as Olivier's "heir" and this comparison continues up to the present day. Many, as time goes on, come to believe he surpasses him. The two actors are, however, very different.

Paul's view:

Sir Laurence Olivier (sorry, Lord Olivier). I knew him very little, he was something of a mystery to me as a man; as an actor I admired him inordinately, his magnetism and prowess, his physical courage, his mastery of technical detail, his nerve; but I was not, on the whole, moved by him. I worked with him only as a boss, i.e. as the director of the National Theatre at the Old Vic. He never directed a play I was in, nor did we work together as actors, so I never had the opportunity of a working companionship with him.

In 1982, some two years after the death of Kenneth Tynan, whose dying wish (call it more truthfully a passion) was to write Olivier's biography, Olivier has just finished his autobiography *Confessions of an Actor*. He nearly split up from his then wife, Joan Plowright, who could not understand why he did not want Tynan to do his book, and why he wrote *Confessions*. Theirs was a stormy marriage, and she kept her distance. She did not admire the productions he directed. She could not work with them, she said, they were all frills, beautifully choreographed. She never desired to act with him. The opposite of Joy with Paul. George Devine had told Plowright, when she seduced Olivier away — or rescued him — from his tortured attachment to Vivien Leigh, "Marry him if you must, but do not act with him if you can help it." She never did, not on stage after *The Entertainer*. They did appear together on television in *The Merchant of Venice*.

Paul never acted with Vivien Leigh; she was perhaps alone in that respect among the well-known actresses of the era. He hardly knew her at all, but said she did have impeccable charm, as well as beauty. As an actress he considered her a miniaturist, and as such "contained her own integrity."

"The night I faced him about this thing," responded Olivier's third wife, Joan Plowright, to questions about *Confessions of an Actor*,

I said I'd go to my brother and get a lawyer. If that will make life easier then we'll do that [meaning, to separate]. Then he left notes all round the house saying he was going to kill himself. Then the next night I said, "Well, if I'm not going . . . to get a lawyer because I had this letter to answer, what was the purpose of it? Have you any method of explaining to me?"

We had a whole night with somebody at dinner, when he [Larry] said over the table, "If you were going to kill yourself, what method would you choose?" An entire dinner table of people having to fall in with this, and say they'd gas themselves, and on it went.

After that I said, "We can't go on and on like this."

"What reason, can you think of any reason?"

"Why didn't you tell me it was coming?"

He said, "Would you believe me if I told you I'd forgotten I'd done it?" That was on Wednesday. He must have met the lawyer on Monday. So, you find it hard to believe, but in his state of irrationality you think, "Well, either it's an excuse or it's the truth." And then he sat in there, hoarse-voiced, and said, "What's happening to me?" and he launched into a description of himself: "The fact is that I don't know who I am . . . I've played all these parts and I don't know who I am. I'm a hollow man."

I was very impressed, and then I realized he was quoting Bill Gaskill out of that book that Jonathan [Miller] brought his passage out of. I went berserk, I rushed to the book and saw, "He is a hollow man. He is sum and parcel of all the parts he's played." It wasn't him then, what I thought was rivetingly true. He doesn't even know that he's quoting, when he thinks he's being completely true. It was dreadfully true, and deeply convincing.

"Well, he was always acting other people's words," said Kathleen Tynan, widow of Kenneth and confidante in this dialogue with Joan Plowright, "Unresolved, a character that's somehow unresolved."

Plowright answered, "They go through this kind of accepting identities, on making identities. Creating them."

"Ken entirely invented himself."

"Yes, well, Larry still doesn't know who he is, or who he was, now."

Have we seen the great actor naked with his fear? Of something in himself, of which he is scared? There appears no such confusion of personality in Paul. At any moment. This is in itself a mystery. Why not? He does know who he is, and apparently always has. Does it make him a better actor? A worse? Or just a different one?

19

Gielgud Observed

So far all Paul's performances in London had been in costume plays, not so far distant from his three-year Shakespeare stint. He was hungry to play a contemporary character in a contemporary play. But now he had still another Shakespeare role before entering his own time, in John Gielgud's production of *Much Ado About Nothing*, when he was Don Pedro of Aragon, not perhaps such a luminous role, but it filled in time until he was due, later in 1952 and in 1953, to join Gielgud and Brook in several more productions.

Benedict was one of Gielgud's great parts; he had already played it in the revival at Stratford with Peggy Ashcroft, and now Diana Wynyard had taken over yet again the role she first acted at Stratford in 1949. Even in the role of Don Pedro Paul had no recourse to tricks and, unlike Olivier, was never one to galvanise a performance with impersonation.

During *Much Ado* Joe Mankiewicz, the Hollywood director, came to London with the express purpose of engaging Paul to play Mark Antony in his film of *Julius Caesar*. He saw Gielgud as Benedict and asked him to play Cassius. "But when Marlon Brando's tests for Antony arrived they were so successful that he was booked and Scofield never even made the test."

This is not quite true, Paul adds, the test "actually did take place. I had asked that Peter Brook should direct it, I got myself into the Roman gear . . . we shot the scene 'Friends, Romans,' etcetera, but no sooner had we finished than word came from Hollywood that Brando had already been engaged. So that was that. Disappointment of course — which didn't last very long. Brando was far better than I would have been."

In the summertime he and Joy moved to Edinburgh. Paul opened here in a Festival production of Charles Morgan's *The River Line* which, with a skip to the Lyric Theatre, Hammersmith, then a jump to the Strand, settled down to a long run. The director was Michael Macowen, and Paul played — to our millennium-tuned sensibility — the rather dull juvenile lead of Philip Sturgess, an American, who has escaped down the River Line, the route used by allied escapees through France. After the war he is reunited with one of his fellow users of the route and his wife, the former French agent who helped them. Sturgess is led to confront the truth that their comrade "Heron," whom they suspected of being a traitor who would betray the line to the Gestapo, and whom therefore they summarily executed, turns out to be the older brother of the delightful English rose Sturgess is intent on marrying.

An impressive if flawed play, much of it is intensely exciting, especially the flashback middle act in which the escaping group have, without his knowledge, to assess whether Major Lang or "Heron" is a "faux Anglais" or the genuine if eccentric British article. The characters are memorably drawn, especially Marie Chassaigne, the Madame of the Resistance cell near Toulouse, who is played by Pamela Brown, a magical and powerful actress whom Paul considers a genius. Morgan has a great gift of sympathy: "Hardness of heart," he writes, "is a sterilising sin in literature as in life," and the characters of the now forgotten but then highly influential author exemplify this.

Sturgess, seeking the truth, is appalled by what finally he finds out, that he and the group killed an innocent man. He does not know that the others, reunited with him in the first and last acts of the play, already know the truth — except for Valerie, Heron's sister, whom he now believes he cannot marry.

However, in the end, in some odd, mystical way, Valerie, who now discovers the truth, absolves Sturgess and the others on behalf of Heron, who anyway had a hand in creating their suspicions of him. "There is peace between us and him," she says.

Virginia McKenna, who had to suggest what the *Times* review calls "an intense, secluded grace," met the demand with "enchanting simplicity." But did the final scene of "extrication from a moral predicament" succeed or fail?

It is difficult to answer this, although *The River Line*'s progress from conversational opening, through the daringly conceived episode of the murder ("It has almost no duration at all, and is shattering in its effect," wrote Harold Hobson) to the challenging dilemma of the third act and its revelation, won even Tynan's grudging admiration as "incontestably the finest new play since *The Deep Blue Sea.*" Tynan upbraided Morgan, however, for avoiding direct statements like a saint avoiding Satan: "If Morgan were only less of a master, *The River Line* might be more of a masterpiece."

Peace, stillness, responsibility. Can the savagery of war ever find forgiveness in peace? These are eternal themes as well as especially affecting to an audience in 1952. They explain why *The River Line* attracted such a following. They strike a chord in Paul's heart and, although he clearly used his technical mastery to "earth" some of Morgan's more metaphysical flights, in January 1953, when he had by now left the cast of *The River Line* to open in another play, he told Morgan:

> I have been intending for a long time to thank you for giving me the opportunity . . . to come to grips with a real and true modern person, and to attempt to interpret your incredibly vivid portrait of a contemporary American. It was all the more exciting for me because I had previously only acted in Shakespeare and in plays that demanded a period style — so that to present a character of the same world as my own was a very thrilling assignment — and one that I never ceased to enjoy. These thanks are very inadequate but I want to try to express them.

"Mr. Paul Scofield finely transforms his own quizzically ironical personality into the personality of an ingenuous American resolved not to shirk responsibility for an error into which he has fallen unknowingly and acquiring spiritual stature as he penetrates the inner meaning of his problem," proclaimed the anonymous *Times* critic. Was it Charles Morgan, usually the *Times* reviewer in those self-effacing days when critics had not even a byline, never mind a smudged, ape-like jellygraph?

"Scofield, strained and intense, animated a part that might have been wooden," wrote Trewin, who was not a Morgan admirer?

Early in life Paul had settled into a pattern he was never to lose over the next fifty years. He is now thirty. He likes already to think of himself as "the actor anonymous." He is practical and realistic about his job. He is settled in Sussex, but says he has no time for gardening, much though he would like it. He arrives in Victoria by train every morning to do what he deliberately calls "my job."

Glamour is a trap if you go just for that. It does not develop the ability. At first when one starts acting one is really searching for an identity. Work is really the sole means of an education. I don't mean by that either you or I were not educated properly when we were at school. But perhaps the real knowledge that we have came afterwards, through our work.

When that realisation comes to an actor he has reached the crossroads. Either he becomes an actor of ego, or a worker. He has to choose whether it is the part that is important, and the effects he makes comes from one part, or whether it is his own personal glamour and style that is important.

The temptations of glamour seem strong when Paul leaves *The River Line* to join theatrical royalty, namely John Gielgud's company again at the Lyric Theatre, Hammersmith. Gielgud had just directed Ralph Richardson's disastrous Macbeth at Stratford and he now embarked on his own classical season of *Richard II*, followed by William Congreve's *The Way of the World* then Thomas Otway's *Venice Preserv'd*, a neglected tragedy that once held its own in popular estimation with *The Merchant of Venice* and *Othello*. Pierre, which Paul was to play, is the hero included by Lord Byron with the greatest Shakesperean characters: "Ours is a trophy which will not decay/With the Rialto; Shylock and the Moor/And

Pierre, cannot be swept or worn away./The keystones of the arch!"

Gielgud inimitably records:

> After Stratford I worked with Peter [Brook] again in my own sea-
> son at the Lyric Theatre, Hammersmith, in the year I was knight-
> ed, 1953. We had opened with *Richard II*. I decided I was too old
> to play Richard myself and rather regretted it afterwards — and
> followed with *The Way of the World* and *Venice Preserv'd* which Peter
> was to direct. I directed *The Way of the World* and *Richard II* in
> which Paul Scofield gave a fine performance, though I do not think
> I helped him very much. I was too aware that I had played the part
> myself and that I was not giving him a sufficiently free hand to
> develop it along his own lines. He is a very individual actor in that
> he seldom feels really confident in his performance until just before
> the first night. Peter Brook, who has worked with him a great deal,
> told me that in *The Power and the Glory*, in which he was to give
> such a superb performance, he came to life only at the last dress
> rehearsal when everybody was in complete despair and thought the
> play was going to be a failure.

Paul comments, "It would be difficult to 'come to life' in rehearsal
when you are playing Hamlet every night."

There is no doubt that Paul's Richard was strangely different from the
mellifluous, celebrated artist king of Gielgud fame (he had played the role
famously twice and did so again, once more and unhappily, on tour).
Memories of the director's interpretation overshadowed much of the critical response. But Paul's approach showed, as Peter Hall has said, the
warts and all — by deliberately failing to romanticize the role.

It was a well-considered performance, scrupulously phrased, and
backed by an appearance that was chilly, even prim looking. Paul was
intent on being different, but without being showy, or laddish, or neurotic, or with any of the fashionable attention-seeking tricks that many
might use:

As the King listens to the great dispute between Mowbray and

Hereford, while lending half an ear to the whispering of his painted favourites; as he sits in state before pronouncing the fatal sentence of banishment; as he stands for a while silent before old
Gaunt's upbraiding, the actor presents to us a mask of celestial
composure in which two half-closed eyes glitter with inscrutable
menace. One has the fancy that not only is this King, as is well
known, the most modern of Shakespeare's creatures, but that, by
some such mysterious process as that which the young American
underwent in *The Sense of the Past*, he is revisiting an age which
holds for him nothing but what he misunderstands, disdains, or
fears.

The preparation Paul put into the role was enormous: even those critics who disliked it admitted this. But they baulked at the solitariness
Richard displays, his pitiable sense of isolation that Paul captured
uniquely.

This was not a Richard who moves one, although when it came to the
deposition, Paul did release the audience from his detached vision. Some
attributed the restraint to the proscenium arch with its restrictive picture
stage as opposed to bare boards, although Paul felt at home: "This old
theatre was isolated amongst a sea of barrows selling vegetables, fruit,
flowers, the underground railway was clearly audible during performances and the auditorium had the most perfect acoustics." (The auditorium is, of course, now preserved inside the concrete shopping centre shell,
like an Aladdin's cave.) Others felt, echoing Gielgud himself — his tone
is barbed, watchful — that Paul was trapped, or at least confined, by
Gielgud's own habits, yet that when he obeys his own instinctive impulse
he became remarkably moving. When he tried to shape it to preconceived
notions he — only temporarily — lost his way.

In other words, judgement was strongly divided. Glitzy, vain, peacock Tynan, showing off like mad to "Dear Cecil" [Beaton] in cavorting
mood:

The theatre here had a blow between the eyes with John G's production of *Richard II* — all very stylised, kept under glass, and prettily gilded by that intricate Loudon Sainthill, but as cold and clammy as the estuary of the Ob. Everyone seemed to be sleep walking, even Scofield; and what [with] the doll's house miniatures of the sets, it was rather like listening to an oratorio on the theme of Larry the Lamb, King of Toytown . . .

In fact, the nicest theatrical event happened at Peter Brook's Christmas party, where Binkie sat slowly and squarely down on to (or rather into) a chocolate trifle which he mistook for a tablecloth, is a delightful tableau. As the papers say, he was sponged off by Alec Guinness.

Paul and Joy did not attend the party. Paul hated parties. Joy did, however, act with Paul every night, playing the Queen, and one critic found her perfect ("sorrow personified") but that Paul failed in pathos when saying goodbye to her. In lack of pathos, in particular, his interpretation differed from the usual. He continued to develop after the first night, as indicated in this letter from Charles Morgan:

When my wife and I came to Richard II last night, I deliberately did not come to your dressing-room, partly because I have the remnants of a bad leg which makes stairs difficult, but chiefly because I am always shy of dressing-rooms on great occasions. An actor may perhaps welcome cheerful visitors after a light comedy, but I find it difficult to believe that he really wants to be bothered with them after he has given as much of himself as you gave last night.

I shall not attempt an analysis of your own Richard because you are in the midst of it, you are, so to speak, still composing, and no artist wants to be messed about and interrupted while he is in the stream. I will only say gratefully that your structure of the character (I mean the development from non-sympathy to sympathy) completely held me, and that your set pieces (and I set great store by set pieces and hate them to be thrown away) were to me enthralling music. But what perhaps matters even more than this is that you so often gave me that rare shudder which marks for me the difference between the presence on the stage of a great actor and an actor of talent. It is hard to define, but the effect is that the rest of the stage, in some curious way, becomes transparent and the great actor emerges from it in a light of his own, and emerges in such a way that I know I am seeing and hearing at that moment that I shall always remember.

Although Paul was to be directed by Gielgud again straightaway in the notoriously difficult *The Way of the World*, it is Millamant here who is the main character, and she was played by Pamela Brown. Paul's Witwoud was straightforward, the perfect whinnying fop shrill with admiration of his own wit. He might have been playing the young Kenneth Tynan: "I confess I do blaze today, I am too bright." And Tynan ripostes, appropriately, that Paul's beautiful, gaudy performance is "pitched somewhere between Hermione Gingold and Stan Laurel."

Gielgud was a notoriously demanding director, quick to fire, ruthless and peremptory in sacking those not up to it. Paul comments:

His wit, often unconscious, is legendary; he speaks as he thinks, apparently without reflection, one can be shaken by his candour, and, though his one-liners are sometimes devastating, I doubt that anyone is ever hurt by them. He is full of heart. Richard II was perhaps, at that time, the role he was most honoured for, the play redolent with his style and his music; it must have been difficult for him to direct another actor who was using different tunes, and not as good, but his patience and generosity left its mark on me.

He is still at the heart of his profession, and for us, his fellow actors, and for his public, will always be so. [Written before Gielgud's death in May 2000.]

Paul deeply admired Pamela Brown, who died before the age of sixty, a lifelong sufferer, an ultimate cripple, from arthritis. No one, not even Olivier, has acted on stage with so many hauntingly beautiful, talented, and different actresses. But Pamela for Paul was unique. *The River Line* apart, she had already won acclaim in *The Lady's Not for Burning* and for the past two years, in London and in New York, had played little else. She had mortgaged, according to another admirer, "her body to pay for her art, and she was in great demand."

Michael Powell, the megalomaniac film director of such notable films as *Peeping Tom, The Red Shoes,* and *The Life and Death of Colonel Blimp,* was obsessed with Pamela. In the hundreds of thousands of self-intoxicated words he poured out about himself — some passages, one has to admit, very striking — he described Pamela as his witch, and sensual beauty incarnate.

Arthritis had killed her father, and from an early age it twisted her legs, toes, and fingers. She had only two toes of her right foot to walk on, while her fingers were, to Powell, like a mandrake root. She was tall, but the demon illness now spread to her left leg, which she had to drag.

In Fry's play on Broadway in its second year every performance became a struggle with death and disaster. In order to keep up with Gielgud ("the fastest speaker on the English stage. He never missed a cue, he never lost a line, he never slowed up for a second") during their eight weekly performances she took cortisone and gave herself diabetes. Only her dresser, said Powell, could have told how thin the line was between triumph and collapse.

Powell's wife commented, "I always thought there was a touch of the lesbian in Pamela," and Powell adds his weight to this remark. "All actors are continually experimenting and inventing with their hormones, their male and female genes, and a few have the luck to be evenly balanced between their sexual drives. Pamela was one of these. She was a witch — women adored her, men feared her, and for the same reason — she fascinated them." Similarly, Paul's more restrained comment to me is, "Absolutely fascinating."

Powell employed her four times, and his great ego pursued her into her bedroom about this time at 36 Soho Square. She was clearly a very vulnerable, even hysterical young woman, living between one hypodermic needle and another, protected by her agent, who was also her lover:

I said, "Where does that door go?" She said, "To the bedroom." I said, "Come on." We make love all night. She was a wonderful lover. Her skin was a delicate shell pink, and the hair on her body was as red as the hair on her head. Her great eyes glowed in the darkness like a cat's. They were so large that she claimed that she could always see almost directly behind her, and I think she could, as wild animals do. We could always make love whenever we wanted to, and we always wanted to. We were lovers until the day she died.

Well, maybe. Powell had already tried to cast Paul in *Gone to Earth*, released in 1952, starring Jennifer Jones, which was the first time Paul came into contact with David O. Selznick, the Hollywood producer, and Alexander Korda, who ran London Films. "Selznick thinks big, talks big, is big, but isn't quite as big as he thinks. To keep awake he sniffs Benzedrine, and to sleep takes sedatives." In fact, the stereotypical tyrant Hollywood producer, he had a tragic passion for his star, Jennifer Jones, and he was to say later of Paul, "This man is bigger than Burton and greater than Peck."

Contenders for the important role of Edward Chapman, the innocent Baptist minister, were James Donald, lean and knobbly, with a gift for making enemies, the saintly but highly alcoholic (and slightly old) Cyril Cusack — and Paul, who was by far Powell's favourite. He had learned already much about him from Pamela, who acted with him in *The River Line*. Powell wanted no squabbles or recriminations with Selznick, so he left the final decision to him:

I worked hard at the tests and played no favourites, but I must admit that I kept Paul's test until the last. When the lights went up there was a silence for about ten seconds. Then David said in a low mysterious tone to me, "Is he queer?"

I explained that Paul was not only not queer, but that he was married to a beautiful actress who had given up her career to devote her life to him and their children. David shook his head in disbelief. Exit Paul.

Paul commented later: "Jennifer Jones did the test with me. This was a rather eerie experience."

Powell further insisted — which is why I explore this incident, for even early on there is in Paul a deep resistance to films — that Paul must somehow be missing out. Is this patronising?

After saying he loved and admired Paul Scofield all his life, Powell went on: "I've always wanted to work with him, but never did, and now never shall. He was the most unusual of my choices, but it was the most perceptive. He has had a great career, has played many of the parts that he wanted to play, but I think that if he had played Edward in *Gone to Earth*, and Matthew in William Sansom's *The Loving Eye*, he would have become less remote to the average man and woman, and the public would have understood him better and loved him more."

In this second test, with Moira Shearer, and "as much in the dark as I was . . . we ran about a lot in a garden." Well, two years later, however, Paul was to become "a major screen discovery."

For the moment on stage, as Aquilina, the savage and sexy prostitute who is his mistress, and as Millamant, with her great liquid eyes full of disdain, Pamela was sharing, or flaunting herself, if only in make-believe, with Paul. She is, according to Emeric Pressburger, "the ugliest woman in the world" or the "most beautiful." She is a blaze of light, "blessed with a big voice, a magnificent chest, a long back and lovely legs, and lungs upon which she could strike organ notes. Her eyes were like two flames . . . " etc. Powell went well over the top, adding no wonder his friend Emeric hated her, because she was everything that he suspected about women. Only drugs could keep her going.

I ask Scofield further about Pamela Brown, who was underrated even then and is now largely forgotten. What I suspect is correct: there *was* a special affinity between them. Could it relate to that central mystery in Paul: "The emotions are real, but they aren't me." Was she not, in this respect, a mirror image?

A very remarkable and unusual person, undermined as she was by permanent physical disadvantages — diabetes and arthritis — a lot of pain always, and never a murmur of complaint, no sympathy required. No self-aggrandisement either: she had a luminous and wonderfully ironic sense of humour, she "sent *everything* up (rather a dated phrase); at the curtain-call of a play we were in together, she and I and two other leading players came forward for a special bow; 'Who do we think we are?' she whispered to me. She disliked any form of pretension, and if she ever deflated it, it was with a gentle, if lethal, humour. In performance, however, there was no self-effacement, she flared, like a torch." John Trewin referred to her "'blow-lamp" performance in *The River Line*:

> In life, she had traces of difficulty in walking, in her movement, barely discernible, but on stage, particularly in costume roles, had an ineffably graceful, sideways gliding motion. Quite fascinating, and very sexy. Her odd face was beautiful, wide bones and sloping contours and the most piercingly intelligent eyes. Off stage, on tour for instance, she was fun, observing everything, nothing escaped her — she was, not with vivacity, but with a certain inner bubble of perception.
>
> I miss her — you will have gathered that she was one of my favourite people.

Pamela did not receive good notices for her Millamant, who is "the play." She was charming, intelligent, coquette, she thought too much, and the exquisite barbing had too sharp an edge. Gielgud in his breathless style, like the headmaster at term's end, summed up: "In *The Way of the World* I could not find much to do with Mirabell and was haunted by the memory of Edith Evans' performances as Millamant, which was perhaps why I failed to help Pamela Brown, whom I loved and who had made such a great success with me in *The Lady's Not for Burning*. The success of the production was chiefly due to Margaret Rutherford's splendid Lady Wishfort."

Venice Preserv'd, Paul and Pamela's other play together, is a thrilling play, a "marvel," with two magnificent parts for men, like *Othello*. The text needed doctoring, but Brook was here again with Paul, and added a hair-raising production number or two (one was Pamela Brown's Aquilina flagellating her ancient "keeper," a senator).

Paul's voice, according to Derek Granger, a future Olivier biographer, had never sounded more darkly sonorous. Smouldering under a dark wig this was the "strongest, surest performance" (Tynan) Paul had given since he came to London. Browne, too, recaptured her fluent authority.

In reaction, perhaps, against his own Richard II, Paul had never shown himself more undeviatingly intense for a principle, while he and Gielgud (as Jaffeir), impulsive and too easily overwrought, played out a magnificent partnership:

Rationalizing their grudges, they become crusading revolutionaries — the process is not uncommon today. But Pierre is a cynic and a man of action. Jaffeir is a romantic and a man of feeling, and when one of his fellow-conspirators attempts to seduce his wife, the romantic in him subdues the rebel, and he betrays the plot to the senate. There is another motive for his treachery — his wife's fears for her father's life — but the key to it is private pique, masquerading as public-spiritedness. In the vacillations of poor, uxorious Jaffeir there is magnificent irony. The plotters having been arrested and condemned to torture, he wants desperately to atone. All he can do is to satisfy Pierre's plea for a quick death, and then to kill himself.

All reviewers united in admiration —

I can recreate scene after scene as in a picture gallery: the chiaroscuro of the conspirators' heavy-arched cellar; the senate enthroned against the darkly glowing depths, the distances of Leslie Hurry's set; a to-and-fro by the lagoon's sombre calm, the execution scene suggested without dolorous parade. Byronic lines I remember were of Venice not as revel of the earth and masque of Italy, but as the place where:
"Though all were o'er
For us re-peopled we the solitary shore."

Yet this was the only play in the Gielgud season that lost money.

During one performance of *Venice Preserv'd* Gielgud's knighthood was announced in the Coronation Honours List of the new monarch, Elizabeth II. "My Lord, I am not the abject wretch you think me," is Jaffeir's first line. It was greeted with an ovation of cheering and applause that lasted several minutes. I wonder if this was not a contributory factor, albeit small, when Paul's turn came to be asked, in Paul's decision not to accept a knighthood. This was the kind of recognition from which he instinctively recoiled. Never the actor before the part he plays.

20

Ring Artist Direct

At this moment in time the excitement of two great stage actors pitted against one another, as in the play *Two Shakespearean Actors* by Richard Nelson, would seem a thing of the past. The contests between rival players, the thrill, the danger, of naked, actual exposure with its unpredictability, such as one now celebrates daily in football, tennis and rugby, no longer happen on stage. It is a fact of life that the feat of great acting — playing a heroic role on the stage in front of a live audience — no longer commands the public excitement and attention it did. It should and ought to, but no longer does.

It is a further pointer to a regrettable decline that most West End theatres are filled with essentially an ersatz form, the musical, in which the scale of the human figure, the human component, is dwarfed by technical amplification and enhancement (the visual and sound effects, especially the use of the microphone and synthetic sound mixers). The technological certainty of powerful sound and lighting effects, and their sheer power to dominate audiences, have done much to kill off the immediacy of live theatre, its sensitivity, its immediacy and frail vulnerability. In football the player is still naked, unenhanced, and the contest remains gladiatorial. In the theatre the human protagonist, the actor, has largely been sacrificed. The musical star has a microphone, and carries electronic warning or cueing devices. She or he might not even sing "live."

As a result the isolated actor and actress have lost drawing power. No longer, or not nearly as frequently, do paying crowds go along just to see an actor or actress as they did Olivier, Gielgud, or Paul Scofield. Writing in the *Observer* in September 1989 when Paul was sixty-seven years old, the (appropriately) anonymous journalist of his profile concluded that he was "perhaps the last out-and-out heroic lead actor working in the British theatre." Someone empowered with a microphone and laser beams does not have natural authority, or convey danger. The thrill of many musicals, even the best such as *Chicago* or *Guys and Dolls* (the Royal National Theatre hit of its decade!) is that of artificially enhanced visual or aural stimulus, which is often sexual, derived from or shared with the pop concert, or cinematic special effects. There is overpowering impact, wonder perhaps, nervous excitement, but little contact from the performer loving and wooing his audience. What would we make of world-class footballers if they enhanced their skills in the eye of the spectator by carrying electronic tracking devices, or artificial limbs to increase the power and accuracy of their kicking?

So the human scale has been lost. Audiences have shrunk in a way similar to the shrinking congregations in churches. The greed and profit motive of the producers prevail. Kenneth Tynan, for all his faults, knew well and loved the gladiatorial appeal of the theatre. It existed in the days of the Funambules and the Grand on the boulevard du Temple in Paris immortalized in Marcel Carné's film *Les Enfants du Paradis*.

Football as a game has kept its rules — just about. Theatre, unfortunately, has lost its rules as codified in the sense of its tradition.

When Tynan saw Paul's first Hamlet he not only commented it was the "best Hamlet I have seen," but "I know there is now in England a young actor who is a bond-slave to greatness." Tynan sensed, in the early 1950s, a "fruitful theatrical conflict stirring between Paul Scofield the poet and Richard Burton the peasant." Alas, it was not to be. Paul had already turned down his first Hollywood offer: Burton having graduated with Romeo and Hamlet, had already headed off to California.

Paul was disappointed: he felt he belonged to the Burton generation. "Burton . . . was almost an exact contemporary of mine and we came together through Stratford and the Tennent management. I used to worry a lot that he'd get to *King Lear* before I did, but then he went off to Hollywood so very early and I suppose I was rather on my own after that."

There was to be no competition between Scofield and Burton as there had been a generation earlier between Olivier and Gielgud. Theatre is the art of the live human being in space, of man and woman commanding the attention of a particular group of people entirely through their own resources on a particular text. Its basis is word and gesture. Scofield as the actor exemplifies it, while Brook, as the director, has gone into exile in order still to practice it.

One of the elements Tynan promised himself when he joined the National, giving up his career as a critic, was that

> What we might see at this theatre was that drama should be re-established to the same level of eminence that it attained with the Greeks; that the theatre should be a place where great matters of public concern were presented . . . In these days, when the churches are empty, there is nowhere except the theatre where such matters can be properly debated as the Greeks debated them: matters of supreme conscience, of the highest level of importance, moral concern with great events and the motives behind them. That is what theatre is for.

Well, one good reason anyway.

In the next ten years Paul is to bestride a number of difficult and serious roles as a colossus (a modest one), treating each, which might represent an ultimate summit to another, as a mere stepping stone. There is perhaps the mighty peak lying behind the others to which he is directed, albeit sometimes not consciously. He brings to each challenge a nonchalance and an inevitability, as if like a traveller (to adapt the metaphor) he finds his own way there, inhabits it as his own for a while, and then, without regret, moves on.

For him, nothing, represents the ultimate because his work is not ego-fuelled. He shuns the advice of outsiders; he makes his own way, from within, and with his own resources. He is an old-fashioned theatrical vagabond, travelling light. "There are too many people," he says, "taking advice from agents and friends in this business. Never, never, never. It is fatal. You must work it out on your own."

"Special points to be noted with Scofield, Paul, CBE," ran a BBC Bookings Department memo, "Ring Artist direct with any bookings in the first instance, then ring Agent to discuss fee and send Contract to Agent." The CBE? "An honour without the romantic associations of knighthood and with a hint of hard work about it."

Frith Banbury was Paul's next director, and after a pre-London tour they opened Wynyard Browne's *A Question of Fact* at the Piccadilly Theatre. Browne was a distinguished figure of the now forgotten West End quality play that captivated audiences before the Royal Court and its more committed, kitchen-sink agenda drew attendances away from what is known as the "well-made play."

His *The Holly and the Ivy* had been an outstanding box office success three years before, and was now being filmed with Ralph Richardson and Margaret Leighton. Beaumont was convinced, as a result of Banbury directing *The Holly and the Ivy*, that no director could surpass him, and he was now one of the most sought after of directors.

When they meet, Paul was wary, I believe, of Frith. Here was someone who had followed a very different path. Frith was the most un-neurotic and well adjusted of homosexual men. He never "cruised," like John Gielgud or the much lesser known Denys Blakelock who was influential in that epoch. His background was moneyed and he enjoyed a private income. He belonged to an elite consisting of, among others, Peter Bull, Robert Morley, Pamela Brown and Richard Ainley. He "bought" his way into directing by obtaining an option on Wynyard Browne's first play, *Summer Smoke*, which he directed himself.

He was at ease with himself, and so remained. Homosexuality was, and always has been, tolerated in the theatre. While he was at pre-school his headmaster "interfered" with him and some of the other boys, but he admits that, instead of causing any trauma, it was one of the few things he accepted in his schooldays, as it was sanctioned by authority. Prayer, for instance, he hated, as it was directed by his nursemaid Goodie who, while he knelt, sat on his bed: "I'm afraid she had a smelly [lap], so I never liked saying my prayers." (Banbury was actually more graphic; Paul's comment on this quotation was, "Do we need to know what Frith said about his poor old nanny?")

His rejection of God and his love of the theatre was tied up with his rejection of his father, an admiral in the navy. He was a conscientious objector. Theatre was his passion, a limited faith, as it was for like-minded homosexuals such as Noël Coward and John Gielgud, both of whom much feted him and his productions.

Homosexuality much dominated the theatre, in particular, in the 1930s, and 1940s, through until the decline of Binkie Beaumont's empire. There was a feeling, I detect, towards Paul's talent and good looks, which came down in the end to "Why isn't he one of us?" or even "He must be one of us, and doesn't know it." Both of these suggestions or propositions are, of course, untrue, yet there was a certain barbedness, or wariness, say, in Frith's treatment of Paul, and indeed Gielgud's. The latter was reported as saying that Paul was "a sphinx," that he "won't open up, and you can't get close to him." Banbury himself has spoken of Paul as possessing a "wall" that you cannot get beyond. "You can only get so far."

My suggestion is that the wall, the obstruction, exists in the beholder, not the subject. The wall, the sphinx, existed in Banbury and Gielgud, who liked to imagine Paul was something else, something other than what they saw and heard — something they would perhaps have liked him to be, because, well, they could not believe such talent, something they would like to possess more (either themselves, or by proxy) could exist without an attachment, in some form or other, to their own values and lifestyle. (This is, on my part, pure speculation, but "And my feeling too," concurs Paul.)

Certainly, as impeccable in their professionalism as they are and were, it did not impede good working relationships in that restrained and hierarchical era. Paul was cast as Paul Gardiner, librarian, while Pamela

Brown played his newly wedded wife who confronts, with him, the discovery that, as an adoptee, his natural father was hanged for murder. This haunts him and, as he then finds out that his father at his trial was described as a psychopath and believing that criminal insanity is heredity, he tells his wife they cannot have children.

The play is an examination of the power of imagination. Browne in his preface writes:

> In Act One we see Paul Gardiner's imagination (and to a lesser extent the other characters) working as it were, in a vacuum, with only a single disturbing clue. In Act Two we see the imagination confronted by the facts, objectively reported in a newspaper; and in Act Three we watch the final confrontation of the imagination with truth. The message of the play (and to those who like a play to have a message, I admit, for once, that the play actually has one) is that only by imagination can we grasp the truth about our fellow men but that, if it is not to mislead us, imagination must be used with love and not with fear.

What is the startling *coup de théâtre*, or reversal? It is that Gardiner builds up a picture of his real as opposed to adoptive mother as a victim, impoverished and defenceless, but when he engineers for her to appear, which she duly does, in a superbly set-up entrance, Mrs. Grace Smith turns out to be "an extremely smart, middle-aged business woman, very self-possessed, obviously prosperous and successful. Her slightly common accent is camouflaged by real savoir-faire and humour."

The description could equally be applied to the actress who played her: a real star of the past, Gladys Cooper. "The effect of Grace Smith's entrance, already theatrical enough, must have been heightened still more by the charisma of the player," writes Charles Duff. Grace Smith really puts the cat among the pigeons. It was her husband's charm and power of invention that led him to being a con man — and the subsequent insecurity that brought his fall through murder, as he killed a girl who threatened to reveal his past to his wife. She, the wife, finds Paul Gardiner just the same, while we, as audience, have seen, in his fears, his self-denigration, and distrust, the same destructive imagination at work, misusing his gift to destroy his marriage.

What you have in common with Ron is something good — or it can be. It's all a question of how you use it. Ron became what he was because he was more talented than other boys of his kind, not less. He was gifted like you are. But his gift destroyed him. All along the line, imagination was his downfall. Don't imaginative boys here, at this school, pose and pretend and put on acts? Of course they do. But it doesn't matter. They're safe here till it's all over. But where was he at fourteen? A page-boy in a West End hotel . . . Out in the world, you know, that sort of adolescent posing and pretending doesn't take long to become delinquency, false pretences — crime.

The overall budget for this production was £2,000: only £140 was set aside for publicity. Pamela Brown received a weekly salary of £80, Gladys Cooper £100, and Paul was on the official top salary of £75. All three earned a small percentage of the box-office gross which, given the fifteen week pre-London tour of every major city including Dublin, and then its 332 performances at the Piccadilly, yielded a considerable return.

After his fashion, as described by Brook, Binkie Beaumont contrived, by elaborate machinations, to have 20 minutes cut during the opening week in Oxford. This was initiated and announced by Wynyard Browne himself. Binkie pretended to be aggrieved at the usurpation of his authority (he had previously wined and dined Dido Milroy, the costume supervisor who then had lobbied playwright and director).

Banbury reports the success of *A Question of Fact*'s success with public and critics alike: "I cannot see you getting that sort of cast in the theatre now. By that I mean you wouldn't get the supporting actors. They would only do parts of that length on the box for much more money, without having to go and do them eight times a week. We, in the theatre now, do have a terrible problem."

Paul Scofield was "marvellous," said Banbury, "his imagination so strong and playing on his own ambiguous personality. Pam Brown brought to a part that perhaps didn't have all the character that it might have had, enormous character."

Paul gained positive inspiration from Gladys Cooper. She was what he called "an athlete."

> She loved swimming — Edith Evans had even called her beauty "the real thing, straight out of the bath" — on stage she suggested complete fitness, and health of body, mind and spirit; relaxation and moment-by-moment enjoyment. She was in psychological jargon "centred." For all the talk of her casualness of approach her attitude seems that of the absolute professional. She had no time for Arty Talk, and some considered her a philistine, but acting had originally been a means of putting her legendary beauty to sensible use and she had learnt how to do it with thoroughness. And with the minimum of fuss.

Paul found her always "there" on stage, sensitive to variations of pace or unexpected change.

No dissenting voices were heard about Paul's acting of the central role, summed up by the *Times* critic, who said: "Mr. Scofield treats the hero's perplexity with delightful finesse, allowing a possible tell-tale streak of harshness to peep through a character which is obviously capable of being touched finely to fine issues and has also a great capacity for taking boyish fun."

Trewin was more specific, calling Paul "splendidly right": "Few can look backwards as he does; each crack in his questing voice seems to be another loophole upon the past. It was frightening to watch the man, perplexed in the extreme, as he sought reassurance, allowed his fancy to seek forbidden paths. There were moments of taut emotion that reminded me, without irrelevance, of the lines from a Sussex poem, 'See you our still woods of oak, and the dread ditch beside.' Scofield is an actor as English as his Sussex home."

One can hardly recognise the brooding American of *The River Line*. During May of the previous year, while Paul was in *Venice Preserv'd*, Morgan diligently persuaded Paul to appear in his new play, *The Burning Glass*, giving him a choice of leading roles, but hoping he would choose the role of Christopher instead of Paul's stated preference of Tony Lack: "I wrote the part *loose* and without extreme emphasis because what I was aiming at was the very special excitement which sometimes happens in the theatre when a part, which has not been theatricalised by the drama-tist, is given glow and life by the individuality of a deeply imaginative actor — namely you."

But now Tynan, the Brummie bourgeois rebel, was beginning his campaign to drive the middle-class audience out of the theatre: drama *had* to have a serious social purpose. He picked on Wynyard Browne. He became Tynan at his worst: "I had been promised a skeleton and I got Gladys Cooper." He attacked playwright and director, although both, like him, were socialist pacifists: "He might never have become a full-time dramatist at all had it not been for the enterprise of a private patron, who was sufficiently impressed by his first play, *Dark Summer*, to put the author under contract until he turned out another. The result was *The Holly and the Ivy*, another success; and now we have *A Question of Fact*. All these were directed by the patron himself, Frith Banbury."

Paul recalls *A Question of Fact* in terms that lean towards Tynan's view as:

> A gentle domestic play with the dear old theme of lost and found mother and son — it had charm and humour and for me was chiefly memorable for the opportunity to work with Gladys Cooper, whose power as an actress was often blurred by her previ-ous reputation as a golden girl and consequently somewhat under-estimated. The women in that play were incredibly strong, the magic Pamela Brown played my wife and an exquisite actress, Mary Hinton, her mother. I think the play was memorable for me because in it I worked with these artists — but the play itself had

integrity without real power — a cosiness perhaps, but beguiling in
its sincerity.

During what is, by the above account, this untaxing commitment,
Paul was filming. This was his first film role, that of Philip II of Spain,
the long-ruling despot and consort of an English Queen, who launched
the Armada against England. *That Lady* was based on Kate O'Brien's
novel mainly about the one-eyed Princess of Eboli (played by Olivia de
Havilland). It was filmed at Elstree and towards the end of shooting
Darryl Zanuck, the production chief of 20th Century-Fox, was so
impressed by the rough cut he ordered more scenes to be written. "This
new man has a great future, but there is not enough of him. Build up his
part and we can make him a real star." At another time Zanuck said of
That Lady: "That actor! The best I have seen since John Barrymore."

Two new scenes were duly supplied, both with Vasquez, the chief
royal courtier, played by Dennis Price. Scofield plays Philip at the end of
his reign wearing make-up "like eroded marble. The eyes seem to need
descaling, the voice itself is dusted over, and he walks with the gingerly
foreboding of the acutely arthritic. Yet he remains every twisted inch a
king."

> *That Lady* was my first film, *Carve Her Name With Pride* was my
> second. While filming both I was also playing in the theatre at
> night, and for matinees. I was so busy that I remember little —
> Olivia de Havilland, in the first, was my first experience of a
> Hollywood star — I had had no idea they were so all-powerful.
> Especially the ladies. When filming *A Delicate Balance* [from
> Edward Albee's play in 1973] with Katharine Hepburn, she once
> delivered a clear ultimatum as to procedure, she was addressing
> most of those of us also in the cast. Joseph Cotten, with a distinct
> twinkle, replied, "Whatever you say, Katharine." I think that that
> was the way it was.

Paul was chosen by the British Film Academy as "the most promising newcomer to films in 1955," while an influential critic called his Philip II "one of the small gallery of classic screen portraits."

Who can remember Paul's role of Prince Troubiscoi in Jean Anouilh's *Léocadia*, one of his *pieces roses*, translated as *Time Remembered*? Few I think, yet it again, sustained by Paul, with Margaret Rutherford and a new actress, Mary Ure, who was decorative, cool, self-possessed and had a talent for comedy, enjoyed a substantial run. Anouilh held sway. First in Hammersmith, then in the West End. *Time Remembered*, a frivolity of fascinating theatrical expertness, was a more than usually thin piece of work from the master of fragile artifice. Brook said of Anouilh that, unlike so many playwrights who write plays that are animated novels, he was in the *Commedia dell'Arte* tradition. He preconceived the accidental and called it an impromptu. He was a poet, but "not a poet of words . . . a poet of words-acted, of scenes-set, of players-performing."

21

The Actor As Writer

Undoubtedly, as I view it now — and from an examination of the evidence in all available sources — Hamlet was Scofield's ideal role. Retrospectively we can with some assurance call Scofield one of the best, if not the best, of 20th century Hamlets. Although capable of great passion Scofield is not first and foremost a passionate, stormy, emotional actor. In Shakespeare, Mark Antony, Romeo, Henry V are not his parts.

For Shakespeare himself *Hamlet* was not a passionate play in which he, as a writer, discharged a whole incubus of stored-up feeling: it was circumspect, controlled, beautifully organised (but also flawed); it was also literary and explorative of ideas and motives in the way of a novel.

Hamlet the playgoer would never have applauded *Hamlet* the play. It is too complex. Even complicated. The character fails to find a reassuring simplicity in himself. "Hamlet is only interesting," says Peter Brook, "because he is not like anyone else, he is unique." He rages through every kind of style: obscene, cynical, choric, sublime; he can pass from scorn and ironic incongruity to soul-searching meditation with effortless ease. Can any great actor have been better prepared for the many facets of Hamlet than Paul, on the record of his experience alone? Is anyone ever likely to be so well prepared again?

The pseudo-insanity is both real and assumed: comedy always exists in potentiality (a special Scofield quality), breaking out sometimes in the darkest moments; Hamlet's cutting wit, his cunning and boldness, his almost supernatural gifts of perception of both himself and others — all belie the Romantic myth foisted on him by Goethe and later Romantics, who sentimentalized his goodness to suit their own feelings and needs.

Shakespeare created Hamlet's appeal through his strength as a dramatic character, in which even his victimized traits have their rich and differentiated quality. In this particular *Hamlet* is a joyous play, written by a happy man who in no way felt trapped by the feelings and preoccupations, or even the darkness, he uncovered.

W.B. Yeats noted in verse, correctly, that "Hamlet and Lear are gay" — expressing joie de vivre, gaiety. This is not to assert that Shakespeare had not himself felt and explored the play's darkness and its suicidal moods. But the way in which he depicted them, with such generosity, amplitude, and underlying stability, made audiences secure in their contemplation, as he was himself so that, ultimately, the effect of the tragedy affirms life instead of denying it.

Hamlet has met his match in Paul. More than any other great actor Paul approaches his roles as a writer. He is closest of all to a creative writer building a character. Not as a critic analysing; not as an interpreter layering on the part psychological interpretations such as Freud or Jung might have done. Shakespeare made Hamlet's crime incidental to his perturbation of mind and soul: the accomplishment of the revenge theme is secondary to the exploration of character. The gaps, the delays in action, are caused primarily by Hamlet's need to find himself, by Shakespeare's desire for an answer to the problem of the melancholy man, the new, pre-eminent type of young man of his day. As much as being a study of a specific prince in a court, and an exploration of the primal family with the curse of Cain upon it, Hamlet is a tragedy of reflection — but also a study of genius in crisis.

Judging by what we have already seen of Scofield, is anyone — can anyone be? — more suited to tackle the complexities of this character? His acting is to bring a second time to Hamlet its absolutely personal structure of rhythms, its own instinctive meanings.

Brook was Paul's director again and they had taken the Phoenix Theatre for the London exposure. First they had the tour: they became ambassadors, for they were to be the first British theatre company to visit Moscow since the Revolution of 1917; but also, probably, the first and only company to include Moscow in a pre-London try-out.

Paul was now a joint director of Peter Brook's new venture. "We were supposedly joint director and we used to 'consult,' but with Peter that meant he decided what to do and I agreed. I have no taste for power, but that was thirty years ago [he recalls this in 1977] and the money involved was so much smaller. In those days it never occurred to me that I was going to be a leading man: I just kept getting these rather good parts because everyone else was old enough to be away at the war."

He was to bring all the leading men from his intensely packed young career into play on tackling this summit of leading roles. Yet he had the unique capacity to leave space around himself, around the words: none of his performances was ever crowded. Brook has also said how Paul has in large measure the capacity to leave this space around himself, and equally the quality of resonance, so that "On a simple word like 'might' he will pause, stirred in some mysterious inner chamber, and his whole nature will then respond."

Brook directed this *Hamlet* as a master. As a director who overtly took pleasure in the sexual side of life his Ophelia was no gentle innocent, no wan pre-Raphaelite maiden, but now the sexually forward, if cool, Glaswegian who had had a Quaker education. Tony Richardson, who was to direct her in *Look Back in Anger*, thought she retained a puritan disapproval of performance.

Mary Ure's beauty was to lead her into an Ophelia-like existence of being the foil for the egocentric personalities of John Osborne (she played the first of Jimmy Porter's wives and she married Osborne in July 1957. "She never loved John or knew who he really was") and Robert Shaw. She was to die in the end from illness caused mainly by heavy drinking. Richardson believed that she never much liked acting. As a strong performer she slid easily into a note of harshness.

As Ophelia she was beautiful, with thick, blond hair, sensual lips and body. She was, to Richardson, the first Ophelia who seemed really deranged and therefore believable. Both she and Paul looked perfect romantics, but deromanticized their parts.

In spite of being condemned by most critics as miscast, "a poor reward for her triumph in *Time Remembered*," Ure was offered a film contract by Alexander Korda during the run at the Phoenix. Polonius was Ernest Thesiger, Claudius Alec Clunes, and Gertrude Diana Wynyard. Clunes was formidably attractive, the smiling damned villain except in what he does. Brook's direction was swift, as swift as thought itself, it moved like the wind.

Any *Hamlet* is bound to face a house divided, for as in our key conception of Shakespeare himself, the part, the man, Hamlet also inevitably finds some reflection of ourselves. "What man is living who can present before us all those changing and prismatic colours with which the character is invested?" pronounces Mrs. Curdle in *Nicholas Nickleby*. The most zealous Hamlet-watcher of the 20th century pronounced, "The test of any Hamlet is what remains with us long afterwards when there has been time for reckoning and retrospect . . . After thirty years I have not met a performance less externalized than Scofield's, able to communicate suffering without emotional pitch-and-toss; he had that within which passeth show."

Scofield went at once to the heart. Emotion is not fabricated to fit the words. His urgency is remarkable: "Mother, for love of grace, lay not that flattering unction to your soul." He took you through Hamlet's mind, marked by such hopeless longing in crying out "Father!," his anguish in "O cursed spite!," his homage to Horatio, given with quiet urgency; in the closet scene he inclines his head to rest on Gertrude's shoulder — "When you are desirous to be blest, I'll blessing beg of you," his tenderness, hopeful yearning for Ophelia's good — in these and many other observations Scofield pointed up the affirmative, noble, joyous, if tormented soul.

His repentance, "I do repent," over Polonius's body was deeply heartfelt and affecting, his "if it be now, 'tis not to come" — the growth to maturity, the acceptance of responsibility — assertive of balance, of normality, "maybe Scofield's for history. With his rifted voice, one that can bring an image of light diffused and fretted against a broken classic column [he] has been essentially the man . . . Nowhere has the Hamlet that I know — and can but speak for myself — rise from the text more poignantly." John Trewin's judgement of 1955 remained firm and the same in 1990, after seeing over ninety other Hamlets.

Hamlet opened in Brighton where it played for a fortnight; then to Oxford, Birmingham (a month), then to the Moscow Art Theatre or, to call it by its full title, the Affiliated House of the Moscow Academic Art Theatre in the Name of Gorky, with its famous embroidered seagull on the curtain, and where its feted exposure was wedged incongruously between the Alexandra Theatre, Birmingham, and Shaftesbury Avenue. Brook considered the seagull of Moscow a symbol of the tour: "We never touched ground."

The company was greeted by leading Russian actors and producers bearing chrysanthemum bouquets. They rushed enthusiastically out on to the airport tarmac and everyone shivered while emotional speeches were exchanged in Russian and English. Paul was welcomed with a kiss by Galina Pashkova, Moscow's latest Juliet. Later they were fed on caviar and sturgeon and beef steak; Paul and Joy were settled down in their hotel in an "anachronistic suite, looking like a page from *Anna Karenina*."

For Paul the trip out to Moscow passed in an excited but exhausted blur. He had driven from Birmingham after the last performance to Sussex, then, after a fitful sleep, to Heathrow. He was expected to speak to the TV cameras and mumbled "some inept words about our historic expedition."

> Arriving at Moscow Airport from East Berlin on a snowy evening, we were aware of a blaze of light outside the plane, peering out we could see nothing but this brilliant dazzle. Hugh Beaumont, who was travelling with us, marshalled us into order for our exit/entrance. Me first, very nervous but excited, then the beautiful Diana Wynyard, cool and composed, then Alec Clunes [Claudius] followed by the entire cast.

Paul created a precedent: he had brought Joy with him as his female dresser. "I don't know much about the job really. But perhaps I'll manage an occasional night off to see another play," she told a reporter. But mainly Paul's dresser was the elderly Galia, "a grandmother wonderfully maternal and reassuring."

They found no hoardings with star billing around the theatre, only small, dignified bills announcing the play. On the first night there was not a single evening dress, yet the excitement and enthusiasm were intense, the jostling crowds outside huge, the newsreel lights blinding for the arriving dignitaries, diplomats, and Soviet theatrical hierarchy. Inside, the Union Jack and the Hammer and Sickle flag hung side by side on opposing boxes. In the front row of the stalls sat Olga Knipper-Chekhova, Chekhov's 86-year-old actress widow: frail, white-haired, and reverently welcome, she was still on the acting list. The English cognoscenti had turned up too. Kenneth Tynan, for instance, who took a good look at the Moscow theatre and came away with respect for the large choice of 150 plays and for the securely employed (and often ancient) actors in the established companies like the Moscow Art. The city reminded him of America without the neon, and he bemoaned the lack of it, "symbol of salesmanship and hence of ingratiation." On the whole he found he missed "the *pizzicato* of the spirit, the relaxed gaiety which makes work worthwhile."

Tynan found merit in Moscow, which his wife Kathleen skirted over in her biography (the cold war is still on, she wants to flatter the American reader, though Paul says, "There was just then a thaw which was the trigger for our being invited. But that is Kathleen Tynan's mistake"). Tynan was more enthusiastic.: "In Moscow age is a badge of merit, and there is time for certainty and for perfection . . . the masters play together as Stanislavsky taught them and as they can still teach the world."

Although Tynan was fairly cynical about the production ("Why join a chorus of general praise?" might be given as Tynan's motto) he nevertheless wanted to register what the audience felt on the first night. He began by describing how beforehand there were national anthems, formal speeches, one from the latest *Hamlet* director, a reply in Russian from Brook.

> The audience reactions were immensely revealing. Accustomed to constant changes of scenery, they were baffled when the curtain rose again and again on the same grey permanent setting. Nor, in a theatre where doubling is unknown, could they comprehend why so many members of the cast were playing more than one part apiece. During the interval one critic expressed his delight at the subtle stroke of interpretation whereby the same actor played the Player Queen and the Second Gravedigger, and I had not the heart to tell him that the reason for this was not theatrical invention but economic necessity. Some of the older Russian actors were shocked at the speed with which the verse was spoken. "Cinema technique!" moaned one. "Is Shakespeare not allowed to draw breath in Britain?" The admiring comments made by many people on the relative cheapness of the production must, I imagine, have fallen rather brutally on the ears of the producer, Hugh Beaumont, for it was one of the most costly shows he had ever backed. Physically, the acting looked wooden and inexpressive beside the rich mobility of Russian players; but if the audience thought so, it kept its counsel, and the applause at the end was long and stormy.

There were nearly twenty calls when the curtain came down, and for a quarter of an hour the clapping grew more and more rhythmical in its enthusiasm: the company responded finally by clapping the audience. "I spoke a few halting Russian words," Paul tells me.

There had been one incident: a photographer, who has been banned from taking pictures by the management, set up a tripod just before Paul was due to deliver a soliloquy in the first act. Brook left his seat, took camera and tripod out of the auditorium, to fling them down the corridor. "This was a brave thing to do — I still feel gratitude for Peter's determined action."

Brook later commented: "I have now discovered something in common between the Soviet Union and the United States — the behaviour of their photographers." Otherwise the audience was praised as wonderfully attentive: "It seemed to hold them and they moved with it."

In subsequent reviews the *Daily Mail* critic, Cecil Wilson, was to call Paul's performance "finely tempered" in its strength. *Pravda's* critic congratulated Scofield on seeing Hamlet as a positive, dynamic hero rather than as a pessimistic weakling. The director of the Maly Theatre called it a "three-octave performance."

There was a reception at the British Embassy afterwards, given by Sir William Hayter, the Ambassador. Paul, always miscast as a fêted star at a party, and desperate for a glass of water, took a great gulp of a colourless liquid he found in a jug, only to experience a searing sensation in his throat: vodka.

He responded gratefully to the warmth of the Russians, and during the fortnight they were there they were besieged by autograph hunters, televised, photographed, and he earned the nickname of the Johnny Ray of Moscow; he was filmed playing a scene as Hamlet in English with a Russian Ophelia in Russian, likewise Mary Ure with a Russian Hamlet. Apart from official presents Paul received from fans "a wallet, a penknife, and from one girl, a photograph of her cat and dog." On his return to London he promptly received his CBE — too quickly, it would seem, to be turned down. At the investiture he was asked by the young Queen, daringly attired in a blue lamé frock with elbow-length sleeves and a mink bolero, about the Moscow visit. "They were very hospitable and they seemed to enjoy the play very much. We got the impression they knew the play well, and they seemed to understand the English better than we expected."

It was a turning point, Paul recently tells me, although "turning points never reveal themselves at the moment of their happening, so it is difficult to assess their gradual influence."

It was my first encounter with an audience who spoke another language, and Russian people have very particular qualities; they have stupendous warmth and immediacy of contact and understanding; as theatre-goers they embraced wholeheartedly the performance of a play with which they were familiar but had never had the opportunity to see and hear in its original language. They followed effortlessly every nuance of our performance, in terms of artistic endeavour and human compatibility they made the great ideological divide between Eastern and Western Europe seem unimportant. It was an experience of kinship. The breaking down of barriers and an awareness that we are none of us as our political leaders proclaim us to be.

He vividly recalled the many receptions they attended after the performances: "This was truly exhausting, but made possible by the unfailing kindness and openness and generosity of our hosts. It is the custom in Russia on such occasions to raise your glass and say a few words. In this I speak for myself, our hosts were not so economical, they made speeches, long speeches, wonderfully articulate and practised, very spontaneous and emotional — a standard of eloquence difficult to match. And the tiredness of which I have written melted away in the warmth of these occasions."

The Moscow *Hamlet*, as it is now known, chalked up 124 performances at the Phoenix, the third-longest unbroken run in English stage history. As all those 124 performances were different — some deeply assured, some leaning towards a tentative probing, or recalling the part, some asking the way, some showing it — I balk at the critics' first-night judgements. "We were not at our best. We did feel something of an anticlimax."

Some mourned the passing of the younger, 1948 Hamlet: others felt he lacked the daemonic, brutal quality of the Renaissance man. Tynan found the outline of the role "impeccable" but that the filling-in, the "brushwork," was crude. This contradicted other views that it was too measured, too carefully studied.

Paul is an actor for audiences, and with his Hamlet, as with virtually all his theatre roles, he established a special bond. In 1999 I find a small leather-bound notebook in which Kenneth Tynan had jotted down anecdotes about Olivier for the biography he hoped, just before his death, to write. It is hard to decipher, scrawled in almost illegible pencil by an emphysema sufferer whose handwriting has become decidedly wobbly.

Oddly enough the note was about Maggie Smith and it ran roughly as follows: "She [M.S.] said of Scofield that *he* has the quality I [Tynan] see in her: When he comes out on the stage you sit back . . . and you feel that it's all going to be all right from now on. He's in complete control so you don't have to worry."

This was what the public above all warmed to and applauded in Paul's Hamlet and why they filled the theatre upwards of 200 times (including the earlier performance). Here is the most complex, difficult role, the most famous in history, and here was the actor who put you at your ease with it, made you sit back and reassured you as he revealed all the character's different facets. Half of the enjoyment is Hamlet's self-torture; the other half is Scofield's pleasure and composure. You are in safe hands.

Hamlet has met his match. Now Scofield has done it, he will never repeat it. He above all applauds his Gertrude and how their mother-son rapport grows during performances: so much for the "discovery" by Freud of the Oedipus complex that some latter-day critics claim Freud owed to Shakespeare.

> Diana Wynyard's Gertrude was definitive I think, she had beautiful maturity, in the best sense of "maturity," she played the "mother" but her Gertrude did not convince us that she was genuinely maternal — she was distracted by her infatuation with Claudius and filled with guilt by her swift desertion of her husband's memory. She was also very much a Queen, so that it crossed one's mind that she also needed that pre-eminent position, needed to remain close to the source of power. She was lovely to work with, and our relationship as Hamlet and Gertrude was troubling, though not, I repeat not, incestuous — except to the extent that mother and son can often be drawn to each other in a way that they would not recognise.

This is all, or most of it — retrospective and with hindsight. The actor himself is working through, but looking forward with part of his mind to the interval, the scene change, the moment he can leave, rush off, catch the train from Victoria to Haywards Heath. Get back to exercising the dog, baking bread or sitting by the Aga. Cut himself down to normal size with comments from wife and family, reveal an ache or pain, or something broken. The balance he had achieved was extraordinary, the two sides in harmony, creating no friction, at least as far as we are able to judge.

Here as elsewhere I write sometimes in the present tense as a means of registering if possible, what it is like to be in his shoes, to be at his rehearsals and on stage, giving one after another of 124 performances as the Prince of Denmark.

22

Paul in Grimland

He was playing Hamlet at night and Brook was rehearsing him in his next role, that of the Whisky Priest in Graham Greene's *The Power and the Glory*. The part of the humble Mexican whisky-sodden priest attracted him greatly, Brook observed during rehearsal, and although in his imagination he saw the character with absolute clarity, somehow "this never descended into his body."

Paul had to struggle day after day with one hurriedly written scene, with its threadbare and inadequate lines. Towards the end of rehearsals Denis Cannon, the adaptor, became conscious of this weakness and brought them a new version that was infinitely better. Paul and Brook were delighted, but after they have tried it out Paul shakes his head. "I have now found all the strands that lead me from one line to another in the old version. These fibres now exist and through them I can make the old pattern real. The new scene is better, but it won't be as good to play."

Even so, during the last performances of *Hamlet*, as they drew near to the end of rehearsals, the writer was desperate, Brook grew alarmed, even Paul was worried — "the alchemy of his secret art was failing, and he could not even achieve a convincing external imitation of the part." (Paul, however, later dismisses this: "Don't understand this, I was not worried, I knew that I could not physically be the priest until I'd finished playing Hamlet, which was the Sunday dress rehearsal in Brighton after the last Saturday night. Then I changed my appearance. I always knew this would be so. It's inconceivable to me that 'they,' Greene, Brook, et cetera, couldn't perceive this. Perhaps to them Hamlet no longer mattered.")

Something is blocking his normal process, and neither of them can discover what it is. *Hamlet* closed on a Saturday and they were due to open the new play on Monday, two days later.

"Did you know Greene?" I ask Paul.

"I got to know Graham rather well, a reserved man. I liked him — he was often present at rehearsal. I remember he was concerned that I might look too 'romantic' as the Whisky Priest, but since I was still playing Hamlet at night I couldn't help feeling he was being a little short-sighted."

Brook was more and more worried. "I spent Sunday in the auditorium with the sets and lights, preparing for the dress rehearsal." Paul seemed unconcerned and Paul went straight to his dressing room, where a barber had been called in to cut off the splendid, romantic Hamlet head of hair.

They were seated in the stalls. Greene, Denis Cannon and Brook. The curtain rises on a seedy wharfside shack. Through a window they glimpse a rusty steamer, a polluted river, a Mexican sky. In the foreground a dentist is pulling out a peon's tooth.

At the back of the set the door opens. A small man enters. He wears a black suit, steel-rimmed glasses and carries a suitcase. They gasp. Brook said,

For a moment we wondered who this stranger was and why he was wandering on to our stage. Then we realised that it was Paul, transformed. His tall body had shrunk, he had become insignificant. The new character now possessed him entirely. The obstacle had been his, or rather Hamlet's, noble head of hair. All through rehearsal his actor's instinct had told him that something was wrong [to which Paul emphatically says, "No!"], that the image he was carrying was false; intuitively he sensed that his silhouette was the antithesis of the role. It took only one lightning glimpse of his shorn head in the mirror for all the thoughts and feelings he had accumulated over the weeks instantly to be distributed to the right places inside him for him to discover the person he had been seeking in vain.

Scofield explains,

I had cut off all my Hamlet hair and appeared with a sort of bedraggled, dyed-black crew cut — no more was said. Greene was not optimistic, I think, as to a successful outcome for this production, and Peter Brook also had his doubts. The actor, however, cannot have doubts, and is thus more philosophical and fatalistic — in the event we had a huge success with this strange, wandering and tormented play. And Graham was pleased.

Paul explained at another time the freedom he felt in Greene's character, for it was a very episodic book:

The diffused structure allowed me to wander with it and to find a kind of freedom from being too bound by technical precision. Within the security of the character I could do anything. It was like improvising, except that I'm not an actor who can improvise without a script. It was like life. I was free to respond to suggestions and influences from other people.

I think I found at that point that effective acting wasn't what I wanted to do, that I didn't want to make effects, that I wanted, as it were, to leave an impression of a particular kind of human being or create an atmosphere in a scene which an audience would take or leave to a certain extent as it wanted to, but not to be too definite, not to say that this is what this person's like, this is this kind of man, this is what this story means — never to say that.

The wonder to subsequent play-goers was that Paul showed himself as such a brilliant character actor. A "superb performance," Gielgud abruptly dismissed this performance, with, a few lines later, "I begged Brando to play Hamlet." Actors (exception Scofield) are envious as well as mimetic creatures. Olivier, the supreme actor of effects, sees Paul's Whisky Priest several times. In a single reference to Paul in his *Confessions* he called the performance one of his favourites: "The evilly catalystic

Peasant, digging into the Priest's inner life, asks him if he has any children and in his fascinatingly chosen Birmingham accent Paul, in a way I have never been able to forget in twenty-five years, replied. 'Ovva dawtah.' In 1963, on 10 January, to my incomparable joy, I was able to repeat that line with the utmost rapture." Paul, in retrospect, wonders if the accent was Birmingham.

Earlier, before he had had the chance to sew it into the patchwork of his own self-serving memoir *Confessions of an Actor*, Olivier commented, "I think it was the best [ever] performance I can remember seeing. I was acting at the time in something else in London [*The Entertainer*] and I went to see one matinée, and I went again to the next matinée, and I don't often go to see things more than once. I was floored by his performance. It was wonderful."

Was it Paul's activity of mind that so fascinated Olivier? In 1961 he taped the same part in eight days for a CBS television production. It was shot in Brooklyn. It was a shabby performance, with Olivier, according to Roger Lewis, "trying to be humble and determined simultaneously . . . The impression we get, when the priest is on the run, sheltering in a banana warehouse or concealing his identity, is that Olivier is acting a man acting abasement. He only pretends to be meek."

But no mention, anywhere in Olivier's *Confessions*, of Paul's Hamlet, his Lear, his great National Theatre performances after Olivier leaves — Voigt, Salieri, Volpone, for instance. How Olivier in real life acted Iago to Paul's Othello — but playing on modesty rather than jealousy — is another, later story. Alec Guinness said to me [over lunch in the White Tower, in 1989]: "You know . . . Larry, I liked him, and he was very nice to me, but I knew how to survive him. He completely destroyed [Michael] Redgrave. He tried to destroy Scofield, not deliberately but by animal cunning, instinctively."

This "prodigious success" of Paul's as the "trudging, wizened hero-victim" won the *Evening Standard* Actor of the Year award. The Brook-Scofield season of "Sin and Damnation" entered on its "last anguished lap" with

T.S. Eliot's *The Family Reunion*, in which Paul played the upper-class neurotic swinging "on the metaphysical high trapeze," in a "has-been, would-be masterpiece . . . magnificently revived," with Sybil Thorndike and Gwen Ffrangçon-Davies.

Tynan commented that to "Mr. Scofield, who has hardly had a cheerful line to speak in the past six months, one's heart goes out." To Eliot's Orestian hero he "bestows a sleepless mien gently haggard, and an anxious warmth of utterance . . . As he is softened by Mr Scofield, we almost come to like Harry. Almost, we believe that he might exist."

Tynan was at his most entertaining — he makes you want to see this final Brook production. (Sadly, it was Brook's penultimate one with Paul on stage.) Eliot's gift is for imposing a sudden chill, as they say ghosts are supposed to do when they enter a room:

> Mr. Eliot can always lower the dramatic temperature, he can never raise it . . . Images of vague nursery dread insistently recur — the attraction of the dark passage, the noxious smell untraceable in the drain, the evil in the dark closet (which was really, as Dylan Thomas used impiously to say, the school boot cupboard), the cerebral acne in the monastery garden, the agony in the dark, the agony in the curtained bedroom, the chilly pretences in the silent bedroom. (One of these phrases is my own invention. Entries by Ash Wednesday.)

23

Murder and Adultery

Paul was tired at the end of 1956. "No man should agree to play Hamlet every night. It is far too demanding. At that time I drove myself right to the limit of my endurance. I was studying the priest while forced to the utmost of my capacity, working in a state of nervous tension which was exhausting. Yet it showed me how far I could go. To that extent it was useful."

He took a holiday. Martin was eleven and Sarah, his sister born in August 1952 was four. They were at a good age, an enjoyable age. Paul was thirty-five on January 21, 1957. He was looking for the next play. He would like a comedy. He regrets petrol rationing, which is in force because of the Suez crisis. His application for extra coupons to travel to work is turned down flat, but even so he resists the temptation to have a flat in London.

He knows where he is as an actor. He continues to make a conscious effort of making himself go "as far as I possibly can in every possible direction and being, in a way, rather foolhardy and not believing there was any area I couldn't go to. I don't mean I thought I could do anything, but I thought I could try."

He essays almost all the great radio roles he is asked to do over the next few years. The BBC Drama Department was run by Val Gielgud as if it was still in the days of Henry Irving. Who was its Irving? Paul, no less. The plays included *The Duchess of Malfi*, *Pericles*, *Lazarus*, *Henry VIII*, *The Seagull*, *The Diary of a Madman*, *The Prisoner*, *Rosmersholm*, and — for television, his first performance — Luigi Pirandello's *Henry IV*.

He excelled (I pick an example at random) in a ninety-minute *Edward II* (Marlowe), of riotously energetic beauty.

Mr. Paul Scofield, who put iron into Richard II's soul at Hammersmith a few years ago, found in Edward's — in spite of his obsessive passion — the iron already there; and one can think of no actor whose voice has inherently more of the pure Marlowe metal than Mr. Scofield's. He gave a resonant and mounting indignation to such lines as:

> "Nay, then, lay violent hands upon your king,
> Here, Mortimer, sit thou in Edward's throne:
> Warwick and Lancaster, wear you my crown;
> Was ever king thus over-ruled as I?"

Pamela Brown played the Queen: Paul Rogers, Mortimer. "A deep, quavering note rounded off Mr. Scofield's beautifully accurate radio performance." Long before David Lean's epic film he took the active and controlling voice in an ambitious two-part adaptation of Pasternak's *Dr. Zhivago*: "His playing was a remarkable exercise in the use of the voice to show the changes made by suffering and age."

Paul's next West End theatrical success had an unusually tortured conception and birth. Frith Banbury and Christopher Taylor were at dinner with the playwright Rodney Ackland and his wife Mabbie at their flat on Putney Hill. Also present was Moura Budberg, whom Taylor considered "an arse-licker." Banbury more delicately observed, "She was inclined to say what one wanted to hear."

Banbury started to talk about John Whiting, winner of the 1951 Festival of Britain playwriting competition with *Saint's Day*, condemned when acted as obscure, but hotly defended by Gielgud, Tyrone Guthrie and others. Paul knew Whiting slightly because they had played in Gielgud's *Much Ado About Nothing*. He said much later of *Saint's Day* (the Royal National Theatre asked him to play the main role in 1998) that it is "An extraordinary play, immensely powerful, though it is hard to say why — many of the characters and situations are apt to strain credulity. I think I have missed out somewhere."

Banbury began talking about Whiting and what bad luck he had suffered in life and in his plays (his marriage broke up, his mistress committed suicide, and not much later he was to die from cancer). Thomas Mann, a writer whose darkness was comparable in some ways to Whiting, in a notable passage called cancer "foiled creative fire," and remarked how all illness is "only love transformed."

Ackland, who according to Charles Duff, chronicler of *The Lost Summer*, resented anybody's luck being worse than his own, suddenly exploded, "He's had bad luck, what about me?" and then launched into a tirade of bad luck competition with Whiting. "Every time he said how disgracefully he had been treated by the world, Moura Budberg sympathetically agreed, 'and by Harold Hobson in particular.' So Rodney became quite hysterical. Eventually Mabbie rose from the table, picked up the doll, and threatened to smash it unless he stopped — which he did. But it had been a terrible manifestation of the anger and self-pity which were to cause him so much distress from then on."

This was the background to Frederick Seddon, the real-life murderer that Paul played next in *A Dead Secret*, the work which in his fury and frustration Ackland subsequently wrote. It was not an ordinary thriller: Ackland did not set out to create tension as a conventional "whodunnit" — and Seddon actually didn't do it, although sentenced to be hanged. Its theme is that all evil stems from the spiritual sickness of self-imprisonment, of "people unable to extend imaginative sympathy to those close to them by locking themselves up in their own egos, by being emotionally unapproachable."

Complete schizophrenia, Ackland suggests, is the end result for those whose sense of separateness impels them to concentrate on the self alone — with Dyson (the Seddon character) being in danger of succumbing to this. In fact the murder is committed by another character, the maid Henrietta Spicer, who is already mentally ill. The simplistic message is that we are all part of one another, while the dead secret, the secret of human personality, is that secretiveness, and a concentration on the self (in the individual in his or her sense of separateness) leads to the death of feelings and is an illusion.

Dyson is wrongly hanged, yet he finds salvation. His wife Margaret confides to the innocent man's father: "He was such a funny fellow, you know Pa — he never let you really see what he thought about anything. [She raises her head and, her cheeks still wet, gives her nervous, flickering smile.] One thing, though, he showed he loved me, didn't he — he did show he loved me in the end."

She has been unfocused and frightened by being excluded from his thoughts and feelings: when he says to her that no one can know what it feels like to be someone else she replies: "I don't see why not, Fred. I mean religion and that, we're not supposed to be shut away inside ourselves like, but sort of 'part of one another,' and I mean if only we *could* feel like that."

And later, when in the witness box the revelation is clearer to her: "In a way, I was outside myself and there was this person called Margaret Dyson being cross-examined there; but I couldn't feel it was me . . . I've always felt frightened of everything . . . but standing there in that police court today with heaven knows what hanging over us, I felt *safe* . . . just in this moment when I sort of stopped being myself, I suddenly got the idea — well, like as if I *knew* — that whatever happens, even dying, there's nothing to be frightened about at all."

Banbury reports that when Paul first comes to see him at his flat in St. James Terrace, Battersea, they sat on the balcony in the sun: "Well Paul," Banbury (on the basis of *A Question of Fact*) opened cheerily: "I think I know you pretty well by now and — "

"No you don't," answered Paul straight back. Banbury said that in spite of this unpromising start, and with his own solecism forgiven, rehearsals were subsequently always "good-humoured and enjoyable." At first Paul was doubtful over the casting of Megs Jenkins as Margaret Dyson, but they prevailed over his doubts.

Paul's opinion of the play was, "Very powerful and atmospheric and full of psychological insights into criminality and its essential pettiness and short-sightedness." In rehearsal he found a way of inhabiting Dyson. As he saw it this was a full-length study of a vain, self-confident businessman who believes he is a match in cleverness for anybody, and whose own conceit and weakness lead to his downfall. The play only accompanies him as far as his committal to trial.

Paul assumed a strong, consistent northern accent. Banbury also recalls how he gave an "absolute character performance rather than playing on his own ambiguous personality as he had done in *A Question of Fact*." He wore hardly any make-up: "just a waxed moustache and slicked down hair, and the inner transformation was complete. His imagination was so strong that he converted the illusion into the reality as you watched it at rehearsal. What seemed *unreal* was when he stopped rehearsing, and what was *real* was when he was acting. It was like a light going on — I've never had this feeling quite with anyone else. When he started to Mr. Dyson a light went on and it went off when he became himself." Again I notice this absolute command of separateness in Paul — of himself from the role.

On the first night, instead of the customary round of applause the leading actor might expect, Paul, unrecognised, went without one. The reviews without exception were full of praise, both for the atmosphere and Ackland's macabre humour, and most of all his "study of Seddon, or rather Paul's study of Seddon," for unfortunately for Ackland the critics confused the acting with the role. Although it was the role that Paul acted truthfully they applauded "Paul Scofield [giving] an extraordinary complete picture of this unctuous rascal."

Succumbing himself to the paranoid element of schizophrenia (but not the passive symptoms), Ackland himself took great exception to Harold Hobson who, under the heading of "Master of Repose," devoted one of his longest reviews ever to the subject of Paul's acting. Only in the tenth paragraph did he come to the play, missing entirely, as did most other reviews, the arresting theme of *A Dead Secret*: "The development of Seddon's character is slow, and there is an impossible Dickensian servant;

but otherwise, Mr. Ackland has dramatized the story — and it is a highly interesting story — well."

This toppled Ackland over into ungovernable rage, and he foolishly (although it is easy to say this now) indulged in "Hobsonphobia" which, unlikely though it may seem, apparently contributed to his creative death. He wrote only one more original play after *A Dead Secret*, and this has never had a professional production. Ackland constructed, wrote Hilary Spurling on his death in 1961, plays of "imaginative strength and emotional delicacy" and produced a "bright, clear, unflattering glass" in the mirror he held up to nature.

What Ackland sadly failed to appreciate was that praise for Scofield *was* praise for his character Seddon: the two were inseparable.

A Dead Secret ran for 193 performances from the end of May: with rehearsals and previews it occupied Paul for most of 1957. He was to have played Brother Martin in Otto Preminger's film of *St. Joan* in this year. "It took me only one rehearsal to realise I had made a mistake. I asked for my release and Mr. Preminger was most understanding."

He also rejected, together with fourteen others, the leading role of Souvorin, in Wynyard Brown's final play, *A Choice of Heroes*, about Russian revolutionaries in the 1880s. Now he was to expand his wings — for the first and only time in his career into a musical. It was the year when the West End became alive with the sound of music — by the century's turn it was to be drowned in it. Sheridan Morley recorded in his book about Robert, his father, how word had come from Broadway that Rex Harrison had decided to sing Professor Higgins in *My Fair Lady*, while in London Paul Scofield was about to undertake *Expresso Bongo*. The hour of the non-singing musical star had arrived.

I find that Hobson's *Sunday Times* article about Paul *is* really curious. It begins, "Of English actors under forty, Paul Scofield is the most outstanding." It goes on to ask, "but is he a great actor, or only a very good one?" He then lists various qualities of the great actor, with Paul's rating in each of these.

The first is repose. Paul is a master of this. In *A Dead Secret* he demonstrates this several times, as he had in *Ring Round the Moon*, when he is mistakenly reproached as his brilliant brother by Isabelle, and he stands motionless, "With one arm hanging unquivering [sic!] at his side, a figure carved out of stone, yet feeling the most bitter pain." In particular, Dyson turns out on to the street an old lodger called Vokes, who savagely abuses him. This time Scofield holds a cigar. "He shows no resentment, no anger, no surprise . . . it is this nothingness that is his triumph."

The second quality of the great (as opposed to good) actor is that of expressing through his personality a vision of life unique to himself. Scofield here rates highly: he demonstrates a basic non-understanding of the universe, the man who looks at the world enquiringly, quizzically. "Behold," he tells us, "I show you a mystery, a mystery that makes uncomfortable." The energy in stillness, the mysterious ability to cut himself off from the pain of identification, both of these I can validate.

The third quality, which Hobson believes Scofield has not yet achieved, is that of a voice that by various means, creates a "sharp unease which can be satisfied only by the utterance of another and completing word, as a bar of music can make us long unutterably for a second, complementary bar."

Olivier has it in *The Entertainer*, Hobson continues, but Scofield does not have it yet. But he has something else. His power of imitation is masterly. Too precise, however, for at the end of *A Dead Secret*, when in the moment of tenderness he puts his arm round his wife and utters a few broken words, Scofield releases no emotion: "Here is exposed the failure of realistic acting." This is, reading it now, an unconvincing assessment.

Well now, after Larry's Archie Rice we have Paul's variety agent, Johnnie, in Wolf Mankowitz and Julian More's *Expresso Bongo* that, after touring, brings Paul into the cavernous Saville Theatre. Paul loves the music and sings four songs lustily, and otherwise gives an "anxious and beautifully timed performance," somewhat breaking the bonds of the satire imposed by Mankowitz. With Millicent Martin as Johnnie's girl-friend and Susan Hampshire as the dolly debutantes, James Kenney as Bongo and Victor Spinetti playing all and sundry, it is set to run and run, and of course it does.

"We are eagerly looking forward," commented another reviewer "to seeing Sir John Gielgud playing a theatre press representative, Dame Edith Evans a dresser, and Sir Ralph Richardson a cinema doorman." Little does he know — "Dudley Moore's Butler Dead" runs the *Sun* headline on the death of John Gielgud in May 2000. The actor's fame is transitory.

Paul loved working with the orchestra. "Light-hearted, delightful company, backstage laughter constant," he recalls. "That kind of high-spiritedness is born from the permanent sense of emergency we all feel in the theatre during performances, and which fades when the danger is past." "Permanent," and "fades": note the paradox, almost an oxymoron.

During *Expresso Bongo* the Moscow Art Theatre company came to Sadler's Wells. Paul was particularly impressed by Vasily Orlov who played Vanya in *Uncle Vanya*, and by Stepanova playing the governess Carlotta in *The Cherry Orchard*.

I was deeply affected by the ensemble playing. Here were actors who had worked closely together for many, many years — rather than becoming so acclimatised to each other that they took themselves for granted, tending to give solo performances, they clearly developed such a comprehensive psychological understanding of each other, that the spontaneity of their interplay was enhanced in a way that English and American companies could not begin to emulate. Familiarity bred empathy.

Paul took time off to repay some his Moscow hosts for their previous hospitality. He and Joy invited his dresser Galia and two colleagues to lunch at Balcombe, and some forty savoured *Expresso Bongo*, Paul's western decadent offering.

Expresso Bongo ran and ran, but Paul moved on. He was now cast as the lover in Graham Greene's *The Complaisant Lover*, which promised a formidable encounter with Ralph Richardson. This was to prove an invaluable learning experience, undertaken in the midst of many other offers for that very reason.

During the Piccadilly run of *A Dead Secret* Paul made his second film,

Carve Her Name with Pride, at Elstree Studios. The film tells the tale of Violette Szabo, a half-French, half-English espionage worker who was dropped into occupied France twice; on the second mission was captured by the Gestapo, tortured, and finally, as the Allies were freeing western Europe, executed. The main performance is that of Virginia McKenna who, with her Roedean accent and her independent school games prowess, is somewhat unconvincingly in the company of Billie Whitelaw (long before her seduction by the dashes and repeated dots of Samuel Beckett) and picks up a Foreign Legion officer in Hyde Park. His name is Szabo and Violette takes him back to meet her French mother.

P.C. 49, Jack Warner, plays her understanding father, an odd family mix. He gives the pair permission to marry after three days of knowing each other, and Szabo, leaving Violette pregnant, disappears into German-occupied territory. Later he is pronounced dead at El Alamein. Revenge on the detested Boche and a desire to buy her daughter an haute couture dress in the rue La Fayette fire Violette to train as a resistance courier; in the course of this she meets Captain Tony Frazer, an unlikely Intelligence hero, played by Paul, who is sought all over France. The distant Scofield character, whose stiff posture reminds me of Michael Portillo, the Conservative politician, hovers on the edge of allowing himself some romance with Violette.

Danger keeps them well polarised, as does the wooden dialogue, such as Tony's, "I'd like to ask you something."

Answer: "No time like the present."

There are forty-four minutes of such tedious preparation until the war action starts and then neither McKenna nor Paul have much more to say to each other. In this 1958 film Paul notably lacked flexibility of feature and too often his face is blank and impassive, although it is true that he is trying to give little away. On screen the stillness does not register. There is no vibrancy under the skin of the face, no tension in the eyes, and while the hands make gestures more suited to the theatre, the way he takes up positions on the set is histrionic. It is evident that Paul hated shooting it piecemeal, under Lewis Gilbert's direction, and found it hard to achieve flow and continuity, in spite of some tender and painful good-bye scenes.

McKenna is at her best in the torture scenes and in her earlier confessions of fear. Paul finds her a very different kind of leading lady from Olivia de Havilland, "calm and sweet and generous." Paul's most memorable line is "I don't like heights. I get airsick on the top of a bus." All the heroism filmed by Gilbert is cool and understated, and genuinely motivated to pay tribute to such courage. But the most moving scene is the last one. Tony goes to meet Tania, Violette's daughter, when she is summoned to Buckingham Palace, wearing the dress her mother bought in occupied Paris, to be awarded her mother's posthumous George Cross by King George VI.

There is no dialogue but Paul's voice delivers the commentary in voice-over, paying tribute to Violette's bravery. The fullness of emotion he projects, entirely absent from the film, catches the throat and brings unexpected tears to the eyes. As Voltaire said, the ear is the way to the heart.

When Paul first read Greene's *The Complaisant Lover* he found it altogether different from *The Power and the Glory* — that is, "Very soundly theatrical. To me its chief comedy theme lay in the title — that in a three-sided relationship it is not only the husband who is required to be 'complaisant.' The faintly bitter aspect of this leitmotif got faintly lost, I think, in performance."

Greene wrote the novel first, then adapted it for the stage. It might be claimed it became a comic hit because in rehearsal they believed it was a tragedy. Richardson played Victor Rhodes, his wife Mary was acted by Phyllis Calvert, while the name of Paul's bookseller lover is Clive Root, who cuckolds Rhodes. This was an early but celebrated *ménage à trois* story that seemed in real life to become de rigueur for such literary figures as Kingsley Amis and indeed for Greene himself, reflecting perhaps the difficulties some writers enjoy in their primal relationships.

24

Interlude — Encounter With Merlin

Richardson takes Scofield to the Savile, one of the three clubs he visited in circulation; asked why he had so many, he said, "You mustn't go to a club more than once a week." (The others were the Garrick and the Athenaeum.)

Paul reports that Richardson told him, "How right I was for the part, because of the line which says you look like a gypsy — and you *do* look like a gypsy." Paul goes to the text of the play to seek this line — but never finds it.

Richardson has something of the same vocal unexpectedness as Paul, who in playing this role finds it difficult to adjust. "Ralph was an actor of rhythm — he had a beat, a pulse inside him which dictated to him; and playing opposite him one had to learn to respect that rhythm. I am inclined to syncopate a little, and coming in one night with a line a shade later than usual, Ralph clapped his hand behind his ear as if to say, 'What was that?' His rhythm had been broken — I had let him down. It was the discipline of music."

They didn't get much direction from Gielgud, who arrived a week late for the beginning of the month rehearsal period. But so experienced were they all that they had the play ready to open in two weeks — and then Gielgud said, according to Phyllis Calvert, "I'm going away, if I'm not going to go away, I'll ruin it." They just ran it over and over again till the opening. Later Gielgud, refusing a further rehearsal, came back and commented, "You're all exactly as I left."

From Richardson, Paul learnt that the trick *is* a trick — in this play it was the feet: he would enter trotting in comedy — this made him a fool, a cuckold. He was well cast — he performed bits with trick cushions, denoting a sudden switch from comedy to betrayal. Paul found Richardson's collapse in this scene from fun and joke-playing to the grief of betrayal "poignant and disconcerting," and the tension between the two men grew and grew. Paul said later: "Playing my scenes with him, I found the gradual hostility, which grew in him throughout the play, almost frightening. Something very hard — an iron in his soul — something dangerously combative, very masculine; and very consistent throughout the run, no change of voltage, just sometimes more alarming."

Paul was by no means the first to notice this hostility: it may have been repressed rivalry, it could have been boredom. Acting may be dreaming to order, as Richardson said, but there are no rivals in the self-directed repose of sleep. This was one of Richardson's finest performances but, as Paul aptly comments, "Perhaps the faintly bitter aspect of his leitmotif — it is not only the husband who is required to be complaisant — got faintly lost."

Clive Root is about Paul's own age, and later he realised it was the nearest he had approached to using his own voice. "If someone did ask me to play myself, said here's the script of your biography, I wouldn't know how to."

During the run of *The Complaisant Lover* Paul read the script of *A Man for All Seasons* by Robert Bolt, and was offered the role of Sir Thomas More. He responded at once to the play "by a contemporary playwright written very much with 20th century dilemmas in mind."

It was, in a sense, another *Adventure Story*, but of a different calibre.

Heaven and Earth was also made at this time, a film directed by Peter Brook; Paul's memory of it is hazy, but he does recall to me that among other members of the cast were Richard Johnson, Marjorie Stewart, who had been parachuted into France during the war while pregnant with her daughter, and Lois Maxwell, the Miss Moneypenny of the earlier James Bond films.

The entire film took place on a plane, which crashed: the role played by Paul was the sole survivor, "A sort of Billy Graham — pious and perhaps obsessed by his zeal to bring us all back to God."

In the final scene, an enquiry into the accident, his character appears much changed — more human: "This last scene was revelatory — but I can't remember why!"

25

A Bad Play?

I am faintly shocked when Richard Eyre, who directed Paul in *John Gabriel Borkman* in 1996, describes *A Man for All Seasons* to me as a "bad play." It is generally regarded as a masterwork by which Robert Bolt chiefly is, and will be, remembered. It began as a radio play some nine or more years before its opening at the Globe Theatre, Shaftesbury Avenue, on 1 July 1960. Few scripts have undergone such critical and loving nurturing as it did in these nine years, during which Bolt also wrote, or reworked, more than twenty plays for radio. Cultural expectations were different: the inscription in the lobby hall of Broadcasting House, Portland Place, just north of Oxford Circus tended to be followed — at least some of the time — "That the people, inclining their ear to whatsoever things are lovely and honest, whatsoever things are of good report, may tread the path of virtue and wisdom."

A Man for All Seasons over those years of script development benefited from the editing skills of Val Gielgud and his deputy Donald McWhinnie, a thin, haggard Scot with a love of the bottle, and Barbara Bray, a distinguished French translator. The suggestion to turn it into a stage play came from Peggy Ramsay, Bolt's agent, after a television version had been transmitted on New Year's Day 1957, with Bernard Hepton as Sir Thomas More. This was criticised as a static version of the radio play.

When the script arrived in Balcombe, Paul, perhaps inevitably now, was turning much down. On the threshold of his fortieth year, he was now old enough for me to ask who exactly was he?

Not Oscar Wilde, it seemed. Hollywood wanted to film the trials.

Everyone expected Robert Morley would be chosen, but Irving Allen, the American film executive said, "Robert Morley as he was 20 years ago would be OK. Today my Number One choice is Scofield. He's a fine actor. He'd be just great." Paul commented, "I have no objections to playing Oscar Wilde because he was a homosexual. I don't have any feelings about that. My main worry is that I am not the right shape . . . I don't look like him at all."

Since 1958, when, after a mixed start to his career, Peter Hall was appointed director designate of Stratford-upon-Avon, due to take up the appointment in 1960, Hall had been wooing Scofield. They had already worked on John Whiting's ill-fated *The Gates of Summer*, which the producer, Donald Albery, never brought to London. In March 1959 Paul had agreed to be in Hall's crucial first season, playing Shylock opposite Dorothy Tutin's Portia in *The Merchant of Venice*, Petruchio opposite Peggy Ashcroft in *The Taming of the Shrew*, and Pandarus in *Troilus and Cressida*.

On 25 November 1958 Paul queried Pandarus: "I'm wondering if I have enough variety — but I will read it again." On 2 January 1959 he wrote again, suggesting — to Hall's offer that he play Jaques in *As You Like It* — Thersites. Further, he tactfully mentioned that Joy could play Julia in *Two Gentlemen of Verona*. Scofield, according to Stephen Fay in his study of Hall, "also thought his wife would be a splendid Cressida, and wanted to know what Hall thought. Not much, was the answer to that."

Joy had recently been working at the Arts Theatre, London, in *The Imperial Nightingale*, yet clearly Paul's own success had come to put her career in his shadow, a not uncommon situation in the life of an actor married to an actress, or other worker in the theatre — or vice versa, as in the case of Glenda Jackson. "They suffer from the fact you're famous," the level-headed Tom Conti tells me. In Glenda Jackson's case it led to bitterness and divorce from her director husband; in the case of Pamela Brown and actor Peter Copley, amicable separation. There is, says Conti, an unspoken reaction on the part of most directors to any suggestion your lesser-known wife might take a role, even if she is very good and the role is unfilled. "A director might ask: any ideas for this role? You might say, after an un-aspirated sigh, 'Hell, Kara's free.' The response is generally a polite refusal, but really they think, 'Well, you can't both be good,' or they'll think you'll fight and there'll be trouble.'"

Paul and Peter Hall politely said nothing of this incident again. Paul commented on Joy's giving up the theatre, particularly from 1952, when they moved to Balcombe and when Sarah was born in August: "Martin, my son, was six years old and now we had a girl, it was of course joyous. And yes, Joy did act less and less from that point onwards, reluctantly, she has always missed the comradeship of work in the theatre, but she has found compensation in her writing and drawing, especially the latter, and has published two books for children and is presently working on another."

The plot, however, thickened slightly when in the winter of 1959-60 Paul wrote, according to Fay, "a strange letter to Flower asking for an advance on his whole salary for 1960. This was refused. Subsequently Scofield wrote to Hall saying that he felt he could not play Shylock, Petruchio and Thersites — a shattering blow, since they were the star male parts of the summer."

Hall received his letter a few weeks before rehearsals started. It was "Reasonable, well argued — and devastating. He [Paul] said he knew he was committed to Stratford to lead my first season, knew the contract was agreed, but now found he just couldn't face it. Something deep inside was telling him that it wasn't right. He had to be released."

Hall was greatly angry, had even a desire for revenge. They had a big row. "It nearly stopped the RSC opening," says Hall to me today, amused but forgiving of their difference. "I said, I'll never work with you again — until I need you. If actors change their mind there is nothing you can do about it. They have to do what they have to do and, when the crunch comes, nothing else matters."

Paul never gave Hall a reason, but outside his own comprehension at the time there could have been one. He was about to take a risk well beyond that of three principal roles at Stratford. They were safe, they were predictable. But he himself has little sense of risk. Presented with the choice between Thomas More and the Stratford season — which Paul today does not remember as the alternative — "There would have been no doubt my choice would have been to play More . . . I had no doubts, certainly no sense of risk other than the knowledge that anything can fail."

He was unusually, consummately, in charge of himself and his decision. "Paul has," Hall notes picturesquely (and wryly) "a private god which tells him what to do."

So who was he now? And who or which god is it? Certainly not success, Mammon, sex, or all the usual ones. Scofield is good for us, wrote Bernard Levin in a sermonising mood a short while after his next three roles, calling him "The Man For All Seasons" not simply because we have been able to enjoy his acting across such a variety of parts, but because "The balance and integrity he has displayed in his choice of parts as in his work on them have added an element of dedication, without the striking of attitudes about it, to a stage that on occasion seems sadly short of the first, and wearisomely full of the second."

Elsewhere Paul said of the choices he had made that they reflected on how he wanted to be remembered: "If you have a family that is how to be remembered." As a man, "I do not have any envy or contempt for people who have done one thing or another in their careers. Envy is such a waste of nervous energy, and I have a resistance to regret." Of competitors, "I do not tread on people or try to bruise them — and the first not to tread on or bruise are your children." Of the role of Sir Thomas More in *A Man for All Seasons* he admitted simply, "The most difficult part I played."

Bolt identified the difficulty of his role and how, in its slow, almost implacable formation, it came in the end to avoid the obvious and the cliché and how much, equally, he had left out. Largely, even on the stage, it is a role of silence, of the unstated, of gaps in the expected, of saving, of salvation. More is the great goalkeeper of English history and the clean sheet he keeps is that of faith, of integrity. But theology is eerily absent, for Bolt was a self-confessed atheist.

> I do *not* want it to be turned into a play of "conflicts." It is a play of one man, and its vitality no more depends on the clash you mention than the clash between Christ and Pilate. If it hadn't been Cromwell, it would have been someone else . . . the play is not a whirlpool but a river running stiller and deeper until it plunges over a cliff. The last thing I envisaged was the "conflict" with Cromwell . . . I think there is ample drama in the beauty of More's behaviour, the tragedy of his position, the sordid violence of his end and the pathos of those who were left, so to speak, at the foot of the Cross.

It retains the simple. It is plain. Frith Banbury, as Beaumont's Number One director, read it once, then read it again. "I have reread *A Man for All Seasons*. I am now ready to burn my boats and say there has been no play in this genre written in English to compare with it since Shaw wrote *St. Joan*. It demonstrates what I have always suspected, that Bolt has nothing to fear from Messrs. Anouilh, Fry, let alone the Osbornes and the Mortimers. The man who wrote it will be able to make his own terms with the theatre and the rest of us will have to like it or lump it."

Banbury had to forego the direction and instead take on Bolt's other play, *The Tiger and the Horse*, with Michael and Vanessa Redgrave, which opened only shortly after *A Man for All Seasons*. Sensitive as Banbury was to the intentions of authors, Bolt, who owed to Banbury and Ralph Richardson the success of *The Flowering Cherry*, believed he was "too unobtrusive, too naturalistic." Banbury was disappointed, but invested money in the play anyway.

Instead, Noël Willman, the actor who directed Fry's *A Phoenix Too Frequent*, was engaged. He had also worked as an actor with Paul, in *Adventure Story*. His most recent acting role was as Alec Guinness's interrogator in Bridget Boland's *The Prisoner*, so he was ideally versed in the genre of political interrogation and faith. He was now perhaps a year or two older than Paul. He has been described to me as a melancholic homosexual, a hard-drinking Ulsterman, a director with authority and experience.

Reading Bolt's own job description of the role, it almost sounds that Paul was to play himself. Both author and actor shared a detestation of labels and of movements. New anti-Establishment movements disappointed Bolt. He told *The Times* (in 1960), "I seem to find just as much personal spleen and materialism there as anywhere else. There are plenty of people who are courageous — and noisy. But there are not many who are active — and quiet. They interest me." This is what attracted him to More. More was misunderstood.

> He was not a man who set out to be a saint. He was a worldly man — that is, in the world of society and politics. He never regarded himself as martyr material. But he kept one small area of integrity within himself. And once the powers that be found out, they could not rest until they got at it. So he became a martyr against his desires, because he would not do what the authorities wanted. They assumed that he must be in with the Catholics. In fact, he was fond of the King, as they all were at the beginning, and scrupulously loyal. When he was attacked, the Catholics thought he must be on their side. He was not. Both sides had the wrong end of the stick throughout. I think there are many parallels in our own day.

Could anything be closer to the man we are attempting to define? Beware, however. Paul is never the part he plays. The two, in his mind, never become confused: "I have never identified with any of the characters I have played." Yet even so there has to be a transference, he has to find the writer's voice: this is the crucial element, the literal way Paul means "voice."

It's the voice, because it's the spoken thought that the writer has asked us to pass on to the audience. This is why it's almost always the most important thing to feel that your voice is responding to what he's written in a way that offers you a positive characteristic of a human being that you can recognise. Then other things follow. They just fit in, almost by a kind of thought influence. You find yourself doing things that you hadn't planned to do at all, simply because they're the sort of things you'd do if you were speaking in that sort of voice.

This passage should be fervently underlined. Three times. Paul immersed himself in Thomas More, got More inside him (and not the other way round), and the vocal appearance could then be worked out. More is a lawyer with a dry voice, so Paul elongates the vowels, but More is also a warm man with a wife and family, so everything has to be rounded. "You just don't put on a voice like a hat." He found achieving a combination of the harsh and the ascetic difficult. More is "full of contradictions." When he achieved one he seemed to lose the other.

When I first read the play I saw at once the danger of More being played over-piously, but it was not written that way; Robert gave him humour and severity and obstinacy as well as goodness. As always, my final guide was the writer. I agreed at once to do it.

The first time I met Robert must have been at the first reading. He had a smiling, rosy, clumping and always friendly manner. I use the word clumping because he walked like a farmer. Robert attended some of the rehearsals though the director's policy was, I think, to debar an author from directly talking to the actors or making suggestions or criticisms to us — a wise stricture because a production can only be coordinated by one person. I think Robert's experience of actors was limited. At that time he seemed instinctively to mistrust us — he once complained of my "insouciance" at rehearsal which I hope was merely a pretence of light-heartedness on my part, which covered a multitude of anxieties! I think that at that time he truly didn't understand the way an actor works. The one actor in whom he had complete faith was Leo

McKern. And rightly so.

More refusals hovered in the wings as *A Man for All Seasons* opened on its pre-London tour. It was not expected to run, although even then Tennents could still "nurse" a production for a while. Mankowitz, during the run of *Expresso Bongo*, bought an option on *Gone to Ground*, by John Harrison, for Paul to play the leading role of Saul Tarn, a character based on the now forgotten Malenkov, the Soviet leader immediately following Stalin's death. Harrison's most recent contact with Paul had been as director of Paul's television debut in Pirandello's *Henry IV*, the name role of which he had already suggested he might perform on the radio.

"Paul wanted the low-down on television acting," Harrison tells me. "I said that the main thing to remember was that, however many millions they tell you are watching, you are basically playing to an audience of two or three. But if he wanted to go for the big effect I could pull back and shoot in long-shot: when he wanted to be really intimate I could get between his ears. When George Devine learned what we were rehearsing he wanted us to take it to the Royal Court but Paul said no, explaining, 'It was being planned and rehearsed for television and that's the way it should stay.'"

Harrison and his wife Daphne Slater conferred with Paul on the out-of-town tour of *A Man*, not expecting it to run, although Harrison noted how much Paul liked the part. Unfortunately for Harrison it was his play and not Bolt's that had to go to ground.

Paul found the London first night of *A Man* a grey occasion: "I had then, and perhaps even now, a sense of resentment at the distorted atmosphere of first nights, the imposed need to impress, the feeling of 'now or never,' the pretence of total fruition when we all knew that we still had a long way to go. We were not at our best that night. In the middle of the first act I heard from the stalls a loud whisper, 'Oh, get on with it.' I'll swear it was Robert's voice. Ah well!"

Given this response it is surprising the reviews were as good as they were, most generally favourable if grudging. There was a lot of scholarly

and arcane dispute on the nature of the play, general approval or condemnation of its (fashionable at the time) Brechtian framework and use
of the Common Man figure as a chorus or narrator, played by Leo
McKern, a character whom Tynan described as the "essence of boorish
corruption." It is perhaps typical that the London critics should have fas-
tened on its political and historical content, and ignored the moral and
spiritual themes.

Yet even on the first night T.C. Worsley in the *Financial Times* found
Paul had "an unmatchable dignity and a kind of humble grandeur. It is a
magnificent piece of acting, so tranquil, so composed, so controlled."
Levin, in the *Daily Express*, judged the first night performance grey, with
every line sounding like a platitude, but later he was to change his mind.
Hobson regretted that only at the end was there a blaze of excitement.
"Scofield looks as if the Fellows of All Souls had pooled their brains and
put them inside his skull."

But the first night is only the beginning. At the Globe the play gradually grew by dint of "stealth and perseverance" although, like More himself, it was always in danger of being axed. The play, the role, developed
from inside, and the audience became its soil, its nourishment.

I think I was only half-way there when we opened. By the time we
finished we could, I think, be counted as a success. All performances grow with repetition and with the gathering certainty of simply doing it and thinking it; my understanding of More and his
predicament and his inflexible faith and purpose grew beyond any
initial visualization. In the early stages of rehearsal and for some
time I was stuck with his rigour, his zeal, his intractability, all qualities vital to the unfolding of the story. His humanity came to me
after I had established those qualities firmly for myself. It came to
me bit by bit, facet by facet, and slowly. I liked More finally, after
I had found the sweetness in him, his love for his family, his loyalty to friends, his deep, impartial lawyer's wisdom.

The whole production developed like a forest fire during the
run. I received a letter from Bob, which was intended for John

Perry of H.M. Tennent and John Perry got the one intended for me. The one that I opened in my dressing room said, "I think Paul was a bit better last night, but perhaps that was because the Duke of Edinburgh was in front."

Only Robert Muller perhaps, another playwright, husband of Billie Whitelaw, but writing as a first-night critic, had met *A Man For All Seasons* on its own terms. Calling it a drama of conscience, Muller indicated the universality of the theme and its timeless application. It was a stark play, "sparse in its narrative, sinewy in its writing, which confirms Mr. Bolt as a genuine and solid playwright, a force in our awakening theatre."

A Man did not run as long in London as *The Tiger and the Horse*, next door in Shaftesbury Avenue, although both last enough, well into 1961. Bolt told his parents the *Tiger* was doing better business than *A Man*, although *A Man* is "much the better play." He went on, "A phenomenon which does alarm me is that the takings of *A Man* fell off rapidly the week after *Tiger* opened. It looks as though if you're going to see a Bolt play, you go to see the later one next door with a Knight in the cast. That's all right provided they like it, as in that case they will sooner or later go to see the earlier one. But not everyone does like it, whereas everyone seems to like Sir Thomas."

But finally I return to Eyre's comment. Is *A Man* a good or a bad play? Alec McCowen, who has also played the role of More on stage, inclines to the latter view. He believes the writing is "thin," the characterisation not very deep, and that it would not have succeeded had it not been for the extraordinary authority that Paul brought to More.

The summer of 1961 provided an enjoyable interlude for Joy, Paul, Martin and Sarah. Paul played Coriolanus and Don Armado in *Love's Labour's Lost* in the annual Shakespeare Festival at Stratford, Ontario: Joy returned to the stage as the Queen of France in *Love's Labour's Lost* and Sarah attended school, while Martin remained behind boarding at the King's School, Canterbury, joining them during the summer holidays.

When *A Man for All Seasons* opened on Broadway at the Anta Theatre on 23 November 1961 nearly all the actors were American. Leo McKern no longer played the Common Man, but was to play Thomas Cromwell: "Not exactly a bundle of fun," he says, and he was extremely dismayed to find himself on the pre-New York tour hissed by a majority of the front stalls. Thomas Gomez took the role instead.

The production, the play, and Paul's performance were universally admired and hugely successful. Paul tells me:

The success of the play in New York was exciting, particularly because we opened at Thanksgiving — a notoriously dead time in the theatre there, and at first we felt that no one knew of our existence. Very quickly, though, word got around and we were soon playing to audiences who seemed to respond to the play as having an acute bearing on the present day — rather than as an historical piece, which, on the whole, was how it was viewed in London — with large exceptions, of course. I met some extraordinarily interesting people, Mrs. Carlotta O'Neill (Eugene's widow), Mrs. Claire Booth Luce, who sat in my dressing room and gave me an endless lecture on the Great Schism, and Boris Karloff, Lotte Lenya, Jackie Kennedy, you name them, I'll drop them. (The cat has just ensconced himself on my lap, so my writing is suffering.)

"You're taken over if it's a hit," says Tom Conti. "Everyone in New York wants to be in show business. You find yourself in a maelstrom. But Paul hates people tugging at his coat-tails."

Even in 1961 everyone went for the stars. You feel the total centre of attention. Even then New York was a city of sexual predators. Especially they had their sights set on Paul, of "Such charismatic talent, so beautiful — add high sensitivity — or supercharged sensibility," as one director put it; "Everyone is in love with Paul, everyone wants to go to bed with him," or, as Ronald Harwood confirms, "I've seen young women throw themselves at him."

To such advances, as ever, Paul remained polite. Reserved. Sensibly, if possible, he prefers not to notice them. He continually deflects attention from himself. The gossip-writers get nowhere. He is unhappy much of the time and visits the Empire State Building, riding to the top and staring out over the sea towards England. Dreaming of his family. He would like to be back in Sussex. New York was not really his scene. He missed his family, Joy, Martin, and Sarah back at home: "While this episode was full of heady excitements, professional ones I hasten to add, there was also a considerable angst involved."

A Man for All Seasons was still running to capacity when, after nearly a year, Paul left the cast early summer 1962, his role of More being taken over by Emlyn Williams. Peter Hall and Peter Brook had been to see the play and Paul had been offered the role of King Lear in the autumn season of 1962 at Stratford. Ideally he would have preferred to play Macbeth before tackling Lear, but that is another story.

Joy made several trips to New York, "So that was a big help. (Just in case I sounded a bit plaintive about homesickness.)"

One night Fred Zinnemann, the film director, sat in the Anta Theatre audience: "My flop with a film called *Behold a Pale Horse* taught me that everything had to be made clear to an audience and there was nothing they would not understand if it was made clear. I also noticed that when *A Man for All Seasons* was done on the stage, even though the axe comes down on Sir Thomas More's head at the end, the audience found the story was not a defeat but a victory. They were elated."

A victory. More has won. And so had Paul. The seed was born of a future enterprise.

26

The Big One

The Lear of Shakespeare cannot be acted. The contemptible machine by which they mimic the storm . . . is not more inadequate to represent the horrors of the real elements than any actor can be to represent Lear; they might more easily propose to personate the Satan of Milton upon a stage, or one of Michael Angelo's terrible figures. The greatness of Lear is not in corporal dimension, but in intellectual: the explosions of his passion are terrible as a volcano, they are storms turning up and disclosing to the bottom that sea, his mind, with all its vast riches. It is his mind which is laid bare. On the stage we see nothing but corporal infirmities and weakness . . . while we read it, we see not Lear, but we are Lear.

— *Charles Lamb*

Paul had already been rejected as Satan by the BBC. But 30,000 advance tickets were sold in the summer months of 1962 for the Stratford-upon-Avon production of *King Lear* due to open in September, with Paul in the title role. He had returned from New York much fêted, ill at ease, and thoroughly exhausted. He had been in New York too long. The doctor ordered a three-month rest.

Hall, who had booked Paul, with Brook as director, displayed amazing sangfroid and fortitude. Even after his painful, earlier setback with Paul his respect was boundless. "Paul will deliver what he has ready, no more, no less," he tells me in 2000. A judgement in maturity, but in 1961 Hall was barely thirty. "I am told that at this time I gave out an aura of calm, even arrogant confidence. In truth I was scared to death by what I had started." Yet Hall was still prepared to wait. With him the RSC was growing almost daily.

He approached Donald Wolfit to play Falstaff at Stratford, but when Wolfit learned Scofield was to tackle Lear in the same season, he withdrew. "The disagreement prompted the remark, 'Lear is still the brightest jewel in my crown!'"

More quarrels attended Paul's assumption of the role of Lear. Olivier had been appointed first director of the Chichester Festival Theatre, which was due to open in the summer of 1962. Olivier was at loggerheads with Hall over actors. Olivier wanted — or did he really? — Paul at Chichester, then to join his fledgling National Theatre at the Old Vic, prior to its home being built on the South Bank. Perhaps he wanted him under his thumb, to make sure he would never outrival him.

There was talk of amalgamation between the National Theatre and Stratford. At first Hall supported this. Then backed off. Olivier jealously believed Hall had his eye on running the National Theatre. But for the moment, writing to Hall, he called it a "horribly formidable spectre" and he wanted to put it out of his mind "as a safely locked away black cloud."

Hall, and Fordham Flower, believed that Stratford would be vitiated and become the poor partner in any amalgamation. So did Paul, who writes a strongly worded letter to *The Times* saying so.

Like a royal piece in a game of chess Hall kept Paul — for the moment. "I never knew any of this," Paul says. "Ignorance is bliss!" Olivier writes to Hall

I am so slow and time goes so quick that I have not thought that perhaps I should have approached you before doing so to any of your players . . . I feel you have noticed my approaches to your stars. I only hope you have noticed that I have not approached Scofield, because I realise that he is sac(h)rosant [sic]. For all kinds of reasons. Thank you. I would rather have him than have you have him, and I think the poor sod would rather do it for 10 weeks than

10 months — who wouldn't — but this only offers to show how thoroughly decent I am at bottom (as they will say in our sort of plays).

The Nat. Th. seems to be at a complete impasse, tout laisse, tout casse and fuck me all dandy. I am in a bad way. I can't get a National Theatre. I can't get a cast or repertoire for Chichester. I can't get into my home, and Joannie's baby is bursting out. I can't wake up in the morning or go to sleep at night. I'm absolutely fucked.

How are you, cock!

I expect Hall was worrying more if he was going to get Paul, never mind keep him. Anyway, at last, in September, rehearsals began in the draughty rehearsal room at Stratford: "It was good to be in Stratford again, staying with my old friend Mrs. Denne Gilkes in the High Street."

Paul and Brook resumed their relationship. Perhaps Olivier's apprehension may be more fully understood in Brook's first words to his cast — for Olivier played Lear at the New Theatre during the Old Vic seasons there after the war and was overshadowed by his Fool, Alec Guinness (whose part, even so, he cut to ribbons).

Brook opened proceedings by calling Lear a mountain whose summit had *never* been reached. On the way up one found the shattered bodies of other climbers strewn on every side. "Olivier here, Laughton there; it's frightening!"

Peter had received a note from Gordon Craig, which he read to the assembled actors; the gist of it was that Lear, like the Oriental husband who had lost his wife, knew that she was somewhere and so had to look for her everywhere. Lear, likewise, was somewhere, although no production had ever successfully realized him, and "So we too had to look everywhere."

Brook added, "The work of rehearsals is looking for meaning and then making [the play] meaningful."

The first reading from the company was a typical "under-energized trot," signalling uncertainty. But what a company! Tom Fleming was

Kent, Alan Webb Gloucester. James Booth was Edmund the Bastard, Brian Murray his half-brother Edgar. The Lear sisters, in order of seniority, were Irene Worth, Patience Collier, and Diana Rigg. Peter Jeffrey (Albany), Tony Steedman (Burgundy), Tony Church (Cornwall) and Hugh Sullivan (France) completed the family as sons-in-law, while Alec McCowen (Fool) and Clive Swift (Oswald) provided the lighter shading. This was the first time Paul and the rest of the cast had met.

Paul, having recovered, was aged thirty-nine, just the right age, for he saw you needed the energy of a younger man for the role. He was full of energy, circling Lear from the start like a wary challenger, full of wary resolve and caution — but also attack. Charles Marowitz, Brook's assistant, is our main witness. He describes how Paul threw himself into the reading as if it were an audition before employers skeptical of his talent. He growled his way into the thickets of the text, constantly testing and retesting scansion and stress, "like a hound chasing an elusive hare through densely wooded terrain."

Gradually the company transformed into something of an audience for Scofield's performance. The actors were both awed and frightened by the muscularity of his attack, the unmistakable sense that something difficult and perhaps unachievable was at stake. "In that first reading Scofield set the whole tone of the rehearsal period. 'This is a precariously steep mountain face with a sheer drop below,' he seemed to be saying, 'so we'd all better get out our sharpest picks and our sturdiest boots.'"

Brook's way of working, having developed from the early days, was now wholly experimental. It maddened some, for he believed there is no such thing as the right way. Every rehearsal dictated its own rhythm and its own state of completion. If what was wrong today was wrong tomorrow, tomorrow would reveal it, and through the constant elimination of possibilities Brook arrived at interpretation. He tells Marowitz:

My analogy is with painting. A modern painter begins to work with only an instinct and a vague sense of direction. He puts a splodge of red paint on to his canvas and only after it is on does he decide it might be a good idea to add a little green, to make a vertical line here or a horizontal line there. It's the same with rehearsals. What is achieved determines what is to follow, and you just can't go about things as if you knew all the answers. New answers are constantly presenting themselves, prompting new questions, reversing old solutions, substituting new ones.

The crucial insights into any play would be found by the actors themselves. It was Brook's belief that "The greatest rehearsal factor is fatigue. When you get so thoroughly exhausted from grappling with a certain problem and you think you can't go on — then — suddenly, something gives and you 'find something.' You know that marvellous moment in a rehearsal when you suddenly find something."

Would it work without a leader? I am not so sure. But for the moment there was a leader, and that was Paul, and what better one for, as Hall says, "He doesn't cheat. He tells you where he is."

I am also not sure Brook was right when he said the greatest factor is fatigue. It is one of many. But they are, for the moment, in balance and in harmony.

The communication between them is now so deep it requires few words. They hardly talk together when rehearsals are finished. They never discuss theory or meaning. It is, on Peter's side, "implied, unsaid, and the close friendship that existed between us, never even required social relationships such as lunches or suppers to keep it alive."

As for Paul he, too, was gratefully aware of the accord. "Peter nourishes growth in his actors, he has a prodigious acceptance of their contribution, he literally encourages, not by praise, but by a tacit endorsement . . . When I came to work with him in *King Lear*, he was wonderfully patient, he waited; he waited to see what was on offer, and then incorporated that offering into his own unique conception of the play. There was now a deeper wisdom in his work."

This is carefully expressed by Paul to me, a complex idea that emerges with clarity and simplicity. There is no coercion, no direction as such.

That was not everyone's experience. Alec McCowen tells me he saw Charles Marowitz operating as Brook's "No-man . . . Charles invariably said 'no' — this amused Brook. Marowitz pushed him into doing improvisations with the actors (I secretly admired Paul because he refused)."

At one rehearsal Brook, with Paul there, told McCowen, "I would like you to make Paul laugh."

McCowen was nonplussed. He doesn't know what to do.

Brook begged: "Please will you make Paul laugh?"

McCowen, still embarrassed, looked at Paul. Paul looked back at him. Then Paul started laughing.

"Look, Peter," said McCowen with triumph, "I've done it!"

Most of the cast disliked improvisation. Diana Rigg was asked by Marowitz to improvise her tenuous relationship with the King of France (after Burgundy summarily drops her because Lear disinherits her): "You're driving away from the cathedral in a carriage after your marriage." So she and France (Hugh Sullivan) started awkwardly dancing up and down in their seats, waving at a crowd. Then, says Rigg, Sullivan had a stroke of genius: "A hand came across me and pulled the blind down!"

Brook's way with Paul was poles apart from his way with Diana. "He did a Svengali on me. I fell in with everything he told me to do. I felt trapped."

After arriving at a near empty stage with expensive decor cluttering the wings in *Romeo and Juliet*, Brook elucidated *Lear* in a denuded post-romantic, burnt-out world. It is a merciless vision he has, of an unredeemed and unredeemable world, and Brook cut the text, not ruthlessly but judiciously, to bring it in line with the post-Holocaust theatre of Jerzy Grotowski, of Samuel Beckett's *Endgame*, and with Jan Kott's bleak political reading of Shakespeare as our contemporary. Marowitz viewed it most as *Endgame*.

In discussing rehearsals, our frame of reference was always Beckettian. The world of this Lear, like Beckett's, is in a constant state of decomposition. The set-pieces consist of geometrical sheets of metal that are ginger with rust and corrosion. The costumes, dominantly leather, have been textured to suggest long and hard wear. The knights' tabards are peeling with long use; Lear's cape and coat are creased and blackened with time and weather. The furniture is rough wood, once sturdy but now decaying back into its hard, brown grain. Apart from the rust, the leather, and the old wood, there is nothing but space — giant white flats opening on to a black cyclorama.

If the vision, the slant, given to the play was Brook's, he left the rest to the actors. They had to find their own way. He did not predetermine or interfere with Paul. He, too, as director, learns.

One morning Brook came to Paul with what seemed to him an illuminating discovery.

Lear is someone who wants to let go. But whatever he sacrifices, there is always something left to which he is attached. He gives up his kingdom, but still his authority remains. He must yield his authority, but there is still his trust in his daughters. This too must go, as must the protection of a roof over his head, but this is still not enough, as he has preserved his sanity. When his reason is sacrificed, there is still his profound attachment to his beloved Cordelia. And in the pitiless process of stripping away, inevitably she too must be lost. This is the pattern and the tragic action of the play.

Paul did not react with enthusiasm. He gave a cautious "Mmm . . ." Then he said, thoughtfully, "That may be true. But I mustn't think of it, as it can't help me as an actor. I can't play negative actions. I can't show not having. I have to find a different way to mobilize my energies, so as to be fully active, moment after moment, even in loss, even in defeat."

At this moment Brook saw, unforgettably, the trap of yielding to the intellectual excitement of "having ideas." "One word out of place in the director's explanations and, without noticing it, he can block or hamper the actor's own creative process." Brook added that the same was true for the director's relation to himself. "Ideas must appear, they must be expressed, but he too must learn to separate the useful from the useless, the substance from the theory."

Paul refused, too, to respond to Brook's constant chiding that he was not portraying an old man. He remained himself, but by the force of inner conviction he wanted to project to the audience the exact image he had in mind: "For me," he tells me, "this was a first indication that the theatre is the meeting place between imitation and a transforming power called imagination, which has no action if it stays in the mind. It must pervade the body. A seemingly abstract word, 'incarnation,' suddenly took on a meaning."

The progress to the Stratford opening on 6 November 1962 was slow, especially the emergence of Paul's Lear. Even at the first dress rehearsal Marowitz recorded: "His method is to start from the text and work backwards. He is constantly testing the verse to see if the sound corresponds with the emotional intention. It is a peculiar method that consciously prods technique so that instinct will be called into play."

Marowitz's next comment brings us back to our central debate on the nature of the actor.

27

Interlude — Madness Versus Method

Fashionable at this time, the Method actor, in Marowitz's description of him, starts with feeling and then adds the externals of voice and movement. But Scofield uses externals as a gauge with which to measure the truth of any given speech. He frequently stammered his lines, openly testing inflections and accents, discarding conventional readings, not because they were predictable but because they did not tally with an inner sense of verisimilitude, and his concentration was a model to the rest of the company. He even asked for a prompt in character.

Only when he saw him fumbling for a line did Marowitz glimpse the disparity between Scofield and the character, and then what he saw was a man winding himself painfully into a Shakespearean fiction. "Underlying all the rigour of creative application, one discerns the gentleness of the man himself. Under the stress imposed by a tardy prompt and his own fierce struggle to master the verse, he never loses his temper."

When Scofield was sure of his reasons and his text, he "is firing on both pistons and Lear soars. When he is not, he falls into a studied, wilful over-reasonable rendering of the verse. I pointed out some of these passages to Brook, complaining that they were dry, monotonous and virtually unacted."

Brook explained to Marowitz: "When Paul finds his reasons and his proper level, he will shift from low gear into high, but anything he is not sure of, he will simply mark out drily as he is doing now. He refuses to throw himself into something he does not feel and cannot answer for."

On the ground, away from the theory, as here expressed by Marowitz, the actors were finding it seriously exhausting. McCowen tells me that the first dress rehearsal lasted six or seven hours. Everyone was shattered, and after it Brook talked at length about every aspect except speed. At the end of his address, Paul put up his hand: "Peter," he said. Brook answered, "Yes?" Paul: "You mean faster, Peter?" Brook replied, "Paul has put his finger on it!"

McCowen found the Brook-Scofield relationship "a total mystery. They never talked together. Paul accepted what Peter wanted. Brook realized when Paul was not happy."

But Paul, mostly, was happy: although the rehearsal period is now "dim and hazy," he remembers the wonderful cast, McCowen, Tom Fleming, Irene Worth, Alan Webb.

> It's a grim play and our work on it was grimly enjoyable, actors always find much to laugh about in this kind of play — not that there is any other play quite like it; and there is always absurdity in extreme tragic situations in drama, an absurdity which, if used, can only heighten the tragedy.

At a public dress rehearsal or preview there was a moment which animated an otherwise difficult scene, known as the hunting scene. A photographer had been clicking away in the stalls at the point when, insulted by Goneril's attitude, Lear overturns the table and orders his knights to horse.

Paul marched downstage and hurled his hunting cloak at the photographer. Without dropping his Lear voice he growled, "Please get that thing away from here!," then resumed his blood-curdling denunciation of his daughter. The whole audience breathed in quickly. There was a sharp and sudden silence. The moment is heavily charged with violence.

28

Public and Private Ears

Cosmic melancholy was the rage of the early 1960s. But boredom, too. Stoned flower power and aggressive anti-nuclear pacifism vied with each other under the canopy of "Make Love, not War." Many will never forget that sulphurous passion that Paul ignited. His Lear was a savage figure, animated by a terrible boredom. He was boredom and arrogance united, his scrum of knights a cross between the English rugger team and a bunch of gangsters. Then that gravelly, hard voice right from the beginning in the court scene, a lot of flurry with the waiting on Lear grouped around the map of Britain when he utters from his throne, where he is hardly visible, "Attend the lords of France and Burgundy" — a line much quoted by other actors in imitation of Paul.

There was a special Scofield quality in his Lear, too, which tempered or lightened Brook's vision of the cruel, alien world the play depicts. Although Shakespeare explored fully the emotions, the blindness, the denial of knowledge that make this great play universal in its application, he remains in no way trapped by the feelings, by the preoccupations, or even the darkness he uncovers. For Shakespeare depicts tragic characters with such generosity, amplitude, and underlying stability, that he makes audiences secure in their contemplation, as he was, I believe, himself.

Paul underlined that effect — that tragedy is life-affirming — and there was, in addition, that special bond he had with the audience. As he points out to me:

> The element of absurdity enters into the great tragic characters, Lear especially, and carries them into our field of understanding and sympathy. There is nothing remote in Shakespeare's poignan-

cies and catastrophes. From an actor's professional point of view, playing King Lear could be said to mark the point of growing up. Attempting to encompass this play and this character must be a "rite of passage," a journey into the tragedy and absurdity of human life, a rigorous examination of the actor's perceptions and his capacity to project them.

The real experience of acting begins, Paul believes, after the play opens, and when "a director is often an absentee from the development of its public performance."

Once *Lear* opened they developed their own ways of enriching the roles and coping with the exhausting demands. Paul arrived three hours before each performance to prepare himself: Part One lasted two and a half hours, until after Gloucester's blinding, and Part Two one and a half hours. Paul found Fleming "the perfect Kent." But especially, though, "The relationship between my Lear and Alec McCowen's Fool was at the heart of the evening."

As with Felicity Kendal, who I have already quoted on acting Desdemona to Paul's Othello, McCowen asks, "Lear's affection for me? — or for the Fool?" His lifeline in this complicated, demanding role — the intention, for what the Fool says is often hard to understand — "I thought of myself as a small boy trying to entertain my father, as if he's just come home from work, so I'd perform for him to stop him being bad-tempered."

The word the Fool used, "Nuncle," is crucial to the affection the Fool continues to feel towards Lear, and this avuncular side of Lear's character was what McCowen saw in Paul — he will still write to him jokingly calling him "Nuncle."

Both dreaded the storm scene — speaking against the thunder, having the wind and the rain effect to combat — and so, before playing it each time, to raise morale together in the wings and take their minds off it, they would sing together Arthur Askey's comic "I'm a busy, busy bee" routine.

A game they played when the Fool is in Lear's arms and they whisper to each other: far away from the sublime rhetoric of Shakespeare, they saw how many names they could remember of the BBC Radio Repertory Company:

> LEAR: Marjorie Westbury.
> FOOL : Rolf Lefevre.
> LEAR : Belle Crystal.
> FOOL : Carlton Hobbes.

By such means they found ways to get through these long, difficult scenes.

McCowen ultimately felt that the way the Fool is forgotten in the play was very cruel, very distressing, for apart from Lear's "And my poor fool is dead," he is never mentioned again.

Diana Rigg always apologised when Paul had to carry her on at the end, dead: she weighed nine and a half stone, was five feet eight and a half inches tall, and she breathed in to make herself lighter as Paul lifted her — she stood on a table offstage for him to do this. He holds her throughout the long speech "Howl, howl, howl, howl, oh you are men of stones," then bends down and props her against a piece of metal sheet.

When she played Goneril to Olivier's Lear for television, many years later, she had spent so many hours in the wings listening to Paul's Lear she found his inflections all come back to her, in that particular distinctive phrasing: "The voice always seems to resonate within," she says.

Paul's close relationships in the play are the Fool, Kent, Cordelia — but also Goneril, played by Irene Worth: "Irene Worth is a subtle and extraordinary actress, she played Goneril not as a villainess, but as a wronged and frustrated daughter, an approach which rendered her ultimate cruelty more lethal and more believable."

"His eyes always spoke more than his words and our fury and hurt against each other was fierce," she tells me (see Appendix A).

King Lear's notices were universally good, and over the next eighteen months it progressed to the Aldwych, played in Paris at the Sarah Bernhardt Theatre, came back to London, visited Eastern Europe and Russia, and finally opened the new Lincoln Center in Manhattan, New York. No greater and more prestigious production of this masterpiece was to hold such sway for so long.

The fundamental difference between this production and previous ones was summed up by Tynan: "Instead of assuming that Lear is right, and therefore pitiable, we are forced to make judgements — to decide between his claims and those of his kin . . . For [Brook] the play is a mighty philosophic farce, in which the leading figures enact their roles on a gradually denuded stage that resembles, at the end, a desert graveyard or unpeopled planet . . . for the first time in tragedy a world without gods, with no possibility of hopeful resolution."

Even so, it was the humanity of Paul's Lear that lingered, echoed in the memory, and lived on. It made contact, it reached out, and especially on tour in Eastern Europe, it was received with rapture: the audiences were deeply starved of contemporary culture, but at the same time they revered Shakespeare. Paul tells me how they apprehended the smallest nuance, and laughed at the rare opportunities for humour, listening with the most intense concentration. Lear "appealed greatly to their vision of theatrical honesty and their demand for truthfulness."

Diana Rigg recalls how students smuggled themselves into the theatre the night before in order to be able to watch it; how Paul was worshipped — "The way great actors are treated" — how single flowers were thrown, or presented — "They could never afford more than one flower."

At various receptions or after curtain call line-ups they met Khrushchev, Mikoyan (who insisted on meeting only six of the principals — very elitist, McCowen thought). To Mikoyan, Diana Rigg's breasts "caused a great deal of pleasure." President Tito in Belgrade, on the other hand, met the whole company and greeted everyone. In Prague they met Vaclav Havel . . . the list was endless. One member of the company recalls that Earl Mountbatten was at one performance: his bleak, disparaging comment afterwards was "Albany [Peter Jeffries] has his spurs on upside down."

Then they flew immediately to Washington, to the land of plenty, where the cherry trees were in blossom and they were struck by the contrast. The Americans were offended by the production of *A Comedy of Errors*, which toured with *King Lear*, for they considered it too slight a play but they were enraptured by *Lear*. After Washington, Boston, and Philadelphia they were honoured to become the first theatre company ever to play at Lincoln Center, New York. However all was not well here, and the tour ended with Brook furiously attacking the bad acoustics, while the technicians attempted to rectify a depleted and anti-climactic *Lear*: the designer of the auditorium could not, apparently, be found. As Paul reports, the Center was intended to house light opera and musicals: "An unsuitably wide and shallow stage with the audience seated in long, long rows far to the right and left of our acting areas. It was rather like watching a tennis match and playing tennis at the same time. I think it was difficult for the audience too, because on one occasion I observed a well-known actress, whom I knew slightly, fast asleep in the stalls. I have to say that at the end of that tour I needed a holiday."

29

Interlude: Mr. Lear

(and the Return of Baddie Number Two)

Did Olivier in his letter to Peter Hall really want Scofield in his National Theatre Company in order to give him a great role, or did he want him there, under his thumb, so that he could "'destroy" him, in the extreme language Alec Guinness used?

"For God's sake," Olivier exploded in 1964, "is acting not as important as football? The theater [sic] is the initial glamorizer of thought, it sugarcoats the pill of thought more than any form of teaching."

He explained in this address made to the American nation with his typical bravado, why the United States should have its own national theatre. "I love the masses like every good fellow should." But he feared public taste: the newspapers, the "idiot box" was third-rate. The public preferred what was third-rate.

Why he had made the British National Theatre "my whole life" was to lead the public towards an appreciation of acting, to "watch acting for acting's sake." Acting for acting's sake? What about the play?

Bold though these words were, they did not quite tally with Olivier's jealous hostility towards Paul's Lear and Brook's production. The words he went on to use (and the indirect bitchiness) are revealing: "And now I have a slight, slight feeling of dismay, *slight*. I had planned to do Lear again. If I alter my conception of Lear, it would be because of what Brook introduced into the image. To do a thing for that sort of fashionable reason might carry you through part of the way but would be very schmukky, I think. However, if I now give them my old Father Christmas they might say, 'This is a bit tired, old boy.' So I'm a *leetle* bit bemused about that one."

"Leetle" and "slight, slight" point to an extraordinary, dark passion in the man. Carefully leaving Paul's name out of it — yet clearly it is aimed at him — he attacked Brook, again in this Machiavellian way worthy of his greatest impersonation, perhaps aware he would never himself reach the heights of Lear. "I don't think he would mind if I said I wasn't one of its admirers. He rid Lear of his glamour, kingliness; made him down to earth. People nicknamed the play 'Mr. Lear.' Whether you liked that or not, the fact is that the image of *King Lear* has had its expression slightly changed."

Paul does not say what he feels about being called "very schmukky," but Brook was very angry. He wrote from the Chelsea Hotel where he was staying in New York to Kenneth Tynan, who was now literary manager at the National: "Larry's article . . . has aroused great ill-feeling. It is surely obvious that like a Cabinet Minister, the head of the National Theatre can no longer be just a private individual at the same time . . . However, for his one public comment on *Lear* and by implication on Paul's performance, seems to many people here either very irresponsible, or malicious towards a fellow actor and a rival organisation. I cannot believe either, but I feel I must let you know this."

Olivier replied with a rather insincere and smarmy letter, asking Brook how he, or "any other thinking friend," could imagine he wished to be malicious to a fellow actor, or one he admired as much as Paul. As to whether he was an artist or a cabinet minister, that was a "large and vexatious question" they should discuss later. Brook was still hurt and wrote again. ("I knew none of this, though Larry didn't like my performance. And knew that he didn't want to like it," said Paul much later.)

Olivier's sense of timing to deliver his outburst was, of course, opportunistic — the eve of Paul's opening in New York; he had previously also, incidentally, spurned the master director, dismissing him to Kenneth Tynan in Stratford's Dirty Duck (after the triumphant *Titus Andronicus* of 1955) as being "like an immovable ox — I won't work with him again."

Time itself does tell: in the Hilary Term 2000 issue of *Oxford Today*, a seminar held on tragedy is reported — Olivier is not mentioned, "Finally, the panel nominated the greatest performances they had witnessed. Mr. [John] Peter managed to nominate [Janet] Suzman's Cleopatra and Dame Diana [Rigg's] Phèdre with a straight face. But the winner, revered by all, was Scofield's Lear. 'He alone gave us Lear the king, Lear the man, and Lear the father,' cries Ms. [Thelma] Holt. Quasi-religious revelation indeed."

There is no doubt about what Lear meant and still means to Paul: "The word from your list of possible aspects of our work in the play which leaps out at me, is the word 'sublime,' again and again, during performance, there is a sense of exultation, that we are close to something uplifting and immense, whether or not we succeeded in conveying this to the audience. I have had no larger experience in the theatre."

Confronted with what I tell him, Paul himself tactfully sidestepped Olivier's response to his Lear, bracketing it with John Gielgud's: "I don't think either liked it very much, I think they felt (about me, i.e.) that I was not kingly enough, and I don't think Larry cared much for Peter's work. John loved working with Peter and would have found much in the production that he liked, but I don't think it was his *King Lear*. This is all speculative, but is what I divined at the time."

Paul's consistency of view over the years is remarkable. Back in 1974 he had this to say:

> Lear is a character which encompasses so much of Shakespeare's observations of human nature. He packed an awful lot in, and it is pretty illuminating to try to play it. You are not the same person when you have finished doing Lear as when you started it. It gives you a broader view of things.
>
> I'm not talking about an actor being affected by the nature of the part he is playing. It's a matter of forming a close understanding of what Shakespeare was writing about. If you get close to it, you cannot help being enlightened.

Being an actor is a marvellously educative process. I'm 52 now and I've been a professional actor since I was 18. I have still a lot to learn. The more you know about the theatre, the more you learn about life. I feel a more rounded person because I've been in the theatre so long.

30

Dipped in the Same Dish

I have recorded how Tynan's response to Lear was very different from Olivier's. During these early years of Olivier's tenure at the National Theatre Paul was constantly present in spirit, but never acted on stage. Tynan wrote virtually every day to Olivier, and endlessly high in his priorities was to have Scofield in the company. Paul headed the list in virtually every casting suggestion Tynan made:

> *Crucible/Dance of Death* — Captain (Scofield 1, Redgrave 2, McKern 3)
> *The Outrageous Saint* (Leonido/Christ)
> Vershinin — Scofield
> *Merchant of Venice* — Scofield (Shylock)
> *Winter's Tale* — Scofield or Finney
> Pericles — Scofield or Finney
> Macbeth

Paul played none of these. Here is another memo (June 24, 1964) to Laurence Olivier, suggesting parts for Paul.

> Tattle in *Love for Love* (Nov. 2 or Jan. 4)
> Proctor in *The Crucible* (Jan. 4 or March 15)
> Danton in *Danton's Death* (Jan. 4 — adapted by John Arden)
> K. in *The Castle* (Jan. 4 or March 15)
> Leonido in *The Outrageous Saint* (March 15)
> Landisi in *Right You Are If You Think So* (Jan. 4 or March 15)
> *The Fall* (Camus) — leading role (done on radio).

But Paul was definitely sabotaged. Tynan tried again, four years later, to have him play Havelock in Charles Wood's Indian Mutiny play, ultimately called *H*. This time it was Paul who did not much like the play, although warm and tactful about it. It would be interesting to see "if a wieldy play emerges" from the draft he read. "It seems to me that Havelock is very much on one note, but perhaps this won't matter to me when it's whittled down. Marvellous play for a director I would think."

The following year it was the turn of Peter Shaffer's *The Battle of Shrivings*, a play Tynan called "like a baroque church — decorative fantasies and operatic gestures, tinsel rather than gold leaf." He wanted the National Theatre to do it with (cast) 1 Scofield, 2 Guinness, 3 Hordern in the lead. But he also suggested for the other main role of Gideon, 1 Olivier, 2 Nicol Williamson, and 3 Scofield, "who might play it rather interestingly in a cold, spikey, satanic, style." Shaffer wanted Hall to direct. Tynan agreed with him: *Shrivings* was directed by Hall with John Gielgud, Wendy Hiller, and Patrick Magee. It received universal condemnation and closed within weeks.

By this time Paul was nearer to working at the National Theatre. Only just. Olivier, after seven years, had been feeling the strain, and there was pressure on him to give way to others, and much speculation that Paul would be his successor — that is, if he wanted to be.

Meantime, Paul had five or six other major roles to play.

31

Interlude:

General Filth and Green Virginity

Up to the time Paul played it, Lear had been generally interpreted as a doting father, an excessively loving man whose fault or foolishness is to entrust his kingdom to his greedy, selfish daughters. It may perhaps be going too far to align Paul's success in this role as similar to the success of Thomas More.

In Shakespeare's plays the undermining of all legitimate authority is a recurrent feature. It occurs with the authority himself actively or positively collaborating in that undermining process. The succession of roles at which Paul most excelled show a characteristic and similar propensity for self-destruction. In other words, his comic gifts apart, Paul does not play winners.

Among these "winning" roles in Shakespeare — and more rousing if less interesting, perhaps, for it, are Henry V, Benedick, Mark Antony and even Richard III, although he of course gets his come-uppance, but not from inside himself. Paul has never played three of these, and did not much shine in the fourth, Henry V. Can it be that, instinctively, he has felt they are not for him? Paul's great roles are the losers and self-destroyers, the victims of passion or envy.

This is perhaps where he shares a deep affinity with Shakespeare himself. Shakespeare had no position in life. He had no title, apart from that of gentleman, which, it is believed, he acquired for his father. His entire theatre is founded on the self-destruction of authority in all its forms. For Shakespeare, in contrast to the narrow but natural inclination and mind-set of most modern authors who imbue and enhance power with demonic intelligence and will, all authority is flawed, weak, and beset with interior contradiction.

Shakespeare shows power constantly threatened, as it was in his own time, its control slender, constantly tottering on the edge of the abyss yet fascinated by its own destruction.

Olivier's greatest roles were Archie Rice and Richard III, in their way both absolutists who never change. Olivier himself, for all his philanderings and insecurities, his vulgarity and tasteless ambition, was, as a pillar of the establishment, an absolutist who never changed. Whereas, according to Paul, Vivien Leigh "took any kind of pre-eminence with a pinch of salt . . . he took it seriously."

Does Paul instinctively feel sympathy with Shakespeare's abdication of power? I suspect he does. He stands outside. He stands alone. Like Timon of Athens who, again, echoes Thersites (a part he has wanted to play and suggested to Hall as an alternative to Pandarus), he may not feel as strong in his violent curses, but even so, one feels he yearns (as did that visionary Richard Jeffries) for the vast, uncivilized space in which he can — well, not exactly spend his frenzy harmlessly — but on a mundane level exercise his dog, read and reflect at his leisure — and in the company of his wife and family. He prefers the anonymity.

The fascination in Timon did not lay for Paul in what he developed from. Compared with Lear, whose "emotions, his environment and relationships, are all clear, Timon has nothing." He is enigmatic: "It would seem that he gave for what he could get in return. It's ambiguous." The performance had to resolve itself "into an abstract picture of disillusionment."

Not surprisingly, then, Paul excelled as Timon and today considers it one of the roles which most fascinated him. One should, perhaps, remind oneself how violent these causes are, yet how the warmth of Paul's voice could invade, fragment and illuminate them:

> Let me look back upon thee. O thou wall
> That girdles in those wolves, dive in the earth

And fence not Athens! Matrons, turn incontinent!
Obedience fail in children! Slaves and fools,
Pluck the grave wrinkled Senate from the bench,
And minister in their steads! To general filth
Convert, o' the instant, green virginity! . . .
         . . . Maid, to thy master's bed,
Thy mistress is o' the brothel! Son of sixteen,
Pluck the lin'd crutch from thy old limping sire,
With it beat out his brains! . . .
         . . . Thou cold sciatica,
Cripple our senators, that their limbs may halt
As lamely as their manners! . . .
         . . . Itches, blains,
Sow all th' Athenian bosoms, and their crop
Be general leprosy!

There is no doubt in my mind, that quietist as Paul is, unerringly polite and courteous — and at the time even prepared, moderately, to air an anti-Vietnam War opinion — Paul is an outsider. As he himself tells me when I ask him:

> The need for equality is important to me, but I know that we are none of us equal with each other. Equality of opportunity we need, but that of purpose or achievement, or desire, or of aptitude, even of the capacity for thought, is surely a nightmare vision.
>
> I don't have political leanings or a bias to right or left, am seldom drawn to the arguments or policies of politicians of any party, and there have been, and are, very few for whom I would gladly vote.
>
> We are governed, it would seem, by fantasy, by ideas that remain out of reach.

Timon was a triumph when Paul played it at Stratford in 1965. The director, John Schlesinger, looked at the psychology of Timon's hatred, showing that his initial open-handedness is the subconscious means by which he protects his inability to give love, and protects also his morbid but moral introspection, which erupts in the end with savage self-loathing. "Not since the famous Brook-Olivier *Titus Andronicus* has a long-underrated play revealed such unsuspected depth."

Although Paul told someone he spends on Timon only a fraction of the agony he discharged on Lear, he deliberately missed the first night party. He went home early "with my wife and son, talked a little, then bed earlyish. You can go physically *down* after a first night that has turned out big." The reviews were unstintingly full of praise, but Paul was worried that they might not reach the same pitch on the second night. Good Timons don't go a-partying!

All that "powerful philosophical stuff pours out of him," says Clive Swift, who had been in the *King Lear* company, and seen him as Timon "just as if he was making it up." The animus, as directed in *Lear*, as in *Hamlet* — in the future, too, in his Macbeth, Othello, Volpone, through indeed to Salieri, is, however grimly and barbarically displayed, one of tortured self-seeking. It was now frequently winning him the accolade "This actor for our times," and soon would be winning another, frequently bandied about, which he was to find a bit absurd, if not embarrasing.

He was credited as appearing in the Peter Brook film *Tell Me Lies*, based on the stage production of *US*, the anti-Vietnam War protest drama in which Brook's *Marat/Sade* company, or many of them, appeared. His contribution consisted of appearing on a platform with Peggy Ashcroft. Both read poems. Paul, ominously wearing dark glasses and sporting his Lear beard, looked quite like Che Guevara himself, the darling of that period:

> Alas we, who wished to lay the foundations of kindness
> Could not ourselves be kind . . .

After reading, he was interviewed and looked rather tentative, fidgeting as he was challenged as to whether *Tell Me Lies* would do any good. "I don't know," he said, "it's a voice. If it's heard it might be worth while if it joins up with other voices."

Glenda Jackson, in Trafalgar Square, possessed much more ferocious conviction as she denounced, from a text she read out, the forces of imperialism. "What were you reading?" asked an overawed member of the crowd. "Che Guevara!" she replied proudly. It should send a shiver up the spine.

32

More Trivial Pursuits

It is 1966. The secretaries at Broadcasting House were competing to type a version of Tolstoy's *Anna Karenina* for Paul to read on the radio, in anticipation of his "voice and unique combination of dramatic intensity and subtlety." Lorna Pegram wrote to him they are desolate that he has turned it down. Can they postpone? Will he lunch? Will he appear on *Woman's Hour*? And so on.

The reluctant celebrity will not oblige. *Woman's Hour*, he tells Teresa McGonagle, is one of his top "listen while you drive" programmes, and if he were to do an interview he would love to do one with her. "It is something, however, I don't like doing, by which I *don't* mean that I disapprove, or have any strong attitude towards interviewing as such, but I simply don't enjoy it, so please excuse me."

One lady journalist issued a paean of praise for his looks, and took her own picture of him backstage after the show.

The best thing about Paul Scofield's good looks is that there are no others quite like him. He isn't a type. You could never confuse his face.

Although undoubtedly handsome 20 years ago, he is even better-looking now. Lines suit him. Those great deep lines which cut down his face give it distinction and enormous strength. But for all its strength it is a sensitive face. I photographed him in his dressing room with no make-up.

Paul Scofield is an example of a handsome man who is not classically good-looking. His features are not perfect. But the whole composition of his face is striking, calm and intensely original. And there is a great quietness about his face which is barely disturbed, when he changes his expression completely, by the merest flicker of a face or eye muscle.

A few of the sort of faces Rembrandt used to paint appear in each generation. Paul Scofield's is one of them. It is more than just good-looking. It is magnificent.

This from Angela Huth's School for Flatterers. But as Donald Zec wrote a year later in the *Daily Express*, Paul "rejects the whole personality package . . . Crowning no beauty queens, opening no fetes, illuminating no foyers . . . [his] genuine passion for self-effacement led him and his attractive actress wife Joy Parker to avoid the cocktail bars at Stratford-upon-Avon in favour of the quiet pubs on the outskirts."

Yet at one of these he was recognised. "Here we go again," mutters Scofield hopelessly. "Didn't you once play cricket for Warwickshire?" It might have crushed other actors. It brought a grateful smile to the "sphinx."

"Sphinx" refers, Zec reported, to the time Gielgud delivered the judgement, "He is withdrawn, remote, a sphinx without a secret." To which Scofield, with equal respect for the judicious phrase, cordially retorted, "All balls."

"Personality," Paul tells Zec, "has no place in the craft of an actor. It is best seen by other people."

Zec mischievously suggested, "Admittedly Sir Larry, Sir John, Sir Ralph, Sir Michael and Sir Alec have had their great and shining moment . . ." Great they are, but the greatest is "*Mr.* Paul Scofield . . ."

"The rumour was, that Mr. Scofield had already refused one offer of a knighthood, his first, made to him in Moscow, when *Lear* was played there. 'I'd rather be known as Mr.' . . . he is reputed as saying." In fact, the offer came when he was playing Macbeth in Moscow — see Chapter 35.

Zec made the point that at close range Paul "dominates from the head. It is a large head, carved in the rough, weatherworn, and storm-proof. When the defences are up, the expression absent, and the Asiatic lids half-closed, you may feel you are in a the presence of a hanging judge. Extreme shyness does this to certain people. In fact, Scofield is as gentle and as congenial as the horse he rides down on the farm. The weighty pouches under the eyes, the deep clefts flanking the mouth, reflect the intensity with which the facial machinery responds to the signal from the master switch."

Concluded Zec:

"Biographers who burrow away in search of the bizarre anecdote or the racy incident in the forty-six years of Paul Scofield find themselves alarmingly short of material."

Aha!

33

Self-Deception — Continued

"Khlestakov was for me, in every performance, a weird dream; as of surf-boarding or flying," Paul tells me in 2000. Peter Hall created a grotesque style for the 1966 production of Gogol's *The Government Inspector*. Two years after the visit of Paul's Moscow friends who played *Dead Souls* at the Aldwych, Hall (and Paul) repaid the debt.

From our vantage point it could well seem somewhat like a nine-teenth-century version of Blair's Britain: cringing and bribery, spin-doctors, incompetent officials, bloated new notabilities, and in their midst, the visiting inspector (of the Millennium Dome, perhaps?), a conman who is taken for the real thing (their self-deception blinds them to the reality of others).

Paul sailed through this with genius, ably foiled by, and duping among others, brilliant caricatures from Brewster Mason (the boring Judge), Paul Hardwick (the pig-like Charity Commissioner), Paul Rogers (the blustering Major), and David Warner (the elongated Postmaster).

He slipped effortlessly (to begin with, using an outrageous mock-gen-teel cockney accent — "loife" for "life," "sympathyair" for sympathy) to establish his façade of St. Petersburg manners, from reaction to reaction. The scene when he gradually realises the Major has come, not to arrest him but to honour him, was as brilliant as it was subtle. The master touch was that Paul shows Khlestakov to be just as stupid or self-deceived as his victims, so the comic absurdity became double from the collision of two fantasies.

From the cockney mock-genteel Paul expanded the accent, until it sounded as polyglot as Babel: "Every voice he has ever heard seems to have left an imprint on his memory and he tries to imitate them all simultaneously — changing from crisp Sandhurst tone to Parisian affectation, and — in the drunk scene — revealing an aggressive streak that comes out in a wild parody of American Method acting."

This unearthly comic sound following his exquisite and meticulous descent in blind paralytic drunkenness was followed by, as Bernard Levin recorded, "the longest and loudest exit-applause I can ever remember, and justifiably so."

If the theme of personal integrity in politics was evidently felt urgently when the film of A *Man for All Seasons* was shown later all over the world, here was its very opposite, disintegration or dishonesty, comically exploited.

Ian Hogg says that he can still hear Paul's inflections when he delivered the first line of Charles Dyer's *Staircase*, as the camp hairdresser, balefully staring out into the Aldwych void: "'Funny day, Sunday." This duologue of bickering homosexuals may have carried metaphysical overtones, but was equally an exploitation of the new freedom to treat taboo subjects that the dramatist, in this case a popular dramatist, could now enjoy. Some say that at one performance, at least, there was a live butterfly, left over from the previous production of Brook's *US*, meant to symbolise the fragility of life, fluttering over the stalls. It was on this that Paul fixed his gaze before speaking.

The ageing man, the defeated outsider with overcharged imagination ("Me being artistic"), the tired, bitchy homosexual, panto routines, spent stories . . . Paul spent two hours in unbroken dialogue with his foil, played by Patrick Magee, whom the Scofield character bullies, for he is vulnerable, soft, paunchy, bespectacled.

Paul loved it: it is "very effervescent and hilarious," but also quite sad and, above all, he enjoys playing off Magee, whom he calls "a treasure, a marvellous and idiosyncratic actor, and a very delightful man. Your own observation as to the intention of the playwright is absolutely correct. He once, during rehearsal, pointed out to Pat and myself that he had not intended the two main characters to be homosexuals. This was a bafflement because there was no other way for them to be presented."

Continuing the identification with animals, one critic said Paul's stiff, corseted walk was "like a starfish on points." Paul articulated certain words (stuffed otter, *salon des dames*, Muswell Hill), to rank alongside Edith Evans's "handbag" or Maggie Smith's "Judith." I remember, in Dyers's meticulous attention to details of speech and his inexhaustible succession of good lines, the voice Scofield assumed:

A voice that now grates as if a stick has been rattled across iron railings; now twangs as if a harpist is plucking uncertainly at the strings; or else moves of a sudden to a peevish, almost rusty vibrato. The voice can curl glutinously round unexpected syllables. It can leave a sentence in tattered shreds, or flare upon a final syllable as though a tired peacock were displaying its draggled fan. The owner of the voice, the peacock, knows at heart that the world is not particularly interested; but the display has become a habit.

This remarkable purple passage demonstrates that Paul could discover, in the "intoxication" of playing these comedies, what he calls the "glorious pretentiousness" and "sublime stupidity" of their characters, what others find in being celebrities.

34

Saint, Homosexual, and Regicide

By the time I came to the film I felt I'd digested him, as far as I ever could. Intellectually, I never could. It was more than playing a man, it was playing a whole spiritual theme. But at least in the film I knew what I was doing, which is very rare for a stage actor.

Sam Goldwyn, when he produced a film he liked, would say, "I don't care if it makes a dime, but I want everyone in America to see it." But when the veteran director Fred Zinnemann had spent three years preparing André Malraux's *Man's Fate*, and the film was cancelled in rehearsal a few days before lawyers and accountants were replacing showmen as heads of the studios, cost-efficiency was king and "a handshake was no longer a handshake."

By his reckoning, Zinnemann's film of *A Man For all Seasons* was the last of the best, for the old motion-picture chiefs knew about the irrational side of the business they had created. It was experimental, it was low-budget, it benefited from the fact its production company, Columbia, did not much care if it made money or not. In addition, it almost never came to be made.

20th Century Fox in 1965 wanted to make a film about General Custer and the Sioux Indians, with Zinnemann directing. But the script was mostly on the side of the Sioux, and Zanuck wanted Custer portrayed as the traditional hero. When the budget turned out to be three times more expensive than anticipated, Zinnemann no longer had a film to make.

Mike Frankovich, a Columbia executive, suggested *A Man for All*

Seasons. Zinnemann said yes, and in five weeks Bolt wrote a script. Bolt, however, had trouble finishing it, and was also preparing a film version of *Dr. Zhivago* for David Lean. Zinnemann was pleased with the result but, after an exhaustive study of the draft, asked for a second script. "I'm liking work with Freddie very much," Bolt told Lean . . . "he's more in love with the play than I am, so that the comic situation arises of him wanting to retain things for their 'beauty,' which I want to pitch out in favour of speed. But I think it'll be good, though I can't see it making a penny."

Calling Bolt's screenplay "one of the finest I had ever read," Zinnemann regretted Bolt had cut Matthew the "Common Man" (the Leo McKern role) whose only ambition was to "keep breathing." But," Bolt told him, "it's a *theatrical* device."

The film did not augur well from Columbia's point of view. As the reader might well by now have come to expect of this book, it had very little action, let alone violence; no sex, no overt love story, and, most important, no great film stars. Hardly, Zinnemann noted laconically, "*any* actors known to the U.S. public."

In spite of his considerable stage success in the role of More, the Columbia executives did not want Paul. They wanted Olivier, with Alec Guinness as Cardinal Wolsey, and Peter O'Toole as Henry VIII.

Zinnemann was loyal, and had sound judgement. He did not want Olivier, who was mad keen and coveted the part if only to eliminate Paul as a rival, and to attempt to obliterate his acclaim in this role. Bolt agreed with Zinnemann, but even so both men had to go through the motions of meeting Olivier and politely turning him down. Richard Burton was also a preferred star, but too busy at the time. He would have wanted £1 million, while the film's whole budget was a relatively tiny £600,000.

Columbia finally fell in with Zinnemann's wishes.

"I was surprised and honoured to be chosen for the film," said Paul, "being almost unknown in the movie world. I missed the *Common Man* as a potent link between More and the working man, but accepted that a film is not a play. My own task was unaltered except that I now focused my thought on to a camera instead of an audience."

(TOP LEFT) Paul, "the short fat one with brother Jack." (TOP RIGHT) On Brighton front with son Martin and elusive mother "attempting as always to avoid the camera." (BOTTOM LEFT) E. H. Scofield, Paul's father, in his school's playground. (BOTTOM RIGHT) As Juliet in *Romeo and Juliet* (with a darn in the big toe of his sock).

Polar Bear took his temperature and was
cheerful and brisk. 'Not very ill,' he said,
'just a chill.' And he filled a hot-water bottle.
Henry was a bad patient and fussed about
his pillows.

(TOP LEFT) As Donald in *Three-Cornered Moon*, with Joy (Elizabeth Rimplegas). (TOP RIGHT)
Joy's illustration for Henry, *The Story of a Mole*. (BOTTOM) Alexander in *Adventure Story*, with
Joy (Roxana).

(TOP LEFT) As Alex Morden in *The Moon Is Down*, with Lewis Cason (Mayor Orden). (TOP RIGHT) As Jack Tanner in *Man and Superman*, with John Harrison (Octavius Robinson). (BOTTOM) As Stephen Undershaft (left) in *Major Barbara*, with Margaret Leighton (center left, Sarah Undershaft), Margaretta Scott (right, Barbara Undershaft) and Basil C. Langton (Adolphus Cusins).

(TOP LEFT) As Philip Sturgess in *The River Line.* (TOP RIGHT) As Richard in *Richard II.* (BOTTOM) As Tegeus-Chromis in *A Phoenix Too Frequent,* with Hermione Hannen (Dyhamene).

As Hamlet, with Mary Ure (Ophelia). (INSET) A drawing by Irina Kadina of Paul as Hamlet in 1954, on the Russian tour.

(TOP) Me in *Expresso Bongo*, taken in Soho during rehearsals. (BOTTOM) A priest in *The Power and the Glory*, with Alex Scott on the left and Patience Collier on the right.

(TOP) As Thomas More in *A Man for All Seasons*. (MIDDLE) Off the set with Orson Welles (Cardinal Wolsey). (BOTTOM) With Fred Zinneman.

(TOP) As King Lear in the film. (ABOVE) Lear with Alec McCowen (the Fool). (LEFT) As Lear on stage, with Diana Rigg (Cordelia).

(TOP) As Timon of Athens. (BOTTOM) Timon with Elizabeth Spriggs and Janet Suzman (Alcibiades's mistresses Phrynia and Timandra).

(TOP) As the Clerk in *The Government Inspector* with Paul Rogers (the Mayor). (BOTTOM) As Charles Dyer in *Staircase* with Patrick Magee (Harry Leeds). (OPPOSITE) As Macbeth.

(TOP LEFT) As Alan West in *Savages* with Michael Pennington (left, the Missionary) and Tom Conti (Guerilla Leader). (TOP RIGHT) As Uncle Vanya in *Uncle Vanya*. (BOTTOM) As Laurie in *The Hotel* in Amsterdam with Joss Ackland (left, Gus) and Judy Parfitt (Annie).

(TOP LEFT) As Prospero in *The Tempest.* (TOP RIGHT) As Othello in *Othello, the Moor of Venice.* (RIGHT) As Volpone in *Volpone*, with Hugh Paddick (Corbaccio).

(TOP LEFT) As Colonel von Valdhcim in *The Train.* (TOP RIGHT) As Verner Conklin in *Come Into the Garden Maude*, with Geraldine McEwan (Maud Caragnani). (BOTTOM) As Zharkov in *Scorpio*, with Burt Lancaster.

(TOP) As Salieri in *Amadeus*. (BOTTOM) As Nat in Herb Gardner's *I'm Not Rappaport*, with Howard Rollins (Midge).

15

In the garden at Balcombe. (INSET) As Captain Shotover in *Heartbreak House*, with Imogen Stubbs (Ellie Dunn).

Paul was contracted for a fee of precisely £26,785. 4s. 3d. (one hundred thousand dollars), plus 10 percent of the net profits. Production was due to start in March 1966. Fortunately Columbia seemed to have washed their hands of the project, while the original producer, Mike Frankovich, moved on to the film of *Casino Royale*, a much larger budget. With Bill Graf now the executive producer it became something of an exemplary piece of film-making, with an exemplary actor playing an exemplary man. It may sound a recipe for disaster, but it gives the lie to the widely held belief that discord, disagreement, conflict are obligatory for successful creative endeavour.

"Hampton Court, I thought, had never looked lovelier. Through the great archway of the outer wall, the lawns gleamed crisp and green in the floodlighting. Beyond them was a second archway, and then more courtyards and more archways, all the way along to the massive door of the palace itself."

This was the illusion the designer John Box created at Shepperton, building a half-size replica of the Court for £5,000. No one could tell the difference between photographs of the set and the real thing, but a few yards to left or right and the illusion was shattered by struts, planks, coils of wire, and ladders.

"Basically," said Box, "it is a very simple set — just four screens, diminishing in size as they get further away, to give the impression of perspective. How did I work it out? Oh. Just by building small models and playing with them like a child. You may think it's a bit extravagant to build such an enormous set for something that is only a kind of lead-up, but that's what cinema is about.

"I call it 'visual orchestration' — it's a corny phrase, I know, but it's the only way to describe it."

They found an old Benedictine abbey, Studley Priory, in Oxfordshire, for More's house (with some kind of appropriate revenge, for it had been "secularised" by Henry VIII). But the most interesting of all challenges was that for the King's visit to More they needed a tidal river representing the Thames flowing past More's house (in whose day the Thames was a waterway teeming with river traffic, not unlike today's motorways). A wall protecting the house and garden had to be built next to the water. This was for King Henry arriving with his courtiers in the royal barge and impatiently jumping overboard too soon, sinking into mud up to his ankles. Furious at first, he suddenly bursts out laughing; his courtiers — the hangers-on of the period — can do nothing other than jump after him, ruining their pretty finery and deliriously aping the King's laughter.

For the mud to be there they had to have a tidal river, close enough to the sea for the tide to rise and fall; but in 1966 every single estuary in England was crammed with modern shipping, cranes, and modern buildings. Nervous weeks went by until Roy Walker, a young assistant architect, discovered that Lord Montague of Beaulieu in Hampshire owned the "bottom" or lower reaches of a small river on his estate. For suitable consideration, yachts at anchor were removed and they had two miles of make-believe pristine Thames to themselves, between Chelsea and Hampton, complete with birds and wildlife; the garden wall was built next to it with steps leading to the top. A replica garden wall was built at Studley Priory, to match it.

The large courtroom set where More is sentenced to death was conceived as a kind of bullring, to convey the feeling that the final outcome had been decided before the victim enters through a dark, narrow passage.

More suitable than Alec Guinness, Orson Welles was pursued by Zinnemann to play Cardinal Wolsey. But he was difficult to track down. Zinnemann finally caught up with him in an apartment in Curzon Street, London, where he was sitting behind a magnum of champagne, complaining of liver trouble. "My French doctor," he said, "tells me that one must surprise one's liver." He agreed, reluctantly, to play Wolsey.

One of the last to be cast was Robert Shaw as Henry VIII. Unknown to Shaw, Richard Burton had already turned down the part. Shaw was offered £15,000 to play three scenes (a far cry, says his agent, from his previous fee of £350,000), with 2-1/2 percent of the producer's profits. He joined an outstanding cast that included Leo McKern (as Cromwell) and John Hurt as Richard Rich (another instinctive, creative risk taken by the director). Hurt was entirely unknown, while the young lawyer's role of Rich, that of an Iago and betrayer, is the most dynamically dramatic in the whole script. Vanessa Redgrave had agreed to play More's daughter, but she had begun to shoot in *Blow-Up* during the day and then was offered the lead in *The Prime of Miss Jean Brodie*, so she implored Zinnemann to release her, although later agreed (without any screen credit) to do a day's shooting for a brief appearance as Anne Boleyn. "We needed an actress," reported Zinnemann, "who, in forty-five seconds, could convince the audience she was capable of changing the course of an empire."

Zinnemann paid tribute to the extraordinary calibre of the crew and the actors. In the first few days the crew did their usual work very well. On the third day of filming, however, when Paul spoke More's words about the law — telling his son-in-law Roper (Corin Redgrave) he would definitely give the Devil benefit of law — and challenging Roper:

MORE: What would you do? Cut a great road through the law
    to get after the Devil
ROPER: I'd cut down every law in England to do that!
MORE [*roused and excited*]: Oh? [*Advances on Roper*] And
    when the last law was down, and the Devil turned round
    on you — where would you hide, Roper, the laws all
    being flat? [*Leaves him*] This country's planted thick with
    laws from coast to coast. Man's laws, not God's — and if
    you cut them down — and you're just the man to do it
    — d'you really think you could stand upright in the
    winds that would blow then? [*Quietly*] Yes, I'd give the
    Devil benefit of law, for my own safety's sake.

Everyone on the set became suddenly mesmerized by the magic of Paul's delivery. From then on it remained that way till the film was finished. "So totally," said Zinnemann, "did Scofield convey the scope of More's character that for months afterwards I couldn't help but look at him in awe as a saint rather than an actor." I would add that Paul allowed you to see More think.

When it came to Wolsey's scene with More, Welles, swathed in scarlet robes, summons Paul to a tiny cramped office. His bulky presence blots out air and light, no furniture but a desk, and the walls are painted in the same shade of red as Wolsey's costume. The scene is short. The King needs a son, Wolsey tells More: "What are you going to do about it?" "I'm very sure," replies More in a dry murmur, "the King needs no advice from me on what to do about it."

As they continued to dispute it was clear Welles hardly knew his part. He was reluctant to play it in the first place and, either from deficient memory or laziness, had done little work on the lines.

Paul was left standing while he struggled. Welles's confidence — with his personality and genius — were so immense he managed in the end to create a monolithic illusion of absolute, corrupt power. He was matched, however, by Paul's patience, equally "enormous," says Zinnemann.

"Welles had a marvellous, endearing sense of humour. We were working on a scene with the Duke of Norfolk coming to collect the Chancellor's chain from Wolsey. During rehearsals the "dying" Cardinal was lying on his cot, puffing the longest, fattest Monte Cristo cigar. We started shooting. Nigel Davenport [the Duke] entered, played his scene and on leaving said, 'Have you a message for the King?' 'Yes,' said Orson, 'tell him the take is no good — there was a plane in it!'"

Henry VIII offered Shaw a great opportunity to excel. The gusto, the exuberance he showed on that first appearance heralded a performance of only twelve minutes' screen time (in mainly three scenes), whose impact remains memorable. In the long scene as he attempts to get More to change his mind over his divorce from Catherine of Aragon, when More responds, "Take your dagger and saw it [my head] from my shoulders, and I will laugh and be thankful, if by that means I can come with Your Grace with a clear conscience." Shaw's King is in turn warm-hearted, roughly jokey, reasonable, frightened, increasingly uncontrolled, and finally despotic as he descends into a tantrum.

Providence played quite a hand, too, in the making of *A Man for All Seasons*: "Another incident: in the course of a scene played by Paul Scofield and Robert Shaw in More's garden, the King was to grow angry; as he spoke a certain line, a sudden violent gust of wind shook the trees, as if on cue. The sudden wind sprang up each time that particular line was spoken — in long shots, reverse shots, close-ups — and we always had a perfect match in the editing." At another important moment,

> The Duke of Norfolk was to ride through a snowy landscape to see the dying Cardinal Wolsey; it was now mid-April and all England was free of snow. Undaunted, Bill Graf and Bill Kirby rented two enormous trucks full of styro-foam (the sort used by airports for fire-fighting) to be spread on the location. Hardly had we arrived there late in the evening, when, lo and behold, snow started to fall. It snowed all night and at dawn the hills looked sparkling white; the styro-foam trucks stayed where they were. Stranger still, just after we had finished shooting and I had said "Cut" for the last time, the sun came out and all the snow melted in less than half an hour, as if on cue.

Zinnemann admired and supported all his cast. Especially he singled out Wendy Hiller who played More's wife who, in a somewhat unrewarding and grumpy role, showed her skill at doing what he calls "a slow burn — her slowly growing anger and indignation and failure to understand why More, by refusing to submit to the King's wishes, is placing himself in deadly peril."

Shaw's agent commented that Shaw's exuberance spilled over into real life. In posing for the press he decided to run through the long grass with Susannah York trailing in his wake. As he ran, the expensively made rings, replicas of historical artefacts, dropped from his fingers. If they were not found it would be a disaster for the film as — with the continuity problem it would create — no further shots would be possible until replacements were made. The whole unit fell on its knees in the long grass looking for the rings. Shaw's cry of "A case of champagne to anyone who finds them" soon got the whole press corps looking too.

When the Columbia executives first viewed an hour of assembled film, there was a sudden change of atmosphere, and a mounting excitement, noted Zinnemann. "Now it was safe others [besides Frankovich and Graf] came eagerly out of the woodwork to pat me on the back and offer advice." It took only seven months from the first day of shooting for the film to open in New York.

Zinnemann's feelings about Paul were fully reciprocated:

Fred Zinnemann was a jewel. A calm, rational man, quietly authoritative and in perfect control of the myriad aspects of film-making. He had a simplicity in his understanding of *A Man for All Seasons* which reflected the simplicities and the complex resoluteness of Sir Thomas More without apparent effort or contrivance. He was a kindly man, he had a core of steel; once having chosen his actors he trusted them, discussions as to how a scene was to be played were rare. As a theatre actor I was initially nonplussed by his ruling that there should be no rehearsal period — having played the part in the theatre both in London and America my misgivings were not for myself, but for the many actors to whom the play was new; when questioned on this point he replied that he didn't want us to get "stale." Though surprised, I never felt, in shooting, that we were insufficiently prepared. Thus I learned a little of the difference between stage and screen performances. And the difference between the spontaneity of the moment and the spontaneity that finally emerges from "repetition" — from practice.

At an earlier time Paul commented how Zinnemann was a strong disciplinarian, but that he had reservations as to how good with actors he really was:

Perhaps you remember the scene that I had with Susannah York on the beach, which is the real crunch of the action of ideas, when the daughter comes to her father and seems to oppose him as an intellectual equal, using her wits that he had helped form, against him.

Now Susannah was marvellous, but she did that scene at first all supplicating and feminine; not as an equal, which was the way I knew that Robert Bolt had intended it. So I went to Zinnemann and said that I thought that she should be told this and all he said was, "I can't do that," and would not be involved. I had to suggest the idea to her myself and I think it worked out quite well.

Just as Paul dominated the stage and brought to the role of Thomas More his own unusual and independent sense of authority, so did his authority bring to the film an extra dimension of truth. When it opened in New York the response was far more perceptive and generous than in England. The British, Catholics apart, tend to balk at the Thomas More story, somehow it has remained unpalatable to Anglicans and the non-religious majority. As people generally will not quite own up to anti-papist prejudice, they prefer to hide it by picking on other faults if they can be found. And imagine the present-day reaction of an audience to this More speech, performed so movingly by Scofield:

"When a man takes an oath, Meg," More explains to his daughter Margaret, "he's holding his own self in his own hands. Like water [*cups hand*] and if he opens his fingers then — he needn't hope to find himself again."

The film was in some ways superior to the stage presentation of the play: the six Oscars it won were well deserved; it had eight nominations. It won the best picture award, Zinnemann's was for best director, Bolt's was for best screenplay and Paul's for best actor. Ted Moore's Oscar was for colour cinematography, Elizabeth Halfenden's and Joan Bridge's for costumes.

The film is now deservedly considered a classic, listed frequently among the very best ever made. It remains timeless and, with its oddly immediate or present-day sense of occasion, was a model for *Shakespeare in Love* some thirty-odd years later. Zinnemann, who died in 1997, was a perfectionist, but in addition a star-maker. It was he who gave Marlon Brando his first film; he cast the fading crooner Frank Sinatra to reinvent him in *From Here to Eternity*, as well as *A Man for All Seasons* he made other, equally distinctive and different films such as *The Day of the Jackal*, with Edward Fox, and *The Nun's Story*, with Audrey Hepburn.

But if the British film critics, such as Penelope Gilliatt, sneered, the Americans were unstinting in their praise. Bosley Crowther wrote: "Zinnemann has done a fine job of putting upon the screen the solid substance of *A Man for All Seasons* and in doing so he presents us with an awesome view of a sturdy conscience and a steadfast heart, with such magnificent settings as only England itself could provide . . . It is to Zinnemann's credit that he has not allowed his excellent cast to resort to pyrotechnics except in the singular case of Robert Shaw's tempestuous performance of the unbalanced Henry Eighth."

Kate Cameron commented in the New York *Daily News* that the film is "a fine work of art . . . profoundly stirring," and above all the brilliant characterizations towers Scofield "who dominates the screen with his gentle voice and steadfast refusal to kowtow to the King even at the expense of his head."

An Oscar is 13-1/2 inches high and weighs nearly 7 pounds. It is 92.5 percent tin, and 7.5 percent copper. Paul was not at the ceremony to collect it, but Wendy Hiller did so for him, and it was posted to him from Hollywood. On arrival in Balcombe the brown paper parcel was opened but the golden statuette was broken — Paul handed the debris to his gardener. "See if you can mend it," he suggested.

The gardener hammered out the Oscar's broken legs, glued together the fractures, and Paul put it away in the corner of his workroom. "I suppose a lot of people would have sent it back and insisted on a new one. Although it was nice to get, it's not decorative, really. I suppose that's why I don't display it. But if anyone wants to see it I'll get it out."

When subsequently Paul wins the top acting award (a "Stella") from the British Film Academy in the same year Edith Evans, also a Stella winner, decided on a romantic impulse that their two Stellas should exchange a congratulatory kiss. In so doing the "kiss" is a shade too passionate. The head of Dame Edith's Stella breaks off, giving, as they say, a wonderful photo-opportunity — Dame Edith gapes in astonishment, Paul holding the broken head.

Legend has it that the day after Paul wins the Oscar all the phones are ringing in Robin Fox's office, the telegrams arriving with offers, and Fox himself, when Paul comes in, is delighted: "We've got the Oscar, we can put up your fees" — to which Paul answers, "I want to go back to Stratford for £12 a week."

The gossip-makers did not have a field day, nor did the sweet smell of success come anywhere near sticking. Paul was mentioned several times as "the greatest actor in the world," but he cringes at the term. He could, they seem to repeat ad nauseam, have been greater than Burton if he had gone to Hollywood. But he doesn't go. He is just plain Mr. Scofield, living in Balcombe, known affectionately to some neighbours over to whom he will walk with his dog as "Mr. Sco." He commutes regularly to London, if at odd hours, and his wife picks him up at the station.

He was "the shy star." "Being a star doesn't mean much to me," he told Barry Norman, the film pundit:

> Once I wanted adulation and fame and all those things. When one is very young they seem terribly important. But a long time ago I realised I should have to choose between films and theatre — and the theatre has always come first.
>
> I'm not an actor because I feel the need to say "Look at me — aren't I clever?" I don't have an inferiority complex that I must disguise with a display of bravura. I don't want the eyes of the world upon me all the time.
>
> I'm an actor because . . . oh, because I'm good at it. I can say honestly and, I hope, without self-satisfaction that I'm happy with my lot. It may be rare but it's true in my case.
>
> If I hadn't been an actor I'd have worked in the country. I'm not anti-social, but I don't like crowds and busy streets and big buildings. The one thing I dislike about acting is having to work in cities.

It was fortunate for him that he saw no point in accumulating vast amounts of money, although *A Man for All Seasons* was to become a steady earner over the next years. Few films make a producer's profit over the production expenses, and film companies usually find ways of denying those actors promised generous percentages the actual sight of any returns. *A Man for All Seasons* proved a deserved exception, so that Robert Shaw with 2-1/2 percent earned, according to John French his agent, well over $500,000 dollars, so Paul may be scaled up accordingly. Virtue and integrity are rarely underpinned by financial reward, and accompanied by a smiling bank manager. Usually they walk alone. Paul and Joy had by then, as their children were growing up, developed a taste for collecting antiques, and their acquisitions were much admired locally.

By no means did Paul abandon radio. He read (twice) the celebrated diary of Nijinsky, perhaps (suitably) the starting point for Colin Wilson's influential study of *The Outsider*. This was a ninety-minute solo. He had time, too, to play Philoctetes in Sophocles's tantalizing study of the gifted healer with the suppurating wound. As if this rich diet was not enough, he read Van Gogh's letters. All the while John Tydeman had been diligently pursuing him to play Vershinin in *The Three Sisters*, and then, more crucially, *Macbeth*, which he recorded in early 1966 with Peggy Ashcroft, although unfortunately, from Paul's point of view, Lady Macbeth was not a role Ashcroft felt happy playing. Paul and she "do not feel," according to Tydeman, "married . . . She didn't get on playing really evil people — she did want to be loved."

The sound production was a great success, and Paul magnificent in it. Not surprisingly he passed on Dostoevsky's *The Possessed* — he had to drop out. But now he was on course to play in "the Scottish play" at Stratford, opening in August.

35

Under Murderer's Report

"The difficulty of working with genius," Peter Hall tells me, "is that nothing is bad." Paul himself speaks of approaching a new role, that an actor's work has no rules, and that with every play and every playwright "the actor starts from scratch, as if he or she knows nothing and proceeds to learn afresh every time — growing with the relationships of the characters and the insights of the writer."

They began rehearsals of *Macbeth* in summer 1967, but from the start it seemed dogged with difficulties. Hall, the director, was in a bad way; his supporter at Stratford, "Fordie" Flower, had just died of cancer. The new chairman, George Farmer, was an accountant. The Barbican, scheduled to open in 1970 with a permanent home for the RSC, was delayed.

Hall was near burn-out. He caught shingles from Christopher Morahan. He carried on but he was far from his best. He had had breakdowns before, notably in 1963 during *The Wars of the Roses* rehearsals. To add to the pressure there was an important film deal in the office for *Macbeth* with CBS. A continental tour.

Rehearsals were delayed, the first night rescheduled first for 26 July then put back to August. Paul was tired himself after the filming of *A Man* and somehow felt the sequence was wrong: Macbeth should somehow have come before Lear, it was the wrong order to do them in.

Disillusion was further heightened by an article in *Nova* about Hall, the headline ran "Peter uses you — Diana Rigg/He's power mad — Roy Dotrice/Yes, I am a dictator — Peter Hall/but the Royal Shakespeare Company doesn't have that lean and hungry look nowadays." Peter

Lewis's article contained a quote from Glenda Jackson that dogged Hall for years: "I do wish he'd stop pretending to be so bloody nice and simple and democratic when really he's very complicated and ambitious and a dictator. You have to have a boss. All right."

Lunching with him in the Arden Hotel, Hunter Davies found Paul nervous from rehearsals, tense, almost shaking.

"I've studied Macbeth for years," Paul tells him, "but I know from experience that if you come to rehearsal knowing every line it means you've already begun making judgements. So you have to start again.

"The sense of evil is everywhere in *Macbeth*. It's pure evil. Shakespeare's knowledge of it is extraordinary. The atmosphere is incredible. This is what we're now getting in rehearsals.

"I can understand why actors have always looked upon *Macbeth* as unlucky. Never quoting Macbeth in the dressing room, that sort of thing. It is there. You can feel it. I'm not superstitious myself. I always walk under ladders. I'm just superstitious about not being superstitious."

Rehearsals hit an all-time low, however, when Hall had to spend two weeks in a darkened room. The pitch of concentration was broken. Progress was slow, for in feeling his way towards the part Paul found Macbeth completely alien to his own temperament. "I have no comprehension of such violence and such evil. But if one only played parts like one's own temperament, it would be very limiting. You must draw on the potentials of human nature which we all share."

Booked to understudy Scofield in the 1967 production of the Scottish play (and to play Seyton), Ian Hogg attended rehearsals. He had not been an actor very long and, unlike most of his generation at the London Drama Centre who had studied with Yat Malgrem and John Blatchley (they included Frances De La Tour, Chris Bond, Amaryllis Garnett, Alison Fisk, and Stephen Fagan — and later Simon Callow), he had joined a major company straight after leaving drama school.

Vivien Merchant played Lady Macbeth. I sat in, as Scofield's understudy, on all the principals' rehearsals. I also played the part of Seyton, who had four entrances. I observed his method of work.

He seemed to let the text go through him and he worked out what the voice was doing when he said a line three or four times in different ways. He would search for a phrase, a sound, an intimation, and when he found it the intuition became a fact in the performance.

Paul showed such dedication; he would come into the theatre two hours before the play began, but not to get into the role, but rather to transfer into the milieu — from the real world, into the tinsel world. He loved gossip.

When I first met him I think he had heard already that I was a pupil of Yat Malgrem's, and he didn't take kindly to that. God knows what Yat had done to him. Yat was an influential figure who came out of the late 50's, the studio theatres and the Actor's Studio of Lee Strasberg; Yat had an open class for dancers in West Street opposite the Ivy Restaurant; Peter Brook took classes with Yat; so did Olivier, Audrey Hepburn and Sean Connery — who incidentally was one of the very best Hotspurs I saw (in this production Robert Hardy played Prince Hal). At this time also Michael Caine (or real name) was beginning to get a stage career, and in many ways he was like Scofield.

I had been in the RSC when Scofield played Lear at the Aldwych, but I had been in *The Jew of Malta*, in Brook's *US* and the ill-fated *Tempest*. I had liked Paul in *Expresso Bongo* — I thought what a good singer he was and he had been very camp, it was part of his game-plan as an actor.

It was that voice, at the beginning of *Lear*, that I could call up so easily. I would never forget the moment at the opening. There was Lear's court, and the whole court grouped round him. A lot of flurry generally. Then there was Lear's huge throne: something inside it moving about — his hands. Then that voice. It was so bored, the essence of disparaging contempt, blasé.

"Attend the Lords of France and Burgundy."

He seemed to find something, a resonance, he gets, when it's right. Very intelligent man, not an intellectual actor. After two or three days in rehearsal near what is now The Other Place, there was a little tea-shop in a temple-like building — it is now a gift-shop.

It was a break in rehearsal. Our encounter went something like this.

Scofield (low, growling voice, quite loose consonants), "You wanna cup of tea . . . ?"

They collected tea and sat looking at each other. "I couldn't work him out," said Hogg, "he seemed a very simple man."

Scofield said, "A very difficult play, this, Ian, have you got any good ideas?"

My immediate response was to ask myself if Scofield was taking the piss. As Scofield's understudy I received little instruction and could not overhear what Hall told Scofield as the pair went away to talk in the corner. All I did notice was that every time they had one of these talks, they'd do the same bit they were talking about. It would be different — but worse. As if, having been given an essay by Hall, Scofield was being driven further and further from that intuition that told him what was right. It seemed also as if Hall was trying to impose an idea of Macbeth on him — cruel, murderous — while Paul searched for a rationale — something fundamentally good in Macbeth.

Gradually I found the production was becoming more and more of a visual exercise, with the play not working.

Vivien Merchant and Sco never got on: she wasn't his kind of woman. Hall kept delivering essays and then stepped back to see if it was working. It wasn't. A dangerous part, Lady Macbeth — Mrs. Siddons was seized with terror on first studying the part.

I found Scofield became my role model and remained so. He never gave in. As Seyton I had four entrances before or after soliloquys. For seven months of playing the part he never gave in. He crept through the piece and began to win it back. It was incredible, the torture he went through pre- and post-murder and he began to get marvellous in the role — a lesser actor would have ditched it. If he makes a mistake, it seems to relax him. He puts out his tongue and smiles.

His acting trigger is so quick; he could turn it off the moment the pros arch is gone; he'd be joking with his dresser. He hated the costumes and set — the costumes all PVC, the fashion at that time (designed by John Bury). He was in metal — it was striking visually, the whole stage covered in thick carpets, redolent of moorland and blood — slippery plasticky surface the colour of bone like stripped cadavers and everyone when they made an entrance would slip, the carpet would ruck up, if you didn't slide you tripped up.

Dealing with all this I found Scofield a man of stoical patience: I watched him go through the show — I watched . . . I myself would have shouted, "I'm not going on in this costume — these costumes are diabolical." But Scofield just put up with it. At the beginning of the play people come off after their opening pouring with sweat and at one point the company had to be issued with salt tablets. Finally the production was re-costumed in leather.

Scofield never broke down, showed heroic, amazing stoicism. "Why doesn't he say something?" the rest of the cast asked themselves.

One night Hogg was in the wings, ready as Seyton: Scofield, due to make an entrance, wasn't there; this was at the Aldwych, stage left down corridor by stage door; Hal Rogers, the stage manager, called again and again, "Mr Scofield, you're off!" [When you should be on]. Hogg realised Paul's tannoy was not switched on, or faulty. He had missed his entrance. He rushed off to fetch him, arriving within a few feet of his door which was closed, he stopped. The door suddenly opened and Scofield appeared, unhurried, no panic, no rush, calmly taking his time he advanced and "as he passed me he smacked one of his hands twice with the other — limp-wristed hand. 'Naught, naughty!' he said, smiling at me."

He could be very naughty on stage and had huge fun at the expense of others. I found the most dangerous time was when you were looking downstage and he was looking upstage towards you. He had a way of dropping an eyelid.

Just after the opening night in London Scofield was off for a week with a bad throat. They rang me up at my home at Hampton Wick about midday and told me I would be performing. I was dead scared. Peter Hall was unavailable, but John Barton came round to the theatre, with a bottle of whisky "Not to be drunk until after the show," and sat with me during the whole play, nursing me through my performance. Scofield's dresser John, his favourite, whom he generally insisted on, and with whom he had a knockabout relationship, whisked me straight into all the changes so I got the flow. I remembered Yat Malgrem's advice — It doesn't matter what you do in the theatre, whether it's Oedipus or Falstaff, it must be based on free flow, enjoying it, loving it — any kind of angst creates what is called "Bound flow" in Laban theory, defined as a "continuous readiness to stop." You had to have zest, be light and free, and Scofield could not free himself as Macbeth.

When Scofield returned I found it difficult to get to know him further. I felt it was because I was a Yat student — or perhaps it was because I was an understudy. I saw Joy once or twice but he never brought children into the dressing room — he was very private, very careful of the integrity of his private life.

He was the opposite of the arm-round-shoulder actor, the feel-ly-feely kind. Without ambition he was the kind "who had Karma, or God empties goodies into."

The RSC took *Macbeth* to Russia, Leningrad and Moscow, where they played at the Art Theatre. "This was where he really wanted it to be right. Russian actors admired him enormously and you felt Scofield was in his element. But they lost the sets in transit and this caused complications. The Soviets made a great fuss of him: if they decided to take care of you they took care of you, but he was ill at ease in his crumpled grey suit with the patronizing diplomats at the British Embassy."

It was during this tour that Paul was offered a knighthood — and turned it down: his agent, Robin Fox, gracefully declined on his behalf, while Paul, at the British Embassy in Moscow, spoke to the Ambassador. ("I tried to explain why I didn't want it. He was courteous but baffled," Paul told me in 2001.)

"When they returned to play again at the Aldwych, Scofield had had enough of rugs: one night, after a soliloquy, he came down the stage and in front of the audience straightened out every rug. He got his revenge on the set. Scofield never succumbed to the Brook-Gurdjieff approach, although he had that kind of dedication, and I felt he was quite mystical — he read all the time: 'Have you read *Eros and Agape?*' he asked me one day. Brook and he were very different. Brook was always close sexually to the women he worked with, such as Helen Mirren, but Paul was not." Hogg found it hard to talk to Brook:

If ever I try it, he gets up. Brook's favourite actors were comedians, and he liked savage extremes and pushing the actors he worked with to the limit of endurance.

While I regretted I didn't manage to get to know Paul as a friend and would have liked to, I admit he was a distant figure, who did not encourage intimacy. He had no close male friends. He never consulted others much. He got on with certain kinds of women, with the stage staff, his dresser, and those he could indulge in naughty camp gossip with, but he never got too serious about the work. And he didn't like praise much.

Above all Hogg summed him up in one word:

Impeccability. Many actors have a fractured nature, they are miserly, have a drink problem, lecherous, conceited, empty-headed and so on and so on . . . Everyone has a fault.

But in *The Seven Samurai,* which so many had held as their favourite in the black and-white epoch, there is one samurai without a fault. He says only twelve lines, but he is the one drawn into the fight with the bully; he refuses and refuses, but in the end can't back down. He is lean and hollow-cheeked like Scofield, and he cuts down the bully without a word, slicing him in half. Shakespeare left no personal account. "Why should I tell you? Why should you want to know?"

Brook said, when you work on a part you find the dream of the play; read it like a storybook, don't tell the plot too much; but it will never work unless the fool persists in his folly, unless the character has innocence. When I came to play Macbeth at the Stratford

Ontario Festival later I couldn't get Scofield's intonations out of my head.

"I know how busy you must be with Macbeth happening and with the Shakespeare film about to happen," wrote John Tydeman to Scofield in late 1967, "but I wonder if you will have time at the beginning of January to go right back to the very birth of things and give us your Oedipus on radio."

Tydeman, with Mephistophelean glee, promised new excitements — stereophany. He tempts him further with the largest of the BBC's studios, usually reserved for symphony orchestras — "I hope we won't all rattle round like peas in a pod, but even so it will be smaller than Epidaurus" — and with a Jocasta played by Irene Worth, how can Paul refuse?

"As for Othello, which we mentioned a long time back, I'm sure you still feel it best to let that wait a while until the other tragic heroes with whom you are involved have had their various says on stage or screen."

Judgements about Paul's Macbeth varied considerably. Perhaps the key to the performance was Hall's observation, "He will deliver what he has ready, no more, no less." In the longer term it became clear that he had more to show than was visible on the first night. W.A. Darlington called it, "a fine performance but I feel there is more to come. When I see it again — as I must — I shall expect to be swept away by it as I never quite was last night."

This, however is just what did happen to Harold Hobson, who was overwhelmed by the beginning:

The stage is hidden by a great white sheet that stretches from the fore-edge to the flies. Suddenly the house lights go out, there is a burst of thunder, the lightning flashes, and across the screen for the sliver of a second only there is thrown the black shadow of the Cross.

Instantaneously the sheet vanishes, wavering momentarily like a ghost, and the three witches are seen in a lurid darkness, on what may be either a blasted heath or a lake of burning marl. They are spattering with blood a degraded Crucifix turned upside down. The effect of this whirlwind opening is enormous.

Hobson's hyperbole extended generously to Paul: "Though apt to crime, this Macbeth is very beautiful. In the central scenes Mr. Scofield is like some great cardinal of the Renaissance, wicked perhaps, but commanding and noble. He is Lucifer, but Lucifer with the light of the morning still on him, and his fall not yet wholly accomplished."

Irving Wardle, in *The Times*, was no less enthusiastic:

The line seems to be that Macbeth, as a man with imagination, is at the mercy of a partner with none. This is the approach Paul Scofield adopted in his radio performance last year with Peggy Ashcroft. Here his partner is Vivien Merchant, who gives a measured and emotionally well-articulated reading, but who does little to convey the actual quality of the relationship. Her florid movement (particularly that wagging index finger) is rather repetitive and there are times when the performance suggests a meticulously drilled elocution exercise.

Scofield, bearish in appearance and like a cat on his feet, shows his usual concentrated attention on the language to which he clings as tenaciously as a man on a rock face. One follows his every step, accepting the unexpectedly disjointed phrasing and the displaced climaxes. It is a thrilling piece of work, but it is limited by a sense of isolation from the rest of the company: cut off to begin with, he can hardly show the decline of a man who cancels the human bond.

For Peter Lewis it was a very good Macbeth, rich with intelligence, but lacking the mystery ingredient that lifts you off your feet with surprise and wonder. Its strength was the Macbeth/Lady Macbeth relationship, but its spectacular failure John Bury's "Woolly, blood-red carpeting like a fun fur designed for an elephant . . . it seems to muffle everybody's movements on the steeply raked stage. I suspected they had half their minds on not falling over." Paul was a "dream-haunted man," hypnotised and dominated by Vivien Merchant's Lady Macbeth. "The more he convinces himself he can still win the more you know he knows he can't. By the time he reaches the 'tomorrow and tomorrow and tomorrow,' he is smiling bitterly at us in the audience as if imparting his secret knowledge of the futility of his life to people who could not possibly understand it." Scofield did everything you would expect with the role, "short of a new revelation of it such as he made with King Lear."

On the tour to Helsinki (six performances), Leningrad (eight) and Moscow (nine), the Russian critics found it "refreshing" and that "it exposes the commonplaces of Macbeth's crime, evoking horror rather than disgust." Paul's performance in *A Man for All Seasons* had just won him the Best Actor award at the Moscow International Film Festival, his performance being hailed as "moving" and "profound," so Paul "is the darling of all Leningrad." Some 300 people waited at the stage door each night. Now they had seen him as Hamlet, Lear, and Macbeth, and you cannot do much better than that.

But the twenty sections of uncomfortably raked platform had gone missing in two lorries between Leningrad and Moscow, so in Moscow they played it on a flat floor: "The Russians are still searching for the missing stage." "Impeccable teamwork," commented the press, while in the audience were ex-President Mikoyan and Yuri Gagarin, the cosmonaut.

When Darlington saw it again — for the third time — at the Aldwych in early 1968 he commended it as "really fine," but was unmoved by Paul's wickedness and not sorry for him in his tragic self-knowledge. Somehow it fell short of the enormous expectation that Paul had then created. Hobson now discovered Paul had been listening to his critics too much, and has toned down his "hoarse and amazing inflections which chilled the blood. The points of emphasis that Mr. Scofield selected were surprising and farouche, and for that reason in a play as hackneyed as *Macbeth*, electrifying and illuminating." The muted impact of a performance which once had "original terrifying power" was noted by Alan Brien, who judged him quieter. Energy, for Ronal Bryden "is lacking." To play Macbeth, an actor must comprehend not only evil but its enjoyment. Scofield confronted it with brave, distressed understanding, but never for a moment grasped or offered its pleasures.

However, when Hilary Spurling saw what had now become a controversial performance it found its true champion. She judged Paul's line on Macbeth had matured and moved now with absolute steadiness to its logical and inescapable conclusion — a performance that would be possible in no other age but our own:

> For the core of Mr. Scofield's Macbeth is a kind of materialism familiar enough in the twentieth century — the brutal, squalid vulgarity of the tyrant for whom other people have no being, or only as disposable objects: "I require a clearness," is the explanation offered to Banquo's murderers, his "absence is . . . material to me." The voice is prosaic, business-like; "and with him — To leave no rubs nor botches in the work — Fleance, his son . . ." This scene with the murderers is remarkably brisk; the tone curiously reminiscent of the rise of Hitler in Brecht's *Arturo Ui* and with the same echoes of *Richard III*; a certain grim humour born of Macbeth's open contempt for his instruments. There is neither flattery, appeal nor self-justification in his instructions; only the macabre flicker of amusement — "Your spirits shine through you" — and satisfaction at the smoothness of the operation. Mass murder has become an item on the agenda; Banquo's throat once safely cut, Macduff takes his place as the next matter demanding urgent attention. Mr. Scofield moves like a man down a corridor, rapid, matter-of-fact, towards the final butchery — "I'll fight till from my bones my flesh be hacked" — when his own body has become, like his victims, stabbed, gashed, slit and bleeding, an object "signifying nothing."
>
> This is damnation, the thing itself. What we see is a mind slowly and inexorably dimmed, crushed, deadened: a mind from the first passive and unprotesting. There is weakness in the shifty eyes which rest on nothing, in the brooding denials delivered with no conviction and, after the first murder, in the abrupt desperate refusal: "I'll go no more. I am afraid to think."

The performance, once planted, seemed to harden into a purposeful life of its own. Paul noted each successive stage of his descent with chill, sardonic humour — with the mind elsewhere, detached:

> This, in short, is that very rare thing, a performance at once horrible and beautiful: appalling in its naked openness to evil, intensely beautiful in the force and passion with which that exploration is accomplished. If, on the first night, there seemed a falling off in the final scenes, some loss of power, it can only be a passing hesitation which on other nights will return, with the same authority as the earlier outline. And the whole is something which only a subsidized theatre could have realised, for this coherence, both emotional and intellectual, was missing from Mr. Scofield's performance five months ago at Stratford. What then seemed forced, garish, unintelligible, is now reshaped in a performance which has grown from its first sketch nearly two years ago for the BBC, deepened and simplified to a hair-raising clarity.

Having missed this performance, but having listened many times to the radio version, I tend to be convinced by Spurling's assessment.

But what of Vivien Merchant's Lady Macbeth? Darkly voluptuous, highly versatile, quick of study she had been married to Harold Pinter for eleven years, and was at the time of rehearsing *Macbeth* increasingly at odds with him. Clive Swift, who played the Porter, tells me that Merchant "couldn't cope with the role — her voice was limited, as was her emotional range." The role-playing between Merchant and Paul apparently did not develop as it might have done, and perhaps the coldness at an acting level between them explains how he seemed alienated and apart: if Paul had played the role with Vanessa Redgrave or Eileen Atkins, if the set had been different, if Peter Hall had not been ill with shingles, and at the end of his tether with the RSC . . . All in all, this was an "ill-starred" production, and for Paul time, after its run ended in April 1968, to leave the RSC, which he had virtually led for most of the decade.

"Paul Scofield says 'I quit.'" This is a personal decision, said Robin Fox, and had nothing to do with Trevor Nunn's succession to Hall's post. Paul remained as wary of permanent attachments as ever. There was some talk of him appearing later in the year in *Prometheus Bound* by Aeschylus, with Brook directing, but this came to nothing. So, too, did the projected film of *Macbeth*, which in spite of agreeing to do it Paul now turned down, giving no reason, but later saying, "I'm very glad that I did it [the stage production], but did not feel that it should be filmed."

Today we arc fortunate in that the earlier radio version still exists, with Peggy Ashcroft as Lady Macbeth and Alec McCowen as Macduff. Although the Macbeths' partnership lacks some electricity and Ashcroft herself partly, not wholly, lacks commitment, Paul himself certainly does not. Especially in the growing sense of horror and affliction of guilt he projects, in the heart-rending and so tenderly, so lovingly delivered soliloquys, in the always rich and unexpected modulations of tone, and in his grim and violent defiance at the end, he conveys an utter and terrifying conviction. It is hard to imagine anyone else ever being able to match it. The sound performance is truly awesome.

36

Four Score and Downward

"A train is like a woman," says Michel Simon, the legendary French actor, in *The Train*. Paul played the two-dimensional character of the Junker German general with a mission to remove the priceless French art treasures from the Louvre to the fatherland. We wait for a further bon mot to complete the observation, but it is not forthcoming. Simon goes on to tinker with valves that erupt with hissing steam.

The German defences are caving in, and in John Frankenheimer's film the French Resistance is chiefly in the unlikely hands of Burt Lancaster who plays the railway official. To keep the train and the art treasures in France he changes all the signals and messages under the very noses of his German masters.

They filmed *The Train* from summer into autumn of 1966. Over to Paul.

We filmed in Normandy with a few interiors in Paris — the Jeu de Paume, for instance. Jeanne Moreau was charming, and formidably professional, but I had no scenes with her, so we met very seldom. Michel Simon was beautifully eccentric [the old railway Resistance man] and one of those film actors who deceptively seem to be doing nothing — until you see them on the screen. Again, I met him very seldom.

Most of my scenes were with Burt L., who had a very broad grasp of all the mechanics of film-making — as an actor he impressed me greatly for his physical efficiency, by which I mean that he could manipulate and seem to be repairing the most complicated piece of machinery that had just broken down — or change the gauge on a railway track as if he's been doing it all his life — an impeccable verisimilitude and coordination. Emotionally I thought his acting had less truth, sincere, but leaning towards sentimentality. As a man he was genial with a touch of severity. I came to like him.

In the final reckoning Lancaster convinces less than Scofield, but neither comes off particularly well. The train itself is given a semi-mystical identity — some effective visual poetry is sparked out of the railroads — but the plot stays too wooden, even the romance that the Lancaster character pursues with Moreau's sultry hotelière.

Paul turned down many film scripts at this time, and if the quality of *The Train* was hardly enlivened by lines such as, "Have you ever been to Germany? You should find the experience interesting; a chance to widen your horizons," one shudders to think what it was like in some of the scripts he rejected.

When *The Train* was first shown I was much taken imaginatively with it. I identified with the story, but on recent viewing I judge that far from being the black-and-white classic I had hoped, it is revealed as clankingly predictable, and from it I can see why Paul does not trust film. The film mainly draws on appearances and these often lie. Paul is an actor who is keen on the truth. In film the appearance, the flesh, tries to become the word in its ambiguity, its uncertainty — its promise. Yet far from the word becoming flesh, flesh tends to assert itself *over* the word (hence, not surprisingly, the obsession with flesh itself) for the medium is the material, its flesh, and flesh itself is more productive of striking images than its covering. Hence the obsession with a nakedness of appearance in all aspects of life. (A camera has recently been invented that can strip clothing from the human body so that anyone however dressed in everyday life, can be revealed naked.)

Paul dislikes the camera, mainly because he dislikes this demand to be revealing, to expose vulnerability, nakedness, frankness in flesh, in visual terms. He resists the prying eye. Even so, his face is very revealing

— not malleable and protean, as Alec Guinness's, who has an ideal character face for the camera — but the face of a Hollywood heavy, a Grant, a Cooper, a Lancaster. For which reason he has rarely played character parts on film.

On stage Paul's face is more of a mask. In the imagination of the audience it takes on the expression and form of what he is projecting from within — the thought. It is his voice that is the true vehicle of imagination, the flexible gift under his control: this identifies him and distinguishes him from virtually all the other great actors of the century (Gielgud and Wolfit excepted).

The tip of Jutland, at Skagen, the bitter months of January, February, March, 1969. They filmed for thirteen continuous weeks in a huge national park, mostly on the fifteen miles of beach. They had a hundred horses in the production and all the cast stayed in a Skagen hotel. This was the final act of Scofield's Lear. The film.

> An extraordinary experience — we filmed on and around a sort of moonscape, i.e., miles and miles of frozen sand dunes topped with snow, lapped by an icy sea. It was cold — we filmed mostly out of doors with an incredible number of layers of clothing and sometimes a rare swig of a violent kind of Danish schnapps. Fortunately our costumes were mainly deerskins. Our only interior shooting took place in a castle designed by George Wakewitch, which looked a bit like Ghormenghast on the outside, with a warren of weird, cavernous chambers within. My make-up was a long job and the make-up artist and my dresser and I would leave our (very comfortable) hotel at about 5 A.M. in order to be ready for the morning's shoot. The northern sunrise on these mornings was spectacular — unreal. We were near the meeting of the two seas, the Skagerrak and the Kattegat.

There was the Irish, convivial drinking group consisting of Cyril Cusack, Patrick Magee, Jackie MacGowran (of these only MacGowran did not drink, he was not allowed to). There was a slightly apart Alan Webb (Gloucester), then there was the younger Brook protegee team, led by Robert Lloyd (Edgar); then the ladies, from Irene Worth, Susan Engel and Annelise Gabold. Hogg reports: "Joy came out once. Scofield was very private; he rarely drank in the bar, although he ate in the main dining room. I rode out with him once; he loves gardening; talked about his cottage in Mull. He loved the riding."

Perhaps Byron's lines in *Childe Harold* were appropriate to his mood:

> I live not in myself, but I become
> Portion of that around me; and to me
> High mountains are a feeling, but the hum
> Of human cities, torture.

He loved, thought Hogg, the windswept, solitary outside. He once wrote to John Harrison about film tests and other professional matters, "But this is all *dull* compared with sea and trees and quietness and things." He told Hogg he did not like the movies, and had not much liked Burt Lancaster, or working on *The Train*.

"I always used to look at his face — and think it was a face that had gone through an awful lot — I thought perhaps between 25-35 something had happened and there had been an awful lot he turned his back on, that he had been dragged through something, an internal labyrinth — something very gathered and contained about a private part of himself." Hogg might speculate, as have others, but Scofield has denied that his tortured face has been caused by anything other than the ageing process.

The actors on *King Lear* were all English, the crews Danish, they had such a different sense of humour, the English actors would all gossip and joke all the time with verbal humoured imitations. The Danes could not work out the humour — "This funny?" they would ask. "Explain." Their sense of humour was always physical, locking you up, or tripping you up, or throwing something at you.

37

Too Strong, Too 'Ard

In Shakespeare and great dramatic poetry it is the *language* that behaves spontaneously, it does the camerawork: the syntax is the camera angle, the lenses, the tracking, the close-ups. In the theatre, on radio, and on the page, in the mind, it is the language, the imagery and words chosen that "shoots" character and story, this is what does the work.

King Lear as a film does not quite work. One has an impression of disparate visual elements. Cordelia has a very French hair-do. Lear appears as a huge, monstrous hunchback in costume of black sitting alone in a dark alcove; the Fool, played by MacGowran, is largely cut. The tundra and ice are alien to this very English play. It is as if Brook did not *see* what is going on — he sees composed, finished pictures, not the ongoing suspense. He needed to create on film that same suspense the language has: dialogue, interreaction between actors, the sudden use of the camera to pick up imagery, the need for the camera to act as its own narrator.

Paul, far from being brought out of himself, giving us some of the introverted power that he has as an actor, is presented visually all the time and, with his great spade of a beard that is disproportionately large for his thin face, as a closed book. His mind, his soul, are visually impenetrable. The efforts to find a symbol in the storm do not find the right equation — they remain theory. There is little sense of spontaneity, only a continuous, growling pain like a bear and it becomes, in Scofield's most monotonous, grumbling tone, sometimes monolithically dull. You do not feel sympathy when he appeals, "Keep me in temper; I would not be mad," and really the sympathy is too much on Regan and Goneril's side for throwing him out. You do not feel he has pared his wits, in the words of the Fool, on "both sides" and "kept nothing in the middle."

As for the riot and debauching nights, far from being a mixture of gangsters and spoilt children, they are like a group of Dostoevskian convicts in a compound. This is Lear in *Lower Depths*, not Lear in middle-class Elizabethan England, nor Lear in abstract *Endgame*. Above all, Paul does not make the madness interesting. The voice is too level and on the same tone.

Something had been killed off between the stage performance and the film; the film Lear of Scofield feigns strength of purpose, appears resolved, yet to quote Lao Tzu, "The hard and the strong are companions of death." Scofield's performance has too much black and white (and it was filmed in black and white too, a mistake). The creative unfolding of Lear's unseeing and denying, then insight, is trampled underfoot. The film Lear controls his fate. His madness has lost the fascinating creative chaos that his situation provokes, and it is preset and predetermined. Something has gone wrong here, and perhaps Scofield's acute yet un-self-conscious, even un-self-aware, antennae sensed Brook was making an unwelcome departure from the one strand in his genius to which Scofield in particular related — that of allowing the actor his full creativity.

So I sense here the beginning of the parting of the ways. With typical understatement Paul told an old friend, who had asked after Brook, during this period, "He's directing the actors." Paul's face fell, the look said it all. "He's *directing* the actors."

Brook later asked Paul to appear in other productions, but with the greatest respect and gratitude Paul said no. In 1998 Brook asked him to appear in a film *I Am a Phenomenon* with Nigel Hawthorne. When he read the script Paul said, "I am not very keen."

Looking at Brook's subsequent work, one cannot ever claim the actors transcend the productions, as Scofield did in those innumerable landmark Brook productions in which he played leading roles. Both matched and partnered each other's gifts, equally and with perfection.

Brook wanted to become, and became in many ways, the Gurdjieff of the theatre — he looked for gurudom and found it. Scofield would not go along with him.

Brook would, at this period and later, attack the unknown bits in an actor, the bits that were dark and painful. Rehearsals became sometimes periods of non-discovery. You could come to the point with him, as one actor remarked of him, that you'd got no soul left: he "dragged" the soul. But Scofield did not believe that you (or he) could get into intensity at the borders of self-control, he did not believe at all "in going mad to stay sane" — or, rather, to become "creative." Brook always left Scofield entirely alone. But Brook, like Gurdjieff in a more general philosophical procedure, had come to believe in administering a scientific shock to the actor's ego — although he never tried this with Paul.

38

Rust on the Leaf

I think Paul may have said, after *Macbeth*, that he was never going to work again with Peter Hall, but Hall famously has a way of getting round people: he fell out, too, with Pinter over the revelations in his diary about Pinter's private life, then repaired the rift. For the moment he had left Hall and Hall had left the RSC. As Hall, laughingly, tells me of himself (quoting Binkie Beaumont) "I'll never work with you again — until I need you."

Paul was now determinedly, whether by design or from outside offer (surely the latter) joining the "opposition," the Royal Court/National Theatre axis of London theatre. He was clean-shaven, a matinee idol doyen. He has, after his two films (and at last getting Lear the right way round), had a rest. He went to Mull, where he wrote to Harrison, "It's wet here and I'm walking a lot and getting soack (dear me!) soaked a lot and the sun is going down in a most ostentatious way, and I'm just going to pour myself a huge whisky." His first Court assignment, and his first contact with the new wave of Osborne, Pinter and so on (Charles Dyer's *Staircase* apart) was Osborne's *A Hotel in Amsterdam*.

The play is a thin one and, according to Robert Stephens, "about all of Osborne's hangers-on waiting for a tyrannical film director who never arrives because he commits suicide: that was Osborne's final pay-off to Tony Richardson!" (Tony Richardson had been the original director and architect of Osborne's fame with *Look Back in Anger*, but the pair had by now very publicly fallen out.)

If Paul, like most people now, found *A Hotel in Amsterdam* little more than a gossipy conversation piece he kept it very politely to himself. Sally

Beauman saw it just before the end of its West End run and before Kenneth Haigh (ironically enough the first Osborne Jimmy Porter) took over Paul's role of Laurie:

> It was a matinée performance, and practically all the seats seemed to be occupied by old ladies. The atmosphere was soporific in the extreme, and Osborne's convoluted conversational platitudes came over as just that and no more. But the play gradually took off, and what lifted it was Scofield's performance.
>
> It really was quite extraordinarily rounded; the "classless" accent, tiny idiosyncrasies of behaviour, the way of putting over a joke: Laurie, in the text, a somewhat two-dimensional character, in Scofield's hands became whole. In a play that I did not like it was nonetheless extremely funny, extremely moving.

But rumour did have it that Paul disliked the play. Sally asked him, withholding her own view. Paul was polite: an interesting situation for a play, he tells her — six people in a hotel room, their relations with someone who never appears. He thinks the love scene (between him and Judy Parfitt as Annie) is "poised, accurate. Maybe he likes it, maybe he doesn't, but is too reticent to let you know."

Robert Stephens was more direct. He watched Paul like a hawk — to learn. "Anyway, you could see that Scofield thought the play was no good, and you could sense his whole ear, his whole being, on the audience, to see if he's still got them. And he would speed up or slow down, speak softly or loudly, accordingly. Scofield, like Lawson, has the ability to be totally attuned to the audience. And of course Richardson had, too. That is what I call great intuitive acting."

The practical jokes the cast, or some of them, played with Paul and he with them provided a whole sub-text of naughtiness — and probably served to keep them on their toes.

Paul came in one night, chatting with a couple of friends: "I didn't notice and went right past my station so I pulled the communication cord and got out." "But didn't anything happen? Weren't you arrested?"

asked David Burke. Paul answered "Oh no, it was perfectly all right."

Hearing the friends turned out to be Laurence Olivier and Jimmy Edwards, Burke at once went off and wrote to Paul an official-sounding letter from the local Haywards Heath police station, saying that two gentlemen who pulled the communication cord of their train had been detained in the cells, claiming they were Sir Laurence Olivier and Jimmy Edwards, and "Would you kindly come down to the police station, sir, to clear this matter up?"

In Osborne's play, Isabel Dean, Susan Engel and Judy Parfitt used each night to arrange themselves in different poses and make little tableaux before Paul's eyes. When *Hotel* transferred to the Albery, then the New Theatre, there was a steel staircase to the adjoining Wyndham's, and some of the cast of that theatre, including Timothy West and Kate O'Mara also used to join in in this little off-stage "happening." One matinée, instead of the usual tableau, Kate O'Mara stripped to the waist and, bare-breasted, knelt down with arms outstretched and imploring towards Paul. He came back downstage looking mightily shaken.

On another occasion, near Christmas, Joss Ackland phoned Paul from his dressing room, putting on a John Osborne drawl, he said, "Jill [Bennett, Osborne's wife] and I wondered if we could come and spend Christmas with you in Mull."

There was a dreadful pause. "Yes, yes, of course — ." Ackland noticed the pain in Paul's voice.

"We won't be staying long — no more than two weeks."

Paul gave a strangulated cry. When they went round to his dressing-room they found him sitting in a fetal position in complete despair.

Burke was being pestered by a man he knew slightly who wanted to meet Paul and asked him if he would introduce him. To avoid him after one show, and to facilitate a quick getaway, Burke changed into his own trousers and took the curtain call in these. Paul noticed; "Oh, wearing your own trousers are you, what a cheek!" "Yes, yes," the flustered Burke replied, "I've got to meet someone . . . " and fled.

A day later Burke received an angry letter from this pestering fellow accusing him of avoiding him, even to changing into his own trousers before the end of the show to do this — he'd never felt so insulted. Burke in turn wondered, irritatedly, "Who on earth could have told him that?"

Next performance, just as the curtain was about to rise, only a moment or two to go, Paul turned to him, "I met that friend of yours, and had a very interesting chat." There was a pause, then as the curtain began to move, Paul casually went on, "Oh, you should have checked that handwriting!"

After the two films Paul breaks for even longer, until March 1970. There were various new projects: one, for instance, was a film about Nijinsky, whose diaries he had recorded for radio, in which Paul was to be cast as Diaghilev. For the moment he was content to rest in Balcombe. "People always ask me what I do down there; and it seems so silly. I mean, there's *everything* to do. There are very good walks — I like to go walking."

He is now forty-eight: "Vanya is forty-seven and when we started I was forty-seven. Then I had a birthday, so I suppose you could say I am one year too old for the part. I have a very strong sympathy for people who have wasted their lives and who get to forty-seven."

It is the humour of Chekhov that attracts him: "Without it, you would not sense the extent of the tragedy. It is not a major tragedy. It is a waste of human talents. And this is where Chekhov is so effective."

The new adaptation, for the Royal Court production, directed by Anthony Page, was especially suited to Paul, although criticized by some as flat and unsentimental. Christopher Hampton based this adaptation on a literal version by Nina Froud. He felt Chekhov was so often sentimentalized and prettified. He asked the translator to keep the original word order in English so he could compare the length of the statements — and found them in Russian much flatter and more unlyrical and even plainer and greyer than he had anticipated they would be.

VOYNITSKY [*alone*]: She's gone. [*Pause*] Ten years ago I used to meet her at my sister's. She was seventeen and I was thirty-seven. Why didn't I fall in love with her then and ask her to marry me?

It would have been perfectly feasible. And now she'd be my wife
. . . Yes . . . The storm would have woken us both; the thunder
would have frightened her and I'd have held her in my arms and
whispered: "Don't be afraid, I'm here." What a marvellous
thought, wonderful, it makes me happy just to think about
it . . . except . . . God, my mind's in such chaos.

One can visualize Paul's wide-eyed, perplexed look. The shifting,
slightly lowered forehead of the loser.

I really have been cheated. I used to worship that gout-ridden old
misery, I worked for him like an ox. Sonya and I squeezed ever
penny out of this estate . . . He was the breath of my body.
Everything he wrote, everything he said, seemed to me evidence of
genius. My God. Now look at him, now he's retired, consider the
full achievement of his life. Not one page of his work will outlive
him, he's totally unknown, a nothing, a soap bubble! And I've been
cheated, I can see it now, like a fool I've let myself be cheated.

Uncle Vanya opened at the Royal Court in February 1970, and it was
generally preferred to the famous Olivier revival at Chichester and the
National. But, typically for Scofield, this production created scarcity
value: it ran only seven weeks as, because Colin Blakeley had to leave to
go into tax exile, Scofield refused to act it with anyone else; although
offered a transfer, it thus had to close.

J.C. Trewin could not have been more enthusiastic. The champion of
Scofield in early years wrote how Scofield, acting the character of 47, a
year younger than his own age, made us immediately aware of the futility of things, a frustrated past, the dim years ahead: this was his flashpoint
— Uncle Vanya's fatigue.

From the first the man had wilted; the rust was on the leaf; everything about him dropped from his eyelids to his speech, apparently a slack ribbon of words. Again and again, in sudden pause, drag-
ging emphasis, a typical downbeat throb on the last syllable, the

actor could make any theatrical point. I think of the moment when, after he entered to find Yelena in Astrov's arms, the pairs separated guiltily, he stood holding his useless bouquet of autumn roses and murmuring, "Not to worry!" . . . Like a dim woman's description of a wrecked liner as "a boating accident," it was a hopeless understatement, and it was in character.

The people in *Vanya*, wrote Desmond McCarthy, are "like loosely agglutinated sticks and straws which revolve together in a sluggish eddy. They long to be detached and ride down the rushing stream which near, but out of reach, they imagine sparkled for ever past them."

To Hampton, then aged twenty-four, this was "of all the productions I've been involved with, the very best." Hampton watched every performance: to him, the scene speech of Vanya's betrayal was especially moving. Page did a brilliant, sensitive job, but was always anxious about what Scofield thought. He did not give anything away, and Page wondered if he thought it was going well or not.

In Nottingham, before it opened, Page asked Hampton to dinner in the hotel: Scofield and Joy were there (she had come up to see the play), and Page took a table near them wondering if Hampton could, by watching the couple's body language, make out what he thought of it, whether or not he approved. The Scofields gave nothing away.

When at the end, after the two attempts at shooting himself, Vanya says to Sonya, passing his hand over her hair, "Sonya, I feel so sad. If you knew how sad I feel," Hampton said, "Paul spoke this so flat, so sincerely uninflected, that it used to make me cry. That's what this man's life has come to."

Anna Calder-Marshall as Sonya was heartbreaking; she was, said Hampton, too beautiful for the part, but they tied her hair back severely and gave her harder face lines. But she was so anxious at first, acting with Paul. She had done a television trilogy with him, written by Alun Owen and called *The Male of the Species*, that had been narrated by Laurence Olivier, and in which Paul played the man she fell in love with, a lawyer.

The other male stars had been Michael Caine and Sean Connery.

Caine said that Paul's first reading of the script was "Like anyone else's opening night . . . Alun Owen calls him 'a grammarian' as the adroit Emlyn, scheming to substitute Mary for his secretary, suggests that 'Miss Leatherhead's tensions' indicate a needed vacation. Watching Paul accent 'Miss Leatherhead's . . . tensions' with a shrug, a clenched fist, folded arms, a different funnier gesture each time — is a cram course in acting." Paul and Anna won Emmy Awards for their performances when NBC broadcast it in January 1969, Paul's for "Outstanding Single Performance by an Actor in a Leading Role." Paul had been Anna's favoured actor and again role model, ever since as a child she had seen *A Man for All Seasons*.

Page said to her, "When you act with Paul you've got to be on the same level": she thought, "How can I?"

When they started rehearsing she found that "He had a way of looking at you when he wasn't speaking which made you feel confidence — a capacity for making you feel a wonderful person — unlike anybody I've worked with."

One day she got something, as Sonya, that she thought was just perfect. "Dismiss it," Paul had told her, "If you're playing a love scene you must play everything but a love scene."

Once *Vanya* opened Anna found, "It bordered so much on things really happening — a chair breaking, a leaking samovar, or the veteran Gwen Ffrangçon-Davies clapping her hands unexpectedly in one scene ('I'm hitting gnats') — that you really believed it. Every night it changed, I've never experienced such freedom. I'd sometimes get really perturbed. It's one of the few things I would still like to be doing . . . And that one night when Sco really cried at the end of the play he said to us, 'Look I've got a tear. Look, that's a real tear.'"

What a happy experience for all concerned: they were to film it, but Anna was called to a film test for *Wuthering Heights* and was offered the role of Catherine, so the film was never made. But all the seats were sold for the seven-week run: it was, as everyone says, more or less perfect.

By May 1970 Paul was filming again, this time in the Herman

Melville short story "Bartleby": now he had left his bearded, secretive, saturnine face behind. He was involved again in a low-budget movie, which he made because he was impressed by the script. John McEnery was suggested for Bartleby, the clerk who opts out of the world under the force of social pressures. Paul was approached for the other main role, the bank manager, completely suburban, who employs Bartleby.

At first McEnery agreed, then dropped out. Anthony Friedmann explains what happened next:

Scofield read the script and wrote back: "This is the most devastatingly simple script I have ever read." Then I just went back and collared McEnery, because I knew he was the right Bartleby, and I knew that the other film was never going to get off the ground. They were bigger but they were bluffing. I just said: "Look, chum, you want to play opposite Scofield? Put up or shut up."

With Scofield, his interest had been secured in our first meeting. It so happened that when we met we got on very well. He saw that I wasn't just out of short pants, that I'd been around, that I had a certain maturity. Anyway, the risk was on my side, not his. He could afford a disaster. I couldn't.

When Friedmann says Paul could afford a disaster he was correct. Why is it that Paul could apparently ride any setback or criticism? The simple answer would seem to be that he did not take any job because he needed a job: he was never, in Leontes' words from *The Winter's Tale*, "a feather for each wind that blows," so he left behind a lasting sense of commitment.

Paul criticised other actors in this period. He admires Anthony Hopkins, but agreed that he was undisciplined. Then almost in desperation, he said:

What has happened to Albert Finney? I welcome his kind of acting; I recognise a skill that I can believe in, that is wholly true and believable. But he seems to be in danger of losing his original gift, because of the power that he has achieved to employ others and the time because of that gift. One so rarely sees him; it seems indulgence. [Paul comments on my typescript, "Oh crumbs. Am eating my words."]

I hope that doesn't sound too unkind, because one only criticizes somebody one admires, because they are the only people who are worth it. But because of our gift actors have to realise that we must get on with the job of acting. The job is what matters; it is our duty. Everything else builds towards that. That is what we are here for.

39

Great Riches

Divitiae grandes homini sunt, vivere parce
Aequo animo.

— LUCRETIUS

In these temporary absences from the stage Paul's reputation was not diminished: he was now more relaxed in films and would be capable in the future to make some of his best film performances, including Tobias in Edward Albee's *A Delicate Balance*, directed by Tony Richardson, in which he starred with Katharine Hepburn and Lee Remick.

But Tynan's preoccupation with him for the National bordered on obsession. Whereas Tynan, in a memo to Mike Nichols, passed judgement on Ian McKellen ("very gifted but very narcissistic"), he had these many suggestions for 1970–1 specifically with Scofield in mind:

J.F. Kennedy play
Julius Caesar Scofield (as Brutus), Plummer, Olivier
T. Stoppard play
Misanthrope
J.G. Borkman
Les Main Sales
Saturday, Sunday, Monday
The Moon in the Yellow River

To which Tynan added, in hand-written scrawl:

Köpenick (This was on Paul's own suggestion)

> *Peter Pan* (Hook)
> *The Iceman Cometh* (Hickey)
> *Murder in the Cathedral*
> *The Critic*
> *Women Beware Women*
> *Bedbug*

In the Birthday Honours List of 13 June 1970 Olivier was ennobled, but on 1 August Olivier was again on one of his many visits to hospital, this time with a "whopping great" thrombosis of the right leg, from his "mid-thigh up to the vena cava." Doctors persuaded him not to return to the stage for three or four months. Peter Lewis in *The National: A Dream Made Concrete*, commented, "The dips in the company's standards all coincided with Olivier's serious illnesses and incapacity." ("You almost have to admire the *energy* of Olivier's illnesses," wrote Roger Lewis in his Olivier biography.)

Robert Lang took over Olivier's *Shylock*, while *Guys and Dolls*, scheduled for December 1970, was postponed. Olivier was to play Nathan Detroit, Geraldine McEwan and Dennis Quilley other roles. But it was ultimately cancelled, which Olivier attributed to a "conspiracy," masterminded by Binkie Beaumont, who "preferred" *Oklahoma!* Olivier could never subsequently bring himself to see Richard Eyre's later production, the "triumph" of the third National Theatre director's tenure, and probably would turn in his grave that *Oklahoma!* should mark Trevor Nunn's assumption of the fourth directorship. The *English* Royal National Theatre?

Olivier's decline could be thought of as Scofield's opportunity. Indeed, many did think of it as such, especially as Olivier was so insistent on an actor rather than a director leading the National. Hall says, "Paul went to see Larry. 'I'm tired, boy, I'm tired,' Larry said. 'You come and play all the parts. You come and play them.'"

However, for the moment Paul was approached to play three roles in 1971, starting with that of Voigt in *The Captain of Köpenick* by Carl Zuckmayer, which, according to some of those involved, Olivier disliked as a play and believed would be a failure. Olivier claimed in one interview that he has "wooed him [Paul] for years to join in the National," which was patently not true, although it was true that he had given in to Tynan's insistent demand for Paul.

Paul was made an associate director of the National. *The Times* suggested to Olivier that Scofield could eventually succeed Olivier as director of the National Theatre, but Olivier's reply was that they had never discussed this. He was sure, however, in the coming season, continued the report, "that if it was a job Mr. Scofield wanted to do he would do it well . . . Mr. Scofield will be seen in three productions, including Shakespeare's *Coriolanus*, in which he will play the name part for the first time in England."

The Captain of Köpenick, adapted by John Mortimer, directed by Frank Dunlop opened on 10 March 1971, and was at once a great popular success. Like Gogol's *The Government Inspector*, it is a satire on how the assumption of a dress code and behaviour (in this case a soldier's uniform) confers not only power and dignity upon him who wears it (the ex-convict Voigt, masquerading as an army captain), but also daemonic sex appeal, for Mortimer expanded the documentary aspects of the play with scenes comically demonstrating the pulling power of a regimental garment. As Voigt remarks, relishing his port and cigar amid police congratulations, "The uniform could have done it by itself."

How did Paul, with little more than a confidence trick to wield, hold the centre of the stage for three-quarters of the play, with our fascinated attention on a man whose basic characteristic is that he is nobody? Or, as many were tempted to ask, "How does a star performer of indisputable magnetism persuade us of his character's nondescriptness?" We are drawn again into the mystery and magic of the actor's art:

> In the mysterious way in which great acting seems to work Scofield can be both nondescript and riveting. There he is — with his dimness, his shuffling walk, and those sentences that start out very boldly but get waylaid somewhere in the back of his throat before their ends. There is the cadging subservience poised on the edge of

a belligerence that doesn't ever quite materialize. There is the deeply ingrained deference to an officialdom that is crushing him underfoot. He gets it all absolutely right, this tired-out and — in life, one would suppose — tiresome man. Yet on the stage there is nothing tiresome about him.

The answer would seem to be, in Paul's words, "The emotions are real, but they aren't mine." Simon Callow recalls to me how Paul "took the man back into his skull." Another critic at the time commented that

The key factor in this contradiction is that Scofield never loses himself in the part, but finds the part in himself. This means that the gaolbird Voigt is always seen within the ambience of the actor Scofield — in Beerbohm's terms it isn't the actor sinking but the part surfacing. And I suspect it is this ability of an actor to find such a character as Voigt within himself that distinguishes the great performance from the good performance.

When Voigt puts on the captain's uniform, marches into the town hall and takes over the entire administration, this is an example of the other kind of acting — which is impersonation. I think probably all actors have something of the impersonator in them, but the best actors have it least. The impersonator really does live the part — as Voigt did in reality, for he was a real person who actually carried off the deception on which Zuckmayer based his play. Being a man used to obey, he had merely to acquire the right authority — bestowed on him by the wearing of the uniform — and then he could give himself an order that naturally he carried out.

Callow picks out this moment in particular. He has read his fable to the girl: "Everything is better than to die." And Voigt becomes a "celebrity" — saucy, sexy, and (with Paul's voice), adenoidal.

Irving Wardle described the successive transformation of Voigt "from vagrant into model convict, and then through boiling anger to his first appearance as the Captain, emerging from the door of a railway lavatory, his bedraggled moustache now bristling with authority and his voice rasping with command." He then observed that it did no justice to the performance to suggest that these changes were slipped on like masks. "The character persists throughout every phase of development, reverting to his old slurred speech even when installed in charge of the town hall, and preserving to the end the sly, almost feline, glances of the old lag. It is a masterly performance that extracts all the humanity and dramatic flourish from the part without the least concession to sentimentality."

Ronald Bryden, too, underlined the protean quality: how Paul starts with a tiny, wobbly, cockney whine — with the big head shrinking into the collar like a tortoise's. His long legs shuffle in small, tentative steps. Then, bang, the transformation as he swings wide the door of a station lavatory as the Captain:

> At once he seems two feet taller. The voice deepens, rasping. The dark, powerful stare which occasionally flashed out of that deject-ed bundle of clothing now rakes the stage steadily. The perform-ance is turned inside out. Now you see that the drooping mous-taches, the bristly prison cut which somehow grew downward, were a parody of Prussian militarism. The joke becomes letting glimpses of the old, fumbling dosser — the broken r's, the shuffling waddle — escape in moments of uncertainty.
>
> The pace of the play, leisured and wandering, jerks into a rat-tle. As Voigt's kidnapped squad of recruits snap into step behind him, the image of a great machine somehow grows on the stage. The lost power of war's old symbol is replaced by its new one.

Bryden rated this performance on a par with Khlestakov: but Paul, as we see, has moved far away from "personality" acting (not that he was ever near it) and — except intermittently — from "impersonation." The unity of the comic performance is how he brings his own integrity to what the writer is saying; he does not see the characters as individuals at all:

236

It wasn't so much a person because in a way Khlestakov isn't a person, but he represents so much foolishness in us all. I was simply interested in making that kind of behaviour real, whatever kind of person I was being. It probably broadened that character quite a lot and probably made him pretty unbelievable, in a sense, but I find myself doing that more and more, being much more interested in finding in a character something that we can all recognize. I can see that my attitude to acting has changed very much. I have become much less interested in myself, in my performance. I am more interested in what the writer has opened up for me and how I can best illustrate it, almost without feeling that I am present, in a way.

It is hardly surprising that Olivier, who represented the total polarity to Paul's acting, had a reaction that was at once fearful and jealous. The first night gave Paul and the cast a standing ovation and twenty curtain calls.

Olivier came round to Paul's dressing room, which was his own. It had a small, carpeted sitting room, with a fridge and colour photos of Joan Plowright and Olivier's children. Invasion? Usurpation? Deposition?

Olivier tells him, "You mustn't worry about our first nights. They're never very interesting." This is also reported to me as Olivier saying, clapping Paul on the back, "Paulie, don't worry Paulie, we'll get it right."

40

Interlude: Prince of the Borgias

On 20 January 1971 Robin Fox, Paul's agent since he had left Christopher Mann, died. Angela, Robin's wife, had taken him earlier that winter to the famous (or infamous) cancer clinic run by Dr. Issels in Germany, but hopes that his chest cancer could be cured were found to be false. She had left in anger at the lack of improvement, bringing him home to Cuckfield, the nearest town to Balcombe. Paul was a frequent visitor to the sick man's bedside, so were others of his adored clients. Fox was hardly ever conscious, but they would, so Angela said, take turns to sit with him and hold his hand. Paul would do this, Angela noted appreciatively, for hours on end. "Paul once said to me, 'He was always such a good-looking friend and now he's dying he's really beautiful.'"

Fox, whose charisma became legendary and who combined "the lethal charm of a Prince of the Borgias with membership of the MCC," numbered among his clients Dirk Bogarde, Vanessa Redgrave, Maggie Smith, Alec Guinness and many other illustrious names. He was, as Angela Fox records in the memoir devoted mostly to him, an extraordinary man, half Jewish, half upper-class English Establishment, who moved between different worlds with extraordinary facility (although by means of a chauffeur-driven Rolls and, if not accompanied by a mistress, with a choice Havana in his hand). He announced to Angela just before the birth of Edward, their first son, "You do know I've no intention of being faithful," explaining men were by nature polygamous, and it was not his temperament to be faithful.

Angela, as perhaps was her right, was always scathing about Robin's mistresses, but Angela's attachment to Robin remained firm, and she was much quoted, before her death in late 1999 aged eighty-seven, for her tolerance towards her husband's mistresses. But Fox was outstandingly sensitive towards, and protective of, his clients and, with Angela often to back him up with her sometimes savagely expressed sense of truth, and often unerring judgement, he proved the ideal agent for Paul. Angela could also be very funny, as well as scathing. The illegitimate daughter of Frederick Lonsdale the playwright, Angela had as her mother *the* Mrs. Worthington whose daughter, in Noël Coward's song, should not be put on the stage.

Angela, who admired Paul beyond measure, could also be quite critical of him and told me she never felt Paul fulfilled his "whole potential," and that he was too much under his wife's thumb. Without having had any chance to find out for myself I believed this and other matters she recounted to me before I began this book. These included him saying that he could not stand the mannerisms of Vivien Merchant during *Macbeth* and he was so irritated "that he wanted to murder her" ("*Not true*," emphatically said Paul, although this would certainly have given a new twist to the Scottish play), and that on one journey into London, when Paul was playing Lear and he and Angela caught the train in together at Haywards Heath, "We were shunted off into a siding or something. He was not the slightest bit worried about missing the performance, but was as cool as a cucumber."

However, as I engaged more deeply with the subject I came to believe Paul had more than fulfilled his potential, which was a rare and impeccable achievement, by simply following the dictates of his heart and conscience, and obeying the instincts of his talent. As he wrote to Angela in 1975, when she proposed some awe-inspiring future venture, "I don't want to commit myself to anything . . . I don't know what I want to do next, and am finding *The Tempest* so all-demanding that I can't contemplate the future, mostly because I don't want to make promises that I might feel differently about when the time came."

Self-knowledge or awareness can often be interpreted by others as undue hesitancy or even lack of courage, but following the dictates of uncertainty can also be viewed as strength. Indeed, I think it may be clear by now that the very uncertainty, the continual return to square one, over the choices Paul makes as to what he is to perform next, is an integral and important part of the process, and a means by which he summons and concentrates energy on the work in hand. When he comes to play a part, as Felicity Kendal says about being on stage with him, "The reality of the moment and concentration is total." This reflects the enormous deliberation that prior to this has gone into making the choice.

This is not to undervalue the perception of Angela Fox, who was herself a unique and extraordinary individual, with a profound love of the theatre and a passion for great acting. As Edward Fox said of Angela, "It has always been my mother's way to speak out frankly, and I can hear every word of it. Indeed, there is no malice in my mother's heart." Right as she was about many things, perhaps her own experience of life as the spurned wife had brought her to an incomplete knowledge of the complex scanners of Paul's own individual methods of choice, or of the way he paid attention to what Peter Hall calls humorously, "The private god who tells him what to do."

Angela looked for bold, heroic outrage in an acting performance, which was not Paul's style. She should perhaps have been mindful of how once he turned down a film idea that Robin put up to him. "I told him [Bob Lewis] *all* depends on casting of other role — but when Kirk Douglas is mooted my tentacles are inclined to retreat into shell."

Tentacles — "a slender flexible process in animals, especially invertebrates, serving as an organ of touch or feeling" — has as well as this definition a botanical application: tipped leaf-hairs, a sensitive filament.

41

Monsters of the Pit

The Rules of the Game, Paul's second play for the National, went into rehearsal in May 1970 and opened the National Theatre's season at the New Theatre (now the Albery) on 15 June. Anthony Page directed, and as a Royal Court director he was a fitting choice because *The Rules of the Game* is iconoclastic. Pirandello, in this early play, is political and not metaphysical; he bitterly sets out to destroy the notion of honour, as exemplified by the idea that if a woman, namely the hero Leone's wife, Silia (played by Joan Plowright) is insulted, in this case by a party of drunken gentlemen, she must be defended by her husband. No matter that the wife is foolish or flirtatious (and has a lover); Pirandello holds up the idea to ridicule by having the husband (Leone, played by Paul) substitute his wife's lover for himself to avenge the insult. That the lover is killed is a matter of indifference to Leone; so too is the fact he will be branded a coward: he laughs, and this laugh is the centre of the play. Social rules and general morality, Pirandello says, are rubbish.

Paul played this sinister perfection of the anti-hero with a "dead-eyes shattered face and a voice of chilling authority," a "perfect marriage between author and executant." Prompting so many animal images, he suggests to Wardle a lizard: motionless and unreachable until he decides to move, and then swift and decisive. The last scene is one of the most electrifying of modern theatre. To goad Leone to fight, Silia taunts him by speaking of shame — on which Scofield hurls Plowright to the floor. "You are my shame," he says coldly. As she goes out to her dead lover, he settles down himself to a gourmet's *petit déjeuner*.

Joan Plowright, however, did not by any means come up to Paul's standard of "limitless distinction and power," as Harold Hobson calls it. She had no charm, according to Irving Wardle, which "brings in lovers" and lacks "enough inner resilience to give Leone a fitting opponent." She fell too often, in her lachrymose, matronly performance, into "languishing poses of boardroom portraiture and hitting her climaxes with many a throbbing vowel and angry flounce."

Because of the Pirandello, plans for Paul as Coriolanus had been dropped by the autumn of 1971. Finally, Anthony Hopkins played the part instead, while the play was directed and designed by members of the Berliner Ensemble. Thereby Olivier was freed from threats of comparison between himself and Scofield.

One of Tynan's suggestions — Paul in *The Misanthrope* — was still possible. John Dexter, who was to have directed *Coriolanus*, wrote to Paul that he was somewhat saddened that they would not be working together as soon as he had hoped.

> I still would like us to meet and discuss general plans for the future, especially with regard to *The Misanthrope*. I still think this is the perfect play for you at this time if we can find a Célimène, and even more important a suitable version. I really believe it is necessary to have one done for us, and I have had what I think (naturally) is a brilliant idea about which I would like to talk with you. Of course this would depend on our doing *Misanthrope* after you have done a film, and this in turn depends very much on whether you really want to come back. It is for these reasons that I would still like us to meet quietly, away from the pressure of Waterloo Road, and St. Martin's Lane.

Ultimately, Paul disengaged himself from the Molière play. Olivier sent Dexter the cable:

> Thank you for your long and trouble-taken letter STOP Please don't think I am piling Pelléas on Mélisande when I tell you that Paul has turned down version STOP Could you advise me if either you can think of somebody else you would find acceptable or if

there is some other subject you would like to get together with Paul on STOP I slid towards conclusion that latter is hopeless quest but will certainly try if you like STOP Feel bound to repeat I think version excellent for some obviously incongruous modernisms and have written adaptor to tell him this STOP Look forward seeing and talking. Love Larry

Dexter later recorded of this enterprise and of Paul's replacement in *The Misanthrope*:

12 January 1973
        The first [Anthony] Hopkins walkout. Discovered on the first day of rehearsal that Oronte was not the lead. That'll teach him not to read the play. Shifty, spineless, Welsh cunt. Has AA helped him? I don't think so, once a cunt always a Welshman.
        And oh my God, the similarity to Burton. The self deceptions, combined with ambition and cowardice. Sexually just as catastrophic a failure.
        ten am Hopkins wedding.
        At least I didn't offer him *Equus* as I had planned. Only New York had that over-emotional indulgence forced upon them, but by that time the play worked. But if we had gone with him first, what then? Total disbelief from critics and public I think.

By now Paul had left the National. He resigned his associate directorship after only two of his three plays. After he left in the summer of 1972 a spate of angry press attacks rounded on the theatre's poor record — typified by the headline, "Panned, pampered and half empty." It seemed that only his two productions had been successful.

John Dexter had left, too. As Joan Plowright put it, describing Olivier's reaction to praise for a close colleague, "Harold Hobson said, 'John Dexter, the finest of the three directors of the theatre.' [laughs] I think, after that, John was out within a year."

Meantime the manoeuvring of those about to follow had continued. Paul, at one time a possible successor, was from his own inclination not a contender. At one point Olivier, acting like "something of an unguided missile," proposed his wife Joan Plowright: she said, when asked by Kathleen Tynan, that she — together with Richard Burton, Albert Finney, and Richard Attenborough — had been asked.

"I think I have said it to him [Olivier], there's no way. I, with my responsibilities as a woman — I'm not just being female or anything like that: that's nonsense. I mean children. *We* all know what that means. And the life I had to live with him as well. There was no way I could have given every waking moment to running a place like that."

She called Larry, asking him: "Suggesting me was in a sort of frenzy . . . it was just carrying on his home . . . It was nothing to do finally with me. I did not agree very often with Larry."

Tynan suggested a collection of people should run it. A school of cardinals — with himself included.

In April 1972 Paul was awarded the prestigious Shakespeare Prize in Hamburg, joining such company as Graham Greene, Harold Pinter, and Janet Baker. It was worth DM25,000.

Later that year Paul read Alexander Solzhenitsyn's Nobel Prize lecture, "One Word of Truth" for BBC Radio 3; Stephen Hearst, the controller wrote to him that he managed to find "exactly the right tone and moral pitch for this exceptional manifestation of courage," a very difficult task. John Tydeman, after failing to corner him as Oedipus some years before (even with the temptation of Irene Worth as Jocasta and the largest BBC studio rigged up for stereophany, "usually reserved for symphony orchestras"), had managed to pin him down for *Othello*. Here, then, Paul was embarked on his journey to conquer the last of Shakespeare's four great tragedies, which he was to play eight years later, in 1980, at the National Theatre, directed by Peter Hall.

By January Dexter was attempting to inveigle Paul into acting in another Shaffer play, the second for which he was approached. This was *Equus*: "The new Peter Shaffer play has arrived on my desk. I have been working with Peter on it for some time and am very pleased with the results. Peter and I have always thought that you would be ideal for the leading role but knowing your commitments I am writing to ask if there is any point in sending you the script? It is not planned to do the production at the National Theatre but in some other agreeable situation. Hope to hear from you soon."

Paul would have been excellent, but Alec McCowen, who ultimately played Dysart (perhaps suggested by Paul), was excellent too. Paul had already committed to Christopher Hampton's new play, *Savages*, at the Royal Court, which started rehearsal in February 1973. Robert Kydd, the Royal Court director, and Hampton had sent the script to Scofield; both were utterly dumbfounded when he said he would like to do the part of the kidnapped diplomat, West.

As for the part of the terrorist, Paul encouraged Kydd and Hampton to take a relative newcomer, Tom Conti, over more experienced contenders for the role. When he first received the script, Conti was about to give up the theatre and return to Glasgow with his wife Cara, who was pregnant, to study medicine. Then the script came through his front door: "If I get this, life will change." He auditioned with the others. In the end Paul said, "Let's take the Scottish boy!"

But they do not enjoy rehearsals. Bob Kydd is a problem — he hasn't a clue and keeps giving them readings that are patently absurd. They have to work it out on their own, says Conti, for Kydd's words, politely received by Paul, go "straight in one ear and out the other. There are a great many charlatans in this business," adds Conti.

When they opened they were not fully ready. Paul does not deliver more than he has. "He doesn't cheat," as Peter Hall says. This time the critics and public did not notice, for the reviews were good and *Savages* ran for nine months, transferring from the Royal Court to the West End.

"Paul's not a first night actor [believed Hampton] — he's not fully there on the first night . . . But he gets better and better — in *Savages* his best performance was on the last night. Every night he is trying out something different, and he has a fantastically accurate self-censoring system."

Conti's character is intelligent. He is a bright man, but single-minded to a degree, "a political nutcase whose complex character comes to like the ambassador he'd kidnapped, although in the end he shoots him dead with a Beretta (the theatre employed an armourer to bring this round each night, and lock it up after the show)."

Paul and Tom met at one moment crossing under the Royal Court stage: they were now, being a week or two into the run, finding their confidence in the dualogues. "Isn't it nice to rehearse the play?" Paul said to Tom.

Paul quickly became a role model for Tom, especially with regard to fame and celebrity. The influence has remained. "He was wonderful to me — here I was, fairly raw, and he was utterly supportive and generous . . . He has a wall round him. You are never close to him. Yet it's a wall not that he builds, but *we* build round him."

At this time Conti was unknown, but with successive plays and films this changed: "You become gregarious or you pull up the drawbridge. I took the same path as Paul, we both became reclusive."

During the run Cara gave birth to Nina. One night Tom, besotted as he was with his first child, brought her in to show Paul. He suddenly realised, centre of his universe as Nina was, she did not, or could not, being spotty and wet and howling, create that marvellous an impression. "Paul was so enthusiastic and so warm: 'Oh yes, Oh lovely!' he responded, and when they discussed fatherhood he told Tom, 'There is nothing you can do about babies crying because you don't have that smell.'"

The Beretta had four blank shots. One night Conti pulled the trigger and the gun merely clicked. Paul instantly roared out with derisive laughter (Hampton: "It shows how quickly Scofield's mind works"). Next time, when Conti pulled again, the bang came.

Conti fired three blanks: the fourth was for emergencies. One night, towards the end of the run, all four rounds went off. Anxiously, Paul, who was chained to the bed for the shooting, asked Tom, "Who fired the other shot?" Another time Paul came in for a Saturday matinee: he looked pale, shattered, and Conti asked if he was ill. "No," he answered. "The most awful thing happened at home. I ran over my little dog, reversed over it and injured it. It had to be put to sleep."

One night he gently admonished Conti: "You were marvellous tonight, Tom, you had that wonderful pace which is so moving," by which Conti understood, "I know you're getting a bit slow."

Paul's authority and influence in the cast were absolute, says Hampton. He had written the poems West composes with Paul's recorded voice-over in mind, but Paul insisted on saying them in person on stage, and asked for another to be added at the final point: "I think there needs to be one more."

At the end of the run, Hampton asked him to go to Broadway with *Savages*. "He was sort of aware that if he didn't go, the play wouldn't go. But he was firm, very polite and refused, saying that he'd given a year or more to the American stage, appearing on Broadway in *A Man for All Seasons* and *King Lear*, and he had no desire to go back there."

Before he told Hampton this, he consulted Conti: "You've got this opportunity," he told him, "what do you want to do?" Conti, with new-born Nina, had no great desire to go. But he thought, "I can't believe he's talking to me: if I'd said 'Oh yes,' would he have gone?"

There were some sour grapes over Paul's choice of *Savages* instead of *Equus*, notably the thwarted director of the latter (though Paul doesn't recall being asked to do *Equus*, which he saw and liked):

Hampton's *Savages*, for example, is just slop. There's no real thinking in it. It's just an opportunity for liberal non-doers to sit back and say how awful and shocking the plight of the South American Indians is/was. Christopher would have been better advised to write a play about how the English got rid of the Tasmanians in twenty years and no one's ever said a word. Larry saw it last night and he thought it was awful too. These parlour reformers may nick society's conscience, goad it into a sliver of guilt, perhaps even effect a few minor reforms. *Cathy Come Home* did that but in no way do they viciously and uncompromisingly take on the society that causes the distress which continues to exist at every level and could I have a cup of tea with some lemon and aspirin, Boddington! [a well-known stage manager]

In this passage can be heard the distant beating of the drums of envy — they would rise to a deafening crescendo with the production of *Amadeus.*

42

Nature and Brutality

> When will it all just go into the past, when memory takes
> over and corrects fact?
>
> — *A Delicate Balance*

Paul had made two more films by the time *Savages* ended. *Scorpio*, for
Michael Winner, was the first, shot mostly in Vienna, in which he was
cast as the sinister Russian secret agent, Zharkov. He liked the screenplay,
he said, because, it was "an action film with subtlety." Zharkov has "lost
the infallibility of what he believed in," yet he has to track down and kill
an American undercover agent, played by Burt Lancaster.

"The Russian agent I play is not like any kind of Russian I've met.
The Russians I know are mostly concerned with the arts and I feel a
tremendous sense of kinship with them."

They filmed his scenes in Vienna. He enjoyed this. He had been waiting for the film of *The Tempest*, to be filmed on a Yugoslav island by Jon
Acevski, a Yugoslav, whose treatment of Shakespeare's play had impressed
him. His Prospero was due to be supported by Patrick Magee and Jenny
Agutter. They were expecting Dmitri Shostakovich to compose the film
score.

It never materialized. So he enjoys Vienna and his big scenes with
Lancaster. He lived in a hotel suite in Habsburg splendour. "I rather like
the grandeur and lunacy of it all." The first scene in which Winner directed him, Winner tells him to do this and that — "And then to piss off."
After the take Paul came over to Winner and said, "I know — I forgot to
piss off." After this they get on famously.

Winner, given to talking in hyperboles, comments over and over again, "I've been living among actors for fifty years. Paul is the only actor I've ever met with real integrity." He could not believe Paul once turned down a TV commercial for baked beans — "Two million or something." Paul told him, "I'd so like to have a million pounds. But I'm afraid I can't do it." "Paul is a man of very strong convictions," Winner tells me.

Sophia Loren, working in London, wanted to meet Paul, so Winner invited him to dine with her. "I'm sending a car to fetch you." Paul answered, "I'd rather take the train." He asked Paul, "Why did you turn the knighthood down? Why wouldn't you take it?" Paul answered, "I'd hate it . . . Would you take a knighthood?" Winner said, "Yes, I'll take anything." Paul asked, "Why would you take it?" Winner said, "It might get me a better table in a restaurant!"

Other praise comes Paul's way from Winner: "He doesn't mind being out of work. He's the only actor I know who's not influenced by fear. He's sailed through the fear barrier. The only time I've seen him unhappy is when they built a development near him. He's lucky to have that wonderful wife: one of the few very happily married couples I've met. He's the only really human actor I know."

Winner's connection with Paul lasted after the successful completion of *Scorpio*, which was a money-spinner, easy to watch as it winds its tortuous, lethal trail through Paris, Washington, and Vienna, although it is sometimes hard to follow, especially in Alain Delon's laboured English (for example, "I am the dybbuk of Cross's labyrinth mind").

"There's nothing more fun than a nicely complicated neurotic," she said. It is a pity that Lee Remick never became as well known as Marilyn Monroe, although she played Cherie, the character based on Monroe in *Bus Stop*. Somewhat prettier than Monroe, although less pouty and voluptuous, she was a much better actress. She never took off her clothes, and she never slept with a President of the United States. "When stripping off became the vogue I had got to the stage where I could refuse!"

Although the star who came to fame in Elia Kazan's *A Face in the*

Crowd, she loathed "bikini-girl-sex-symbolism": in some ways she could be seen as a female counterpart to Paul. When Otto Preminger declared, for instance, when she took over the part of the trollop of a wife in *Anatomy of a Murder* after Lana Turner walked off the set, that she would be the next great Hollywood star, Remick sharply took exception: "What does he know about me? I never wanted to be a great star anyway."

She dismissed, equally, claims that she was America's answer to Brigitte Bardot. "I don't look like her, I don't want to look like her, there's no way I could be like her." No superstar then, but a developing, highly competent actress.

She appeared in much dross: later on in her career she commented, "It would be nice to make films for grown-ups again, and when they decide to start filming them, I'll start acting in them." But two of her best film roles were with Paul: the much-married and melancholic daughter in Edward Albee's *A Delicate Balance*, and, a few years later, the spinster Maria Gostrey in the film version of Henry James's *The Ambassadors*. Tony Richardson was the director of *A Delicate Balance* (he was to be known later as the father of Joely and Natasha Richardson). He died in 1991. He clearly relished the tribulations of filming this play. Scofield was cast instead of Henry Fonda. Katharine Hepburn was considered right to play the wife of the Scofield character, Tobias, who has grown sexually tired of her. As her alcoholic sister, Richardson cast the legendary Hollywood actress Kim Stanley, who had a drink problem herself so Richardson judged the role was perfect for her. The producers, who were more wise, agreed only reluctantly. Paul agreed too, so all that was left to Richardson was to woo Hepburn. The role of imperious matriarch was ideal for her, but she resisted it. She found the play difficult to understand, but now she also resisted Stanley, feeling their styles would be too different (maybe this was, in Richardson's words, "an old trooper's smell of competition").

Richardson found himself under pressure to recast Stanley, but he took the production office complaints of erratic phone calls from her as lies and gossip. He assembled his cast in his St. Peter's Square,

Hammersmith, house; it used to belong to Michael and Rachel Redgrave, and he was now married to Vanessa. At the first reading were Paul, Hepburn, Remick, Joseph Cotten, Betsy Blair, and, of course, Stanley, who was already staying with the director (and always refusing drinks when offered).

He asked them just to read through lightly and get a rough timing; the first act adheres to that, consisting mostly of the marital infighting between Hepburn and Paul's Tobias. Then they come to the Kim Stanley scenes:

> Gradually she started to act, not read. She began to improvise on Edward's text, she crawled on the floor, she sputtered, she cried. Looked at one way it was a parody of the stereotypical view of Method acting. In a London first-floor drawing room, expressing her emotions, her flesh, her bulk, it was almost obscene. "How could you have let that happen to us?" Paul — whom I didn't know — hissed violently at me when we finally broke. But it was magnificent — its reality so compelling, so violently and truthfully exposed, that there was more knowledge of the depths of human experience and of alcoholism than I've seen in any other performance. It transcended anything I'd ever imagined could be in the play, and I knew instantly how to direct it. It had the ugliness, the truth, the understanding of great arts.

But it was clear to Richardson that Kim's truth was at the expense of everything else: the other performers, the text of the play, and the exigencies of the production. If they had had a year to shoot he could have got something so disturbing on film it might have been unwatchable. But they had two weeks' rehearsals and then four weeks to shoot.

All the cast were shattered at the end of that first day. The bombshell followed: Hepburn announced she was withdrawing. In private Richardson argued back, accusing her of trying to ruin the production by a kind of cheap blackmail. Stanley has to go, insisted Hepburn. Paul, "whatever his hidden feelings were, said he would continue to work with whomever I chose." (Paul here wrote on my typescript, "Not quite true — I supported Kate.")

On reflection and on receiving advice from his doctor on the nature of alcoholism — and although it meant turning away his idol — Richardson sacked Stanley. He was feeling hurt, thwarted, but Hepburn helped him. They filmed in an entire house in long-sustained takes, some nine to twenty minutes long. Richardson and Hepburn sparred all the time, and it possibly helped Hepburn to ignore her anxieties of working in real spaces. "Paul, I'm sure, thought we were hopelessly silly and frivolous." (To this, Paul wrote, "I didn't.")

Richardson's reservations about *A Delicate Balance* build up:

I found the play itself, the more we worked on it, unsatisfying in its emotional underpinnings. Edward's mandarin dialogue is fascinating, and modulated with impeccable rhythms — satisfying for performers to handle — but the moral dilemmas at the core seem small in comparison with the intricacy of the trappings (excepting the portrait of the alcoholic sister). The central "betrayal" is that the husband has grown away from his wife — no longer wants her physically. That's not the greatest sin in the world. To me, the effect of the play is similar to the effect of Henry James. When I was an adolescent, I used to think he was the greatest novelist ever; now I find him unreadable — the surface is just too elaborate for the amount of life underneath; the characters become etiolated.

Viewing it now, and with Richardson having restored the character balance, I find it highly satisfactory, with Paul and Hepburn's performances in the major roles carefully and trenchantly supported by Remick in particular, but also by Kate Reid (who took over from Stanley), Cotten and Blair. Reid, a Canadian actress, was Paul's suggestion: he had worked with her at Stratford, Ontario — he'd found her speech patterns as Queen Katharine in *Henry VIII* closely resembled Hepburn's. But on reflection he was not sure: significantly, he says, "This was a witty and emotional actress . . . curiously wrong in the context of the play . . . no sense of a sibling relationship between her and Katharine."

The overall effect is that of a baroque concerto, and a humour, a lightness informs all the performances. In particular Paul gives a gentle, loving, coaxing performance — it is very smooth — which seems to unify, even mould together, the others. It rises to the moments both of present and retrospective passion, and his duelling with the mighty scorn and arrogance of Hepburn is wonderful to behold. All of it where Paul is concerned is so delightfully easy and relaxed. Surely this is the definitive version of *A Delicate Balance*.

Seemingly out of nowhere, in 1974, Paul gave a remarkable performance as Prospero, which also began as a radio performance. He came to Leeds to play Prospero, staying in a secluded cottage on the Farnley estate near Otley. "It's really a story of a chum of mine asking me to work in his theatre. John Harrison, the director of the Playhouse, is an old friend and colleague. Prospero is a part I've always wanted to play and I'm pleased to be doing it with John at the Playhouse. It is one of the major Shakespeare roles — very complex, very difficult. None of these Shakespeare parts are easy, but Prospero is extraordinarily complex."

Harrison wondered how Paul had kept himself available for six months in order to come to Leeds. "I truly believe he has kept faith with that one ambition, confided so many years ago in Birmingham: 'To be a good actor.' So if he likes a script he will do it, even it it's only ever going to be an art movie after midnight on Channel Four."

Art movie after midnight on Channel Four? Times have changed. Paul has learnt the role striding over the Sussex Downs with Diggory, his bearded collie, and confides he often goes on learning roles till four or five in the morning, with Diggory as audience. Diggory, like himself, is large, bearded, and prematurely grey ("Do you think he worries?"), but unlike him "ebullient and obstreperous."

"The role of Prospero is something I've always wanted to do. The poetry is irresistible. It is such a mysterious play. Whoever does it, whether with an intellectually considered approach or an instinctive one, opens up something new. Something new happened each time.

Shakespeare was speaking for himself at the end of his career and at the end of his tether. Prospero gives up his art — so does William."

In one interview he says, unusually for him, that he does not mind being labelled "the greatest actor in the world" — a label increasingly used in some form such as, "*arguably* the greatest actor in the world." But, he asks mischievously, "What about all those knights?"

He also aligns Prospero with Thomas More: "There was a saintliness in Thomas More, of course, in *A Man for All Seasons*, but he was also intractable, harsh. His insistence on personal integrity at the expense of his own family amounted to something like cruelty. Unless you see the fallible in people, always, it wouldn't be true, it would be an artistic lie. Prospero is a good man, but unrelentingly vengeful, unforgiving."

Harrison's starting point for the production was the drawings of William Blake. Blake's Job. "And the drawing in the Tate — the portrait of a man who instructed Mr. Blake in painting and so on in his dreams." Indeed, Paul's Prospero did turn out to look like Blake's Job, and in its four-week run the London reviewers were drawn like a magnet to review it. John Peter called it "A piece of incomplete magnificence: like Michelangelo's monumental, unfinished sculptures. Scofield can face his audience, utter a great set passage like some incantation, and the brooding, cavernous eyes hold each spectator captive in a way no other actor can."

Jack Tinker relished how Paul bestows on "this past master of mysticism the most marvellous humanizing qualities," and how in his first scene with Miranda (Nicky Guadagni) he sets the tone, coating the words "with honeyed paternal tenderness and such protective intimacy." His relationship with Ariel "has an almost tangible quality of affection and caring about it."

Michael Winner tells me he met Paul in the street at this time, who told him about the production. "This is a very good story," enthuses Winner. "I said, 'I'll put it on in the West End.'" And he did. Just like that. With H.M. Tennent as partners. "To my amazement it made money. The longest-running Shakespeare play in the West End up to then."

They opened at Wyndham's on 26 January 1975. In the break Paul and Joy have been away to Mull. His face was tanned from the wind. "*The Tempest* is appropriate. My wife and I have been staying at our cottage on a Scottish isle and there have been gale-force winds, snow, thunder and lightning. Tremendously invigorating."

John Peter rightly judged how much Paul's performance would improve. Frank Marcus delivered the ultimately quotable judgement:

This Prospero is no enslaver. Tall, bearded, and silver-maned, he bestrides the stage with the spiritual authority of John the Baptist. There is much evidence of close rapport between the actor and his director, John Harrison. As an impressionable teenager, I recall seeing them in their early days, often working under the prodigious Peter Brook.

Mr. Harrison rightly puts his trust in Mr. Scofield's imaginative powers. He has avoided distraction. The stage is two-tiered and uncluttered. A highly competent company — among whom Paul Brooke and Ronnie Stevens's Laurel and Hardy double-act and Tony Steedman's fraught Alonso demand special mention — provide a firm setting for the central gem.

Scofield leaves the clue to his interpretation to the very end. A light shines from his eyes as he utters in a rapt whisper the final words "set me free." Here is a man who, like his author, has decided that life must take precedence over art. He does so not with self-pity, but with excited hope.

As Harrison points out, Winner's judgement was actually true. *The Tempest* ran for almost six months, till summer 1975, "the longest recorded continuous commercial run for a Shakespeare play on the West End Stage. And it was still playing to packed houses when it had to make way for the prior booking of Pinter's *No Man's Land*."

Paul had said in the beginning of 1975 he would be, after *The Tempest*, faced with a blank page. A newspaper reported that someone told him of a Zeffirelli new TV series about the life of Christ in which he was to appear, but "that was the first I knew about it." His sights were still set firmly on Othello. There was talk of this at the National, with Albert Finney as Iago, but nothing was signed and sealed.

In the meantime, an overture was made to Paul to play Abraham Lincoln in a one-man play on Broadway for the American bicentennial preparations. Herbert Mitgang (the author) did not think it unpatriotic to pick a British actor to portray the American hero: "Scofield is brilliant," he said. But I have to add it to Paul's list of might-have-beens, which also includes F.D. Roosevelt in a film about the liberation of Europe (Orson Welles was to play Churchill in this Russian film which was all signed up four years before but never made). When you add the unmade Kennedy film, could it be that Americans saw in Scofield their ideal President?

Paul did play, instead, the seedy trickster Nicholas Fennick in *When Greek Meets Greek*, the first of Thames Television's Graham Greene stories in the series *Shades of Greene*. The swindly, eccentric academic, who in wartime fabricates a phoney Oxford College (St. Ambrose's) and dishes out degrees to gullible parvenus and crooks, meets his match in the equally bent "Lord" Driver, played by Roy Kinnear. One day Paul was in a pub with Kinnear and Richard Attenborough: people crowd around them asking for Attenborough and Kinnear's autographs, but ignore Paul. It angers Attenborough. "They simply didn't know him — and he's one of the world's greatest actors," comments Attenborough. Here we go again . . . !

"It is his [Paul's] few unqualified boasts that he can walk down most streets unrecognised."

"When life in a profession is seen with open eyes we must sit up and take notice. Truth matters. Each of us carries his own theatre," Paul wrote in 1975 in an introduction to a book about acting. Two literary plays occupied Paul in this year, one a failure, one a success. The failure was Athol Fugard's *Dimetos* which played the year before at the Edinburgh Festival, and now opened on 24 May at the Comedy Theatre. Before this it had played at Nottingham. Not only had he turned down Abraham Lincoln, but also a film offer from Peter Brook. Yes, he told Michael

Owen, "I wanted to do this play. I didn't take the decision lightly. Peter has been of major importance to me as an actor and I regret missing any chance of working with him."

Owen asked if he might join Brook in his new Indian venture:

It's not quite the same thing for an actor. Peter explores the possibility of theatre in different localities. In non-conventional areas of work. I explore a bit in the areas of subject matter and what the writer and producer have in mind. I haven't got to the point of changing the arena.

I'd like to go to India, not to work but on a visit to see it. Perhaps I'm unadventurous but I don't really want to work except in my own country and to understand the language I'm speaking.

This may be a limited attitude but it is the words that matter to me. I like my working background in the English language and people who speak that language.

Dimetos is an engineer who has a lifetime of acclaimed work behind him. He retreats in disgust from the money-grabbing city to a primitive village with his housekeeper and adored niece. The latter, who is first seen nearly naked at the bottom of a well, rescuing a wounded horse (a symbol of her uncle's fettered spirit), is an irritating, emotionally unstable child of nature. A visitor (played by Ben Kingsley) tries to convince Dimetos to return to the Big City and build dams. The visitor attempts to rape the niece who, realizing her uncle's attachment to his housekeeper, then hangs herself. Dimetos and his partner retreat to the desolate seashore to brood over her death, then slowly he goes mad in some simulacrum of Lear's despair. This was certainly what Paul sympathized with as "Something I'd like to say that the writer says better," but for public and critics alike it simply did not work. "A bearded Scofield toils to endow the engineer with life, but the author never explains the self-doubt at the heart of his mystery. The actor uses a curious rising inflection to add irony, or convey a tortured conscience, but his words never match the greatness of spirit implied."

Peter Hall says that at this time, while running the National Theatre, he had selected some seven or eight plays for Paul to be in and sent them to him, asking "What part do you want to do?" Paul at last agreed to do two of them in 1977. But first there was Lambert Strether to play.

The protagonist of Denis Constanduros's adaptation of Henry James's *The Ambassadors*, a late masterpiece, was ideal casting for Paul.

The main theme of the work may well be to "live all you can" and that the "right time is any time," but James Cellan Jones's direction put the emphasis on the "switch," the ironic changing of places.

The inhibited, fifty-five-year-old Strether is despatched from America to rescue a young American, Chad Newsome, from the supposedly bad influence of Parisian life and, more especially, from the clutches of the Comtesse de Vionnet. However, after meeting the Countess, and himself succumbing to the liberating influence of Europe, Strether gives up his rescue mission and urges the young man to stay. Meanwhile, Chad's attitude has changed. After at first refusing to leave France, he then eagerly embraces the idea of returning to America and engaging in business.

Strether waves him off triumphantly, for he himself has become liberated from his constricting self-denigration and naivety and the "sacred name" of Mrs. Newsome, Chad's mother. "I'm the perfectly equipped failure," and "I'm always concerned with something other than the moment," are lines in which Paul turns on himself in self-vexatious amusement. I can hear them now, so distinctively does Paul voice Strether's innocence.

His scenes with his confidante, Maria, acted by Lee Remick, in which the whole love intrigue is unravelled between Chad and the Countess, convey a delightfully amused contrast, against the unspoken love Maria and Strether have for one another. The layers of irony are beautifully read and registered by both Paul and Remick, who also looks stunning. Paul manages Strether's double-consciousness so finely that we believe equally in his embarrassment and distractedness. We also almost (and here Paul lets us remain in a tantalizing ambiguity which deepens the character as we say to ourselves, "Surely he can't really be that innocent?") believe in his refusal to accept what everyone else knows full well — that Chad and the Comtesse de Vionnet's "platonic" love (as he defended it) was no such thing, and that it had been well and truly consummated.

The *scène à faire* between Strether and the Countess, when she throws herself on his mercy, is deeply tender and moving: Paul as Strether accepts his betrayed loyalty and innocence with such affecting grace and dignity. As the Countess Seyrig, too, is spectacularly beautiful and distinguished. All in all, and with Gayle Hunnicutt as Sara Pocock, Chad's sister, this remains one of the most watchable and faithful adaptations of a Henry James story that has been made.

The "chiastic inversion," the changing of places, may have been crucial to James's later work, as Leon Edel pointed out; "Live all you can, had been central to *The Ambassadors*: man had to learn to live with the illusion of his freedom. Life without love wasn't life — this was the conclusion of *The Wings of the Dove*, and having found love James had come to see at last that art could not be art, and not life, without love. He had become his own Sphinx; he was answering his own riddles."

Paul, equally, took on the opposition in his next play, becoming himself the animal of prey on the gullible and innocent. At last he had agreed to do one of the scripts Hall had sent him nearly a year before. Ben Jonson's *Volpone* is a long play, and Paul headed a cast that included John Gielgud, Ben Kingsley, Paul Rogers, and Elizabeth Spriggs. The casting was as acquisitive as Volpone himself.

I don't think I'd ever really understood the play when I'd seen it performed, and I'd never really been drawn to it, but then I read it and it really did seem very good, and I thought it was encouraging that the National management suddenly wanted very much to stage it. That seems to be a far better reason for a revival than waiting for a Jonson anniversary or anything like that. It's a real performers' play, you know, with a whole range of marvellous parts: when Wolfit did it he used to cut back most of the other characters (including Gielgud's Politic Wouldbe), I think in order to reduce both the running time and the competition on stage. But we're doing the whole lot.

"Great acting," a "magnificent" production, was the general verdict. "Superlative performance," wrote Michael Billington, Paul gave the hero's greed real grandeur. "The Turk is not more sensual in his pleasures than Volpone," he roundly declares, "but he raises sybaritic excess to the status of a heroic passion."

"In the great seduction scene with Celia he ravishes her with language and it struck me that his voice can truly be described as 'Ovidian' since it is capable of instant metamorphosis. When he talks of 'some quick Negro or cold Russian,' his tones change in a second from lustrous warmth to arctic chill. And when cornered in the final act, he confronts the Court with a rigid, poker-backed disdain, refusing to join in the general pleas for mercy."

"The most bushily resplendent of Foxes," agreed Robert Cushman, "his final reckless self-exposure a believable (and thrilling) moment." The audience nightly gasp as, following Volpone's stalking of Celia (Morag Hood) in her white innocence he towers over her, and then throws off his red, luxuriant gown to rape her.

Volpone was followed by another revival at the National. In Harley Granville-Barker's *The Madras House*, directed by William Gaskill, Paul plays the owner of the drapery emporium, a magnifico called Constantine. Paul, wearing a green velvet suit and polychrome waistcoat, acts with splendid flourish, pouring out on the flamboyant eccentric all his most precious essences of comedy: especially a dark, velvet voice, with a hint of foreign vowels ("my grandfather was a Smyrna Jew").

It is almost a relief, in this Tamburlaine-like list of unending triumphs and victories, to turn to disappointment; perhaps it served for Paul, if only at some unconscious level, as this too.

43

Interlude: A Family

I am wrong. It's Ronald Harwood who makes bread, not Tom Conti as I first thought: "Paul makes bread. I make bread. I hope Paul's making his bread . . . His face expresses a triumph over pain: the personality is so unusual — enigmatic. The secret is his marriage. Joy. She is the key. Fascinating walk — he revolves on the balls of his feet so he seems to slide . . . has a wonderful grace to it."

Harwood was amazed when Paul agreed to do his play *A Family* at the Royal Exchange, Manchester, in early 1978: "If you tell other actors he's in it he brings prestige." Joining him in Caspar Wrede's production were Eleanor Bron, Celia Gregory, Harry Andrews and Irene Handl. Paul says, "The reality of family life is in the play. Not my lot. My two children and wife are fantastic, but in the larger family problems do arise. I think my character is a composite one by Harwood. The whole play is clearly observed. Whatever part you play is not yourself but this character is my own age, a modern character, a bachelor. There was a particular situation in the war that was the cause of his being a bachelor. It's true you can't bluff your family. We all know each other so well. This man is surrounded by his family but he's all alone. I suppose we are all alone."

The family is ruled over by a loving tyrant (Harry Andrews). Scofield is the embittered son haunted by a lost love and paternally thwarted. The theme is the self-destructiveness of his family, but it is given thin expression and most of the characters are unsympathetic. They "nag . . . snipe, they complain, they recline, and paint their nails, waiting, like us, for something to happen." When Paula, the bedridden daughter, threatens suicide and runs screaming down the street in her nightdress they make a meal of it. Again, as in *Dimetos*, Paul excels at having more to impart than the lines contain. He arouses, for Irving Wardle, strong hopes of revelation that "steadily evaporated as the evening progresses." But, concedes Wardle, "He is, however, beautiful to watch, and I shall remember his wordless cough of choked bereavement at the final bereavement."

Through Birmingham and Brighton, *A Family* comes to the Haymarket. Harwood is sitting in the stalls scribbling during a rehearsal: Paul comes over to him: "You're writing a play about us, aren't you?" (Harwood is writing *The Dresser*). At another time Paul is washing his hair. "Don't you have a hairdryer?" asks Harwood. "Oh no — I dry it with a towel." Harwood takes Rod Steiger round to meet Paul after one performance at the Haymarket. The star dressing room is high up in the building, up many stairs, and Steiger, who has just had a bypass operation, takes it very slowly. On the stairs they meet Paul. Harwood introduces Steiger. Paul: "Oh excuse me, I've got to catch my train," and rushes off.

But *A Family* had opened at the Haymarket to a chorus of critical condemnation. Jack Tinker likened Paul's agony in the play to a man lapsing into "long trances hoping to wake up and find himself in another play entirely." One journalist asked Scofield if he wasn't offered a knighthood in a recent Honours List, but declined.

Paul did not deny the offer: "If you are offered that kind of honour, and you feel that it's not for you, and decline, then you should shut up about it," he said quietly, adding that he'd much prefer any mention of it here to be as oblique as possible.

Hall tells me recently that he himself was lobbied by the board of the National Theatre to persuade Paul, but he still said no. Hall confesses he still has ambivalent feelings about having accepted his own: "I almost had a nervous breakdown when I was offered a knighthood."

Ralph Richardson says, "You can't catch all the trains," Paul tells his interviewer. He goes off next to read some Richard Jeffries for Radio 3: "The spreading oak gives more shelter as it becomes older."

44

Bricked Up in Fame

I don't believe in labels like success or failure.
— Scofield

We go back to March 1977. Hall noted in his diary on the 10th:

> Lunch with Scofield. I floated over his nose the notion of him join-
> ing a small crack ensemble in the Olivier committed to me, with
> me committed to them. He reacted very well and, significantly, he
> took me aside after the *Volpone* rehearsal this afternoon, and said
> he thought it a most exciting and marvellous idea. But then, as I
> have continually to remind myself, you can never be certain of Paul
> until he's actually there and doing it. He is, though, happy at the
> moment: happy with the play, and I think happy with me.

Exactly two months later Hall received an "expected" letter from
Paul. He won't, after all, commit to the group of actors Hall hopes to
gather for his crack ensemble. He does not want to commit himself so far
ahead, only stay till December when his contract finishes: "Mr. Caution
strikes again. It's a repeat of the same situation I have had with him many
times over the years: initial enthusiasm and terrific warmth; then with-
drawal. But I believe he will do *Othello*."

In August Hall again discussed *Othello* with Paul. He says he still can
not make up his mind about it. Hall suggests *The Cherry Orchard*, but
gets no response: "I mentioned Peter Brook's idea that he do a joint
National/RSC *Antony and Cleopatra*. Paul said Antony was a part he'd

been avoiding all his life, he gave no indication of whether he intended to go on avoiding it."

Volpone went on to 25 January 1978: Hall recorded, "Last night of *Volpone*. Packed house, cheering. It's been a good run. Paul promised to keep in touch. I said I hoped he found what he wanted while he's away from us, and he said if only he knew what he wanted. I said I knew he'd find it, whatever it was."

Shaffer was the Anouilh of the last twentieth-century decades — in Brook's description, "a poet but not a poet of words: he is a poet of words acted, of scenes set, of players performing," added to which there is an element of theatrical terrorism. How Paul came to play Salieri in *Amadeus*, after missing out on two of Shaffer's previous triumphs, in particular *Equus*, is itself a tale of envy, anger and high drama — worthy itself of Shaffer's pen?

Hall read a draft of *Amadeus* in the autumn of 1978; rereading it in January 1979 he judged that, in showing Salieri destroying Mozart, Shaffer had written one of the most remarkable new plays he had ever read. But the National Theatre associate directors did not entirely agree. Michael Rudman, for example, called it "the longest sleeve note ever written." According to his biographer, Hall had "an absolute child's lust to direct it."

Amadeus was, however, at the start, firmly John Dexter's property. On 14 January 1979 Shaffer asked him to direct it. Dexter said he had discussed the idea with him for three years. He had brought Shaffer's previous works successfully to the stage, and directing a Shaffer meant directing the author as well as the actors. For his predicted gargantuan efforts on the script — much editing, reshaping and reworking had gone on under his guidance — he wanted a cut of the author's royalties. When Hall said this was out of order (he had none of Pinter's royalties for directing Pinter, although his productions influenced the way they were performed all over the world) Dexter, an authoritarian and, even at times, a martinet with a stinging tongue, became increasingly hysterical.

Listing how much Shaffer owed to him, he became obsessive and very bitchy: "Shaffer blew it!" he wrote on 6 March, then, next day "Talk to PH re PS and the facts!" Then began an awful row, which Dexter later explained was caused by Shaffer being a twin. "Shaffer's being a twin makes it impossible for him to maintain a creative relationship with me. He's too competitive. So am I. He with me. I with the play."

When Shaffer's agent, Robert Lang, offered the National the play, to be directed either by Dexter or Hall before April 1980, Dexter complained to Shaffer, whom he called "Ruby," "Why do you have to decide *now*? I don't think pressure helps."

Hall, in the middle of directing *The Oresteia*, confided:

The centre of the day was taken up with John Dexter and Peter Shaffer. They came for lunch. John fizzed, and talked nineteen to the dozen without ceasing. I sat and listened. Peter looked troubled. When Dexter went to the lavatory, he — Shaffer — gazed out at the Thames and murmured through gritted teeth, "My dear, during these last few days every one of the hairs in my head has gone white." Anyway, I don't think we did badly, for after two and a half hours the only big worry seemed to be whether or not we could persuade Paul Scofield to play Salieri.

Dexter later had his own explanation for Shaffer's outburst about white hairs: "Because you knew Peter Firth had no chance with me or with *Amadeus* and poor Shaffer wrote it with his curly head in view. Riggs [Dexter's male partner] and I thought Callow would be better. He was."

Dexter seemed to think Hall was manoeuvring him out of the direction, but Hall, in his own account, seemed happy that Dexter should regulate his increasingly vitriolic demand for a share of the royalties: Hall had already declared on 25 October 1978, "I think Dexter is much better for Shaffer than I: sweet with sour, and plenty of bitch."

To which Dexter later added, "Which you, of course, do not possess."

And on 25 January 1979, Hall had written "I want Dexter to stage *Amadeus* at the National. But he doesn't like the place — new building, I mean. He's spent the last four years saying he will never work there. So it's going to be difficult."

Dexter objected: "Wrong. I said nothing of the sort. It was your company I objected to."

But was there some deeper, darker problem between Dexter and Shaffer, a quarrel, a row over a lover that was clearly at the heart of this undignified haggle over royalties? Insisting on calling Shaffer "Ruby" — "she" — Dexter returned one letter unread, then on the phone Shaffer said the problem wasn't about money: "He's *fucking* right," responds Dexter, "it's about *trust*."

To get to the heart of this we have to go back to the earlier triumphant production of *Equus*.

Was this the cause of the rift between them?

In 1972 Dexter agreed, he said, to direct *Equus* because of the speech that says, "You can't take someone's pain from him. He's earned it. He lives with it. If you deprive him of his pain you deprive him of his passion and his life." The attractive idea for Dexter was that personal pain was an essential part of life.

It seemed Dexter was at that time — or could have been — pursuing Shaffer himself: 19 May 1972 — "Dinner, Shaffer. What about? *Equus*? It could have been social. It never is, mean old bitch."

But Shaffer was forever attached to Peter Firth who had created the role of Alan Strang, the ill boy who mutilated horses — Dexter wrote to Shaffer, 3 December 1973, "Peter Firth's talent has been *used* by our play but not extended. He wished to take Firth with him to New York, as a trained professional, not an amateur . . . There is nothing in this for me. I have neither a sexual nor financial interest in him. There is no ego trip involved nor money."

There was, it seemed, precisely that, for both men (or so Dexter suggested) lusted after Firth, Shaffer probably in a more artistic if not physical way, Dexter in a more sexually if veiled sense. "Dear, dear," he wrote to Peter Hall in September 1979, listing great parts he wanted Firth to play, including Prince Hal in *Henry IV* and Andrea in *Galileo*. "Personal reasons for wanting to use Firth I think you can guess." And, at another time, "A talent like Firth's comes once in a lifetime, it needs watching, nursing."

Whether Shaffer *took* Firth from Dexter or not, something still deeply rankled, for on 25 May 1979 Dexter confided, "It's all about money. If it isn't it's all about trust, and when have betrayed your trust as you have betrayed mine by that one act of moral cowardice all that time ago. I have of necessity, since you would not discuss the matter, had to be on my guard, and if I *cannot* have a contract that protects me we *cannot* work creatively together for I can no longer trust you."

What act of moral cowardice all that time ago? Peter Hall says that he was never aware of any sexual rivalry between Shaffer and Dexter. He thought it really was "the power of money."

On 28 May Shaffer asked Dexter to "beg off this one" (the production of *Amadeus*), but Dexter hung on tenaciously and on 30 May, determined to go on: "I would, oddly enough, have no problem working with him day by day. I can look at him. I have nothing to be ashamed of. He has, and knows it, and that is the root of his problem. He has taken his decision and left me with the moral problem, guessing that a moral decision in the hands of a protagonist is safe. I should have remembered he learnt his code of theatrical behaviour from Binkie."

On Friday, 8 June Hall rang Shaffer and told him it would be better if Dexter and he made it up. But Shaffer, according to Hall, went mad, and for three-quarters of an hour categorically denied there was any way he and Dexter could, at that moment, make it up. "This is becoming a disaster: the whole thing," commented Hall.

He had a passing thought for Paul a day or so later — it would be easy, for instance, to get Paul Scofield's *Othello* sponsored. But they would be betraying themselves and the rest of subsidized theatre if they did. Paul had never firmly been in Dexter's mind for *Amadeus*, and one sensed the right sexual (in his case homosexual) frisson was not there in the actor for Dexter, who seemed much involved, always, in his instinctive feelings or desire. Dexter's original choice for Salieri had been Christopher Plummer, to whom he sent the script in February.

Plummer declined.

Writing of one speech by Salieri, Dexter commented, "The speed and venom of this needs LO [Olivier]. Alec [McCowen] who played Desart in *Equus* has no speed and his venom has an antidote, this does not. It must be fatal."

To Hall he wrote:

The question of age and the starriness of the cast seems fairly clear in my mind now as I think it has been in yours from the beginning. If we are prepared to think of JG [John Gielgud] and Paul S [Scofield] as Salieri, then why dismiss Jacobi and McKellen? None of these four is exactly expert in the expression of passion for "tit and slit" but whereas the older suffer either from problems of memory and energy (and saintliness) the other two can produce energy, venom and astonishing vocal variety and are also adaptable enough to be unflustered by the constant changes of text.

But in Hall's mind there had only and forever been one choice for Salieri — Paul.

Hall hoped, expected, that Shaffer and Dexter would patch up their quarrel. He recorded great relief on 13 June that *Amadeus* is really on — but then, on the same day, he was on the phone the "whole bloody afternoon" trying to dissuade Dexter from demanding his percentage. "I wonder how many hours I have spent on this play? If anybody should be getting a share of the rights, I reckon it's me!"

Then he heard later it was "off" with Dexter. Shaffer had, according to Dexter, dillied and dallied, offered rights then withdrawing them. He had, in the course of their rows, even said to Hall, "I would never hold a pistol to John's head. At the moment I would use a pistol to blow his head off. But I wouldn't hold it to his head." To this Dexter later added "too cowardly and afraid of a kick in the balls."

With all this, who could not help but laugh at Dexter's comment, which had some finality about it: "The play doesn't need me. Even Michael Blakemore could do it. It wouldn't be as good though."

Envy was the key to *Amadeus*, Dexter believed, and certainly there was plenty flying about in the pre-production period. He scorned Hall's approach when Hall wrote, "For years I have been praying for a sincere radical right-wing play, and this is it."

Dexter commented: "That's the problem, it wasn't radical. He caught himself in his own trap and missed the real play about the envy of talent for genius, i.e., Beckett and Shaffer."

Envy and jealous greed fought one another tooth and claw to get it on. At the still centre of all this was — Paul. With his mystery. His quietness. His power to hurt that will do none. What a contrast. He comments. "This Shaffer/Dexter story is all quite new to me. Ignorance is bliss."

Rehearsals for *Amadeus* were due to begin in September 1979. Hall rang Paul and told him: "He was delighted and frightened. I think he will be our Salieri." Hall hoped, he tells Shaffer, that *Amadeus* would bring together the two sides of his own talent, a professional puritanism in the theatre, and a desire to luxuriate in passionate and operatic rhetoric. He considered *Amadeus* to be about the uniqueness of talent, its refusal to be other than selfish. "It celebrates the individual and individuality with a Renaissance fervour."

This too (partly inaccurately in my view), is how he viewed Paul:

As all great actors must be, he is deeply egocentric, and deeply instinctive. He does what he needs to do, whatever the consequences — and he should. In this sense he is the most bewildering of men because he is so modest, so genial, so utterly sensible and human, no one can believe that at the last moment he can back out if he's changed his mind. I still remember the nightmare of 1969/70. He had agreed to play Proteus, Malvolio, Shylock, and Thersites at Stratford, and only two months before we were due to start rehearsals, decided not to do it. The hectic rearrangement of the entire repertoire made necessary by this last-minute change is something I shall not forget.

When it came to the play, Hall was worried at once that the story should not be presented entirely through Salieri's eyes: there must be a tension, he says, between this and what the audience sees. The cast was superb, including Felicity Kendal as Constanze; Simon Callow as Mozart; Andrew Cruickshank as Rosenberg; Basil Henson as von Strack; Philip Locke as Greybig; John Normington as Joseph II; Nicholas Selby as van Swieten; and Dermot Crowley and Donald Gee as the "Venticelli."

But Hall began in a desultory mood with *Amadeus*: on 4 September, he recorded: "We started to put *Amadeus* on its feet, cutting and trimming. A whole passage, one of the things which first attracted me to it, is now questionable. It is where Salieri describes his reason for being a musician. Music, he says, has absolute standards: all other human activity is relative, but a note of music is either right or wrong. I think that passage must go. It is too weighty, over-written."

Hall's sight deteriorated (an infection over the pupil of his right eye), and he later needed treatment. He was depressed because of his personal life: he was in love with Maria Ewing, the American operatic soprano, and wanted to leave Jackie, his wife. These early days of rehearsal seemed to weigh heavy with him, although he complimented everyone.

Directing is not a satisfying creative activity (or so Hall observed) but a dedicated profession. This is perhaps why so many directors were uncertain (together with actors, conductors), and needed to have their identity confirmed by being passionately in love; the tension of this, even if unhappy, counterbalanced the fact of always using someone else's talent, always juggling with insecure and unpredictable circumstances and personalities. A truly creative talent "that makes something out of nothing is never uncertain."

Yet Paul had that certainty of a truly creative talent. His resources of theatrical power were secure. Simon Callow was at once aware of this in Paul. "His mind," he says, "works in a circular way, he is not consciously intellectual." As Paul speaks Salieri's lines Callow notices how all kinds of strange things "accrue simultaneously," and become as if reflected in "multifaceted mirrors." His body, face, voice, as acting instruments, become "a filter of such extraordinary originality and a word or two can resound with fifteen meanings." The originality is at the heart of the security.

The anguish of pain and vulnerability, when Salieri yells out "Deo Ingiusto," is real, yet it is not Paul's, it belongs to the character.

Callow was thirty and had only been acting for six years. Felicity Kendal had now been in England for fifteen years. To me she recalls how Paul is "born with it," yet is "incredibly complex getting to a performance." She found the rehearsals electrifying, but of Paul she says, "His performance is not moulded by a director. Vanessa [Redgrave] allows the director in; Paul takes what he needs, but he will not be swayed."

Paul's Salieri is "extraordinary," "special," Paul is "born to play that part" — but there were difficulties. Hall observed of himself that no juices were flowing. "I love the play, the cast, the author. But I don't love me." Paul was irked by Shaffer's additions and rewriting, but he was too patient and polite to say so. "Shaffer describes the process we are going through with *Amadeus* as carving out a play with actors. 'It must be very strange for you,' he says, 'evolving a text with actors like this. You are used to a firm, hard, finished text . . . like Harold's.' Peter must have made far more money, be far more successful in a material sense, than Harold. Yet I sometime think that in Peter's eyes Harold is *the* dramatist."

On 13 September, ten days after they began, Paul did the first dozen or so pages without the book. "Miraculous," commented Hall. "Still too thick and of course slow, but miraculous. As far as Felicity Kendal and Simon are concerned, I almost want them to change roles. I want Felicity to be coarse and common as Constanze, Simon to be refined."

Five days later Hall marvelled at how voraciously the actors ate the play. They loved it. And "Shaffer is being wonderful in cutting, slicing, making it more tasty." Hall himself was the self-indulgent chef whose mind had drifted off to other things.

Callow's observation of Paul at work now deepens, as he describes it to me. Olivier, he comments, never really enjoys acting, but does it (and did it, for by now he has appeared on stage for the last time) for the sense of power; driven with stage anxiety he could never let up. He could never look other actors in the eye. But Paul is very and distinctly different. "I don't think he's fascinated by the mechanics of acting . . . He's interested in enjoying himself."

During rehearsal Paul told Simon he was a great fan of Charles Laughton. Paul was very "circumflexed," is the word Simon uses. He gestures from the elbows, and exotic as he is — with that voice — he grounds his character in an earthy reality. In those parts of *Amadeus* where he is not yet happy, "The complexity disappears, he becomes straight. But that particular place for the fragmentation — where the complexity starts, and transcends stereotype — is to be found in the deep sea of character." His great gift, his secret, says Callow, "is to make complexity so vivid."

Callow wonders, as does everyone else, that he has no sense of self-importance. But on Monday, 8 October, that massive potential power asserted itself. They were gathered round the harpsichord in the first act when Hall gave him some new lines Shaffer had written. "I'm not learning one more line!" he says emphatically. "No more lines, please. They are like nails going into my head." Shaffer swiftly closes him down, "I'm sure it's not necessary." But Paul has spoken.

On the Friday of this week they had their first full run-through. Hall was quite pleased:

The play is still far, far, too long: three hours of solid red meat. The principals did their stuff. They all have to play against their natural selves. Paul must not be too silky and smooth and general. Simon must not sweat as Mozart, there must be no tension in him, he must go for grace and containment. Felicity must not be twee, little me-ish, but earthy and comic. All three made big steps today along those paths. Shaffer continues to be most creative and enthusiastic; never a cross word.

Monday saw Hall taking Paul aside:

Spoke to Paul about the harsh, sour nature of Salieri as narrator. The essential thing is that he should show his brutal self nakedly to the audience, but put on a mask of courtesy and charm to the other characters on stage. Inevitably Paul was sidestepping the issue. I say inevitably because the first instinct of any actor, however great, is to be noble, upright, and charming to the audience. That is exactly what Paul must not be.

They now had ten days of dress rehearsals before the first audience: the technical rehearsal was "like pushing a heavy tank uphill." At the first preview they would find out whether it would work with an audience.

This one did, no question. It's still slightly muddled, slightly sentimental, slightly old-fashioned. But what I like about it is that it accepts the great theatrical gestures, and tells a story of the eighteenth century and the revolution in music. My feeling of relief at the end was enormous. I saw it with Lucy [Hall's daughter] and Peter Shaffer. Lucy, aged ten, asked me in the interval if Mozart was really like that, not a very nice man. But after it was over she said it was very sad. So the play had worked its basic trick upon her. You are made to dislike Mozart in the first act, and then your heart is broken by him in the second.

It is fascinating, the way audiences tell you things. After Mozart's first scene, when he blows fart noises with a virtuosity that delighted the public, Paul goes into a serious speech about hearing a wind serenade. It brought the house down. Amazingly, not an actor, not a stage manager, nor Peter Shaffer, nor I, have realized during rehearsal that that laugh was there. It must go.

With the audiences now, for the first time, Callow found himself over-eager; he tramples, he repeats, lines. By way of contrast he is totally struck by Paul and by the "wave of desire coming from the public. The moment Paul walked on stage the audience lay back, drooled over him. He rose to it, and they to him, just as if he was making love." Callow, playing the scenes with Paul, "felt like a gooseberry."

A little further down the line of public performances, Callow tells me, he realized Paul doesn't in the least bit mind if he himself plugs into the love of the audience and shared it. "He is not at all competitive." When on stage he has a sense of humour, says Kendal: "The line of contact is always there: he is comfortable enough to allow a joke or two to pass between you. It comes with the energy. No edginess, no tightness — the total dedication bleeds out into the rest of the company. He's like an adult. Most actors are like children."

Hall chronicled the next, very critical two nights. After Sunday, 28 October, he thought he had at last clarified the end of the play.

From the moment he knows his behaviour has killed Mozart, Salieri wants to atone. Society doesn't let him. Instead, they pour distinctions upon him. So he tries to cut his throat, and leaves behind a false confession of poisoning Mozart. But he also tells the audience — and this is what I am misinterpreting and have never got right — that most men are mediocre. Why? The audience represents the future, and Salieri tells them that as they come to this earth and fail, as most men must fail, they now have a patron saint of mediocrity, silent Salieri, looking after their interests. Finally those on stage and those in the auditorium have to unite as Everyman.

Hall found the preview the following day the best up to then, and that the end began to climb on to a tragic plane. But there was still something too complicated. He still felt a softness in the play itself — he hadn't yet crystallized the hard centre. But the play was working, and "terrifically successful with the audience." The most interesting reaction in that "very starry" audience came from Milos Forman, the Czech film director, who was extremely excited, and saw it as a great play, the first he had ever seen, about the problems of the creative artist in all ages. Producers, Forman said, still tear up scripts as Rosenberg tears up the score of *Figaro*, and still the creative man can do nothing except rail and blaspheme; originality is always attacked by the conventional; the people who are successful are not the innovators.

Hall worried that while the public would like it, the critics would take exception to its championing of the individual artist.

When Ralph Richardson visited a preview he declared it left him unsatisfied: he was, as many were to become, shocked by Mozart's frequent use of scatology, the "shit-talking presentation." As the opening approached Hall felt the play leaving him. The actors, Paul especially, wanted to be left to develop the play with their audiences: "Paul Scofield said his was the hardest part he had ever tackled in his life. Much harder than Lear because, as Salieri, he was always on stage and had such continuous and alarming changes of tone and concentration."

Salieri is the narrator of his own drama, and he encourages the audience to join in, witness the events as he outlines them. The give-and-take of confession between him and the audience, who like him does not possess the genius of Mozart, integrates them ironically into his own resentment at not having Mozart's gift, while forgiving them their ordinariness.

"Mediocrities everywhere — now and to come — I absolve you all. Amen."

No part brought him closer to his audiences, and it is here that, while Hall felt the play leaving him, Paul feels the director loses his power: "The audience becomes the second director. It is sometimes terribly difficult for a director to accept that this happens, but it does and it is a fact."

45

Completing the Quartet

Michael Winner tells me that Paul turned his back on a second Oscar. *Amadeus* was going to New York. Winner met Paul: "Are you going to do it there?" "No," answered Paul. "I beg you to go to New York. Go for six months." In spite of Winner's pleas, including, "There is no doubt you will get the Oscar [when the film is made] . . . You will have a greater choice of projects for the rest of your life," Paul was adamant.

He had a date set for his meeting with Othello, following almost immediately on from Salieri, and he was determined to keep it. Even now he remains firm in his belief that he made the right decision:

> I didn't want to do *Amadeus* in New York because my schedule with the National Theatre for that year entailed appearing in both *Amadeus* and *Othello*. It was put to me that we postpone the *Othello* production until after the New York season. I felt ready for *Othello*, postponement was an attenuation and weakening of my preparedness for the part; I stuck to our original plan, opened *Othello* at the Olivier Theatre and played it in repertory with *Amadeus* until the end of that season. I have not regretted this.

He had long set his sights on Othello, more than eight years earlier, when he recorded, over seven days, the play for the BBC. Again, as with *Macbeth*, John Tydeman was the director.

It may be that Paul had been keeping himself too much in readiness over these eight years. He was fifty when he went to studio 6A to rehearse what is possibly Shakespeare's most difficult great tragic role. As Olivier had defined it for himself, in May 1964, before playing the role at his National Theatre, *Othello* was badly designed. There were "too many climaxes," "too many outbursts." Then there was "the awful loading against the role by the author's delight in Iago (which is why *Othello* has always been regarded rather as a fencing match between two actors)."

Olivier succeeded triumphantly as Othello, especially in creating a dangerous Othello, a monster of self-regarding vanity whose jealousy was based on narcissism. But was it an Olivier great performance, or was it truly the character conceived and written by Shakespeare? Franco Zeffirelli, the director, called Olivier's performance "an anthology of everything that has been written about acting in the last three centuries," but anthologies do not sustain for long. As virtuoso acting the role was a supreme effort of energy and will power. Olivier himself said after each performance he felt "useless in the office next day — as if I'd been run over physically by a bus."

Without mentioning Olivier, Paul started off his approach to the role eight years before his own stage performance.

> I don't think an actor can allow precedent to influence him. After all, there have been historical performances of many of the great classic roles. No, I have undertaken Othello now because I feel I am ready to do it justice. It is a question of one's maturity and experience. I was forty when I first played Lear, who is an old man. The power the part needs can only be attained by a younger man. But Othello benefits from being played by an actor of the correct age.

For this occasion Nicol Williamson played Iago, Martin Jarvis Cassio, and Peter Egan was Roderigo — a better-balanced cast than that of the later National Theatre production. Tydeman identified exactly the crux of Othello's difference from the other tragedies, especially *Hamlet*: "The characters don't change much in *Hamlet*. The plot's the king. It's a marvellous detective story. But *Othello* is essentially a play of characters rather than of action. All the plot is in Iago's character. And people have to discover their character as we work on it." Paul himself defined a particular difficulty in the part of Othello for a radio production: "There is so little he really *says* in the early part of the play. It is only when his total confidence in his world is pricked that he becomes dramatically alive. Until then he remains a kind of pure centre of the play, a centre of good-ness."

As can be seen from Olivier's and Scofield's statements, both viewed the role very differently: Olivier, as refracted through himself, his powers of performance, and impersonation; Scofield as an objective char-acter created by a playwright: "He is a foreigner, an exotic outsider . . . a good man, but an innocent, and one rendered totally vulnerable by his love . . . we must thrust preconception away, start absolutely empty with the play."

Tydeman's production and Scofield's performance were outstanding and, with justification, richly praised. Even when hearing it many times on my car radio during the writing of this book, its quartet of male voic-es — Williamson's, Egan's, Jarvis's, and Scofield's — offset by the Desdemona of Rosalind Shanks and the Emilia of Hannah Gordon com-bine to create as rich and immaculate a performance of *Othello* as there is ever likely to be heard. For, as Bottom says to the Duke in *A Midsummer Night's Dream*, "Will you *hear* our play?" The effect is like proceeding into a series of interconnecting caves where, as the ominous space of darkness grows larger and more threatening, so more luminous and glit-teringly bright do the poetic and emotional treasures gleam, even dazzle, before being snuffed out. Finally, the biggest and darkest cave of all becomes the ultimate treasure house.

Chief among the treasures is Paul's immaculately voiced Moor, a nobleman of the sand dunes, a West African Arab. But the drive of the production, the "plot," derives from Williamson's equally wide-ranging and versatile Iago who, vocally and in feeling, is like a mirror image of Othello himself, as if each human character is double in themselves. Iago is, as perhaps he should be, the unexplored dark potential of Othello, the side of himself of which, above all, he fatally lacks self-knowledge.

Of course, this radio production should have moved straight on to a stage, and to his credit Michael Winner tried to make it do exactly that. He heard the radio production — "One of the greatest ever shows" — and approached the two leading actors, but Williamson had a precondition, which was that Sam Wanamaker had to co-present it. Wanamaker had made some agreement with Williamson and would not budge (Winner: "He's a wonderful actor but a pain"). Paul, who was possibly suspicious of the pretentiousness of Wanamaker's Globe Theatre enterprise, said to Winner, "I don't want to work for Sam Wanamaker." Wanamaker telephoned and asked Winner to plead with Paul. "Will you tell Paul we have three titled people, two Sirs, and a Lord on the board of the Globe Theatre." Winner did so.

Paul replied, "So what?"

"Well, I said I'd tell you," Winner said to Paul.

It did appear also that Paul, mindful of the energy the part required, wanted to play it in a repertoire, and not every night.

Paul remained set on *Othello*. And, according to Robert Stephens, Paul asked him if he would play Iago with him at the National. They had worked together before only once:

> I recorded Edgar on gramophone records in his King Lear, which was superb. We had a very clever academic producer [for Caedmon records, director Howard Sackler] who gave him detailed and really quite insistent line readings, which Paul might easily have dismissed as impertinent at that stage of his career. But, typically, he took every one and responded positively to all the suggestions. He is incredibly open to suggestion and humble in the execution of his work. He always has been. He has a total simplicity about him, and a real dignity.

But Stephens was on the point of leaving the National.

"Larry's a natural tenor," rumbled Orson Welles, himself a former Othello, "and Othello's a natural baritone." Whereas Olivier elaborately forced his voice down, unaccountably deepening it some of the time to bass rather than baritone, Paul, as the broadcast shows, naturally had the range. Vocally, his performance was in potentially fine shape when they began rehearsals in January 1980.

But Hall, the director, for all his energy and ability, was not focused on Paul's performance. How could he be, after the emotional and financial triumph of *Amadeus* in London with Paul, and *Amadeus* in New York without Paul? There was not the urgency, the hunger for success, about *Othello* when it went into rehearsal, as there had been for Olivier's performance sixteen years earlier, when the new National Theatre enterprise desperately needed to win prestige. There may also, unusually for Paul, have been a sense or feeling in him that, having waited patiently for so long, he felt too committed to do it then. Perhaps he slightly exaggerated the physical effects such a role might have on him (the effort for Olivier had virtually put paid to his stage career, for he only performed one more role on stage): he was, after all, only fifty-eight, a year older than Olivier, yet much better preserved.

There was no doubt that, from the start, Paul's was a very human Othello. But the Iago of Michael Bryant was wrong from the beginning. He was by no means Othello's double, but an entity, an alien entirety in himself. Those who liked him found Paul's Othello lacking, those that liked Paul found Bryant deficient. Highly gifted and intelligent, Bryant would never have passed as twenty-eight, which is the age Iago gives himself in the text, and he was too naturalistically motivated as neurotic, twisted, mentally ill. Iago is a character whose apparently motiveless motivation and desire for revenge needs to be eminently normal and sane to be dramatically effective: "I am what I am." He is a morality figure, "Vice," "Evil," "Resentment," and to characterise him too much is to belittle him, and to reduce Othello's stature. Both need to become locked into one another; as Olivier observed, Iago is a "delight," the audience's darling — sparkly, full of impish mischief — which is why Williamson, who often sounds like Scofield being naughty and mischievous, is so perfect in the radio production.

Bryant was drab, dour, realistic, but also far too honest, "too likeable." It isolated Paul, it failed to ignite him, so he was pushed back on his own resources. It did not, at least at first, catch fire. Robert Stephens called it dismal: "Thought he did the first speech, 'Oh, most potent, grave and noble senators,' particularly well, but I told him afterwards that he had to tell his Iago, Michael Bryant, to get on with it. I never understood why Michael played it with a bald head and white hair; the National has a wig department. Iago's a young man. Twenty-six, in fact, not fifty-six."

The production lasted a long time, three hours forty minutes, and it had, generally speaking, a stately rather than an urgent progress: it gained measure and status from Othello's opening speeches before the senators — which, of course, makes up for the absence of Othello in the early scenes. The natural integrity Paul conveyed was impressive, and his wooing power, recapitulating the inflections as perfected in Granville-Barker's *Madras House*, suggesting the "impossibly perfect English of a cultivated foreigner."

But Iago is "the plot" of this play, and in Bryant's hands this was stillborn: he suggested to John Barber a "wily, lecherous old gardener gleefully cheating himself at billiards in a small back room," while to Irving Wardle, "A cherubic smiler . . . ready to bite his tongue off rather than speak ill of anyone, his kindly manner does something to justify white hairs on a twenty-eight-year-old. There is no change of manner even when he finds himself alone."

He was therefore in complete contrast to Williamson — or a might-have-been Stephens. The penalty, as Wardle astutely observed, given that the relationship between Iago and Othello has now become largely one of music and tempo (and not of character) "is a reduction of contact between the two actors," and as a result Paul's first stirrings of jealousy seemed self-generated.

By contrast, the scenes between Paul and Desdemona (Felicity Kendal) glowed with warmth and passion. Kendal played the role as a spirited, defiant, upper-class girl who could tease and stand up to her suspicious husband (and who was subject to the animal magnetism of his love, for Paul radiated towards her on stage a convincing passion in which she believed totally). Indeed, the production improved considerably as it went on, because he was so persuasive and moving, so the end became very disturbing indeed.

A small shift in emphasis, a different build-up, a different sense of occasion or timing — and this *Othello* could well have taken off. But it remained slow as Paul gathered the momentum to move securely from one precipitous climax to the next. As one reviewer commented, "After the interval the play's greatness suddenly came into view." Too late? Yet as the jealousy began to bite, Paul developed the emotional power necessary to reveal Othello's catastrophic primitive ego and pride: this convinced Milton Shulman, usually a hard man to please. "I have never before seen Desdemona's murder done with such a blend of compulsion and compassion. In his 'I have done the State some service . . . ' he captivated a hushed house with his picture of a noble spirit crushed by jealousy, perplexed by evil and overwhelmed by lost love."

In the radio production of 1972 the equalities are sonorously all-embracing throughout, and the recording remains as moving as when it was recorded, innovatively for the time, in stereo: the vivid complexity of *Othello* fully on display.

The mediocrities stick where they are, the truly gifted move on, going where talent and art takes them. While *Amadeus* ran on and on in London and New York over the next few years, the naturally self-deflatory Paul embarked on less-monumental undertakings. Whereas at the age of thirty he had run in *Ring Round the Moon* for two years, nearing sixty he needed no such underpinning and consolidating of his potentiation and perfectibility. There were to be no such theatrical peaks as *Amadeus* over the next eight or more years, but there was quantity, together with an extraordinary demonstration of undying versatility. Even more astonishing, perhaps, was that in spite of one or two dud productions or plays, his reputation remained firm. Potentiation and the ability to astonish retain their quickness and vitality: and, of course, as before, the volume of parts he turned down continued to be heavy and constant. Day after day from producers, agents, and writers the scripts came thudding through the letter box. "Even if I know straight away that it's not for me, I try to read everything through. You always learn something." And back it would be sent promptly, with a kind or polite, often appreciative, comment.

Paul had been dropped from that so-called arbiter of household taste *Who's Who on Television* as far back as 1970, yet he was still the actor — even more so now, with *Amadeus* — who provided the milestone by which people charted their lives. *The Ambassadors* had been his last television production, six years before, but now he turned his hand to two parts very different from one another, the American Verner in Noël Coward's *Come into the Garden Maude*, and the Hungarian Professor Moroi in *If Winter Comes*, by Janos Nyiri, written to mark the anniversary of the 25th Year of the Hungarian Uprising in 1956.

"I personally get very little from watching myself on the screen, because it's just a repetition of a past experience," he told a reporter sent along to interview him before *If Winter Comes*. Acting for television gave him no sense of identity at all. The character of Moroi did interest him, however, for he is an idealist, a drama teacher, and set as *If Winter Comes* is in 1954 before the Uprising, he finds his idealism crumbling as he asks his drama class to act out the moments of "truth" in their own lives. This is in order, ostensibly, to find in the dilemmas they portray the correct ideological and political posture. But the hope in Communism has gone and it is on the way to becoming a "pitiless monster." "Only God knows when I am lying and when I am telling the truth: and if there is no God then no one knows."

Paul defined his own attitude: "I'm not politically very sophisticated but I'm immensely interested in faiths, and an ideology such as Communism interests me very much because of the involvement of the people who have faith, the reasons for their commitment and the kind of people they are, all of which is in an artist's area."

As such he was very affecting as Moroi, whom he sees as "Somebody who has a very fine sense of balance in a very precarious situation. I think cynicism is inevitably involved, but I don't think he's callously cynical. I may discover that he is. To oversimplify absolutely, the play is about the dream and the reality and the sort of postures that people who pursue an ideology have to adopt or seem to adopt." Moroi drowns his broken idealism in drink, and instead of counselling Karoloi the student to betray his girlfriend for his Stalinist principles, advises him to take her mountaineering to Austria and freedom.

Paul also recorded in that same year the Coward play, which is a gem, as well as *Song at Twilight,* a similar work but of lesser impact. The Buffalo Bill millionaire character of Verner could not be more opposite to Moroi, although both suffer a crisis of conscience, in Verner's case resolved by quitting his nagging, parvenue snob of an American wife and running away with a Sicilian princess (who turns out to be English, and is played with mischievous humour by Geraldine McEwan).

The amazing quality Paul shows in this performance is how American in depth he can be, and again one is put in mind of those "heavy" American film actors who are so real and uncompromising in the roles they play. "These huge men with brown skins (Gable, Cooper, Grant) — they were giants, they looked more like ranchers or oilmen than actors," Olivier once told Kenneth Tynan (in fact, Grant was English). Such acting makes Olivier in some later film roles appear arch and artificial, confirming what George Cukor said of him, "A mixture of a great actor and a spoiled ham actor."

46

Return to Central Park

Come into the Garden Maude benefits from being shot in sequence as a "playhouse" production, while the action all takes place, as did *A Delicate Balance*, in one setting, in this case the elaborate, richly decorated hotel suite of a luxury Lausanne hotel. As Verner, the "worm who turns" — as he says, early on, "I am now going to utter the five most important words of the evening (his party piece), which are 'Garçon, bring me the cheque' — Paul plays both the solid, reasonable foil to the hysterical, extreme woman (acted by Toby Robin with a grating, comic thrust) *and* the romantic rebel who breaks out.

His performance contains the delicate suggestiveness that he so clearly relishes: so relaxed, so assured, so full of naughty humour as when alone he puts on a Beatles record and does a little dance of defiance. It is so ordinary, balanced, yet at the same time contrives to be extraordinary and compelling — and very funny: "It seems to me that people are much the same when you get below the surface," or "I suppose American men must like being bossed by their women, or they wouldn't put up with it," are typical Verner lines — commonplace but, as Paul plays them, tinged or fragmented with threats and glints of other-worldliness, of complexity.

Another film of this period, made for television and screened in May 1985, was *Summer Lightning*. Paul had earlier been cast in *The Shooting Party*, a screen production of the novel by Isabel Colegate, together with Edward Fox and Robert Hardy. They were shooting in Amersham, Buckinghamshire, travelling through parkland in a four-wheeled open carriage with two trotting horses when the driver's seat fell through to the ground and the horses panicked. This had happened nearly two years earlier, in October 1983, and it was unfortunately the first day of filming — "and my first shot," Paul tells me.

The driver vanished beneath the carriage, escaping with only a bump on the head, but the horses careered out of control for a mile through parkland with Scofield, Fox and Hardy clinging on for dear life. Fox and Hardy were battered and bruised all over. Paul, with broken left leg and rib injuries, had to be detained in Wycombe General Hospital, along with Israeli actor Aharon Ipale. Paul was replaced by James Mason.

Paul's attraction to *Summer Lightning*, his first film work after the accident, was that he could act in it from the waist up, using his unbroken half as the narrator, meant to be the Russian poet and novelist, Turgenev, but reinvented as Sir Robert Clarke, the new hero of an adaptation of Turgenev's *First Love*.

The screenplay transplanted the novella into the eighteenth-century Ireland of Wolfe Tone, and featured the savage British reprisals against the Wicklow insurgents. Paul is found (now in his early sixties, bearded) recounting the story as he writes it in his library. He inhabits a dry, cold world, and only the past is fully alive. Feeling his younger self tugging at his sleeve he relives the horror of his awakening to love a young wild girl who prostituted herself to his Establishment judge of a father. The younger self is played by Derek Mayne, with continual interpolations from the older author. The effect and the whole story tend to become superficial, bland and over-prettified. But Scofield's voice underpins the visual performance, lending a background, a secret play, some inner meaning and resonance otherwise lacking in the work.

With the memorable tones of Paul saying, "So it was I bade farewell to my first love," the final awakening is better integrated. Clarke ends by visiting the wild girl as she gives birth and dies in a Dublin convent hospital.

"Strangely, though, I had never seen her before as a person . . . It was only in death that I saw her as she really was . . . I was never to see her again." With its clinching lines, "First love is like a revolution. Youth takes to the barricades," here is a genuine frisson of complexity.

At this time, too, Paul records, among other works, *Scenes from a Voyage to the Indies* by his old friend John Harrison, an ambitious sea tale set in the eighteenth century aboard a ship of the East India Company. Paul plays the philosophical Captain, Josiah Bennett, who is a "remote and enigmatic man." He finds the play very powerful and thought-provoking, and there is some suspicion in my mind that Harrison wrote the play around his own knowledge of Paul, which Harrison disclaims. "In the late 1970s," he tells me, "I asked him what sort of new play he was looking for; in the words of Shaw, what 'struck on his box.' Paul answered, 'What strikes on my box? Something that I'd like to say that the writer says better.'" Paul tried to have Harrison's play staged at the National, but it was turned down by Michael Rudman, and later performed at Nottingham Playhouse, but not with Paul.

The tempo of Paul filming in 1984-5 quickened, and after Turgenev he might well have seemed to be embarking on a whole series of patriarchal figures. First there was Alexander Sherbatov, a Russian aristocrat exiled by the Bolshevik rising in 1917 who, as an old man living in present-day Vienna, relives and reassesses the experience of psychoanalysis by Sigmund Freud, then a rising genius but lacking the money to heat his consulting room. The film was called, with remarkable mundaneity, *Nineteen Nineteen.*

John Berger, in his foreword to the published screenplay, wrote, "It is becoming more and more apparent, as our century nears its end, that the most valid testimonies to its history need to include the intimate, the almost sacredly private, and the gigantic historical currents that have rendered it indescribably cruel. If people speak of the end of ideology, it is because ideology, in its passion for the average and the typical, hates the private."

Well, roll on intimate confessions — but will they prevent war? For Paul, the revelation of the script was "The mystery of history . . . the mystery of accidents which affect lives that seem to have been determined by springs of emotion and will, but which are nonetheless turned in quite different directions."

The film, itself multi-layered, a complicated tissue of memories and feelings, is more Proust than Freud. The doctor off-screen is impersonated by Frank Finlay (who took over the role of Salieri from Paul in London). It starts with the two former patients, who have talked about the master of the ego, superego and id on television in New York, meeting up again in Vienna when Sophie Rubin, played by Maria Schell, seeks out Sherbatov.

Sophie wants to remember, and so she and Sherbatov rake over their pasts, which are intercut with their earlier selves, on Sigmund's couch answering probing questions about their sex or dream lives, and receiving wise words from the father of psychoanalysis. It turns out to be much better than *Lovesick*, in which Alec Guinness impersonates the dogmatist. Thankfully we only *hear* from Freud himself such sentences as, "There are no cures: only the possibilities of converting hysterical misery into everyday unhappiness."

Neither of the ex-patients has children, and both were the victims of unhappy love affairs. Sophie's was a lesbian one with Nina, played by Diana Quick (who conveniently was pregnant). Nina is reluctant to strip down to show Sophie her pregnancy in their bedroom scene (Freud: "In Nina you were looking for your mother and father").

"You made love?" asks Scofield quizzically.

"Yes — what does it matter?" — to receive the disingenuous reply, "I never knew any homosexual women in Russia."

"That was the happiest night of my life."

Freud was very thin, Sophie tells Sherbatov. "I used to think he was the one who was sick. His voice was full of authority. Nothing escaped him."

The newsreel shots of prewar Vienna create a fascinating background to Sherbatov and his Jewish girlfriend Nina's efforts to remain invisible from adherents of the rising Nazi spirit. Sherbatov, now a waiter, went off and indulged his sexual needs with an Austrian prostitute at the back of the restaurant: "The Nazis used to call the Viennese cream cakes." He was unable to bridge the gap between his desire for whores and his need to worship women as he worshipped his sister.

"Ah," sighs Sherbatov at the end (we are back in the present), "Life is very long — I didn't learn that in the treatment." All too true. Both left Freud way behind.

In spite of its many clichés, the mix of black-and-white newsreel, the romantic colour scenes of the past with younger actors playing Sherbatov and Sophie, and especially the duologue of the older pair that climaxes when Sherbatov relives the death by suicide of his Jewish Nina (with whom he could never bring himself to the point of having sexual intercourse; only by suicide does she avoid the concentration camp), *Nineteen Nineteen* creates a powerful atmosphere. Schell and Scofield's acting is of vintage quality.

"He did me no good," said Sherbatov of Dr. Freud, and one may safely speculate that this would be the attitude of Paul who, like Guinness, does not really want to analyse himself, or his acting. Sherbatov says, pointing to his kitchen floor, "this is where she lay — you can't do it with gas any more," a line perfect for the archetypal Scofield inflections that widen the vowels.

Apart from the condemnation of Freud — another notable line is, "He wanted to believe I owed everything to him," which suggests that the beloved transference of patient to psychiatrist worked the other way too — the doctor thought of his patients as part of his own family. Vienna has a strong presence in this family, and perhaps inevitably the pair, who begin to form their own romantic attachment but then break it off, have to fit in an obligatory visit to Freud's house. Ossie Jung was the electrician on this film. Any relation?

Another probing document of the inner life in which Paul appeared just after *Nineteen Nineteen* was *Only Yesterday*, in which he rejoined Wendy Hiller, his wife of *A Man for All Seasons*, to make an elderly warring couple. The writer, Julian Gloag, based this pair closely upon his own parents, his father being an invisible architect and prolific novelist.

Although Paul's appearance is that of stagey patriarch, his lines appear more similar to the Kingsley Amis curmudgeon: "One of the great privileges of old age is being totally inconsistent," or "I never like women writers. P.D. James a woman? Good God." "Mature," and "of the kind of one-off dramas the BBC always used to do best," were the general comments on *Only Yesterday*, in which nothing much happens except Paul's architect son arrives with the news he has left his wife, and his granddaughter later provokes equal agony — finally, the architect dies.

The elegiac tone of Paul's filmed work continued with the portrayal of Anne Frank's father in *The Attic*, screened in the autumn of 1988. Then as the Ghost to Mel Gibson's *Hamlet*, a human and convincing creation giving credibility, at an emotional level, to Hamlet's desire for revenge. Then we come to another eastern European older figure in the film of Bruce Chatwin's *Utz*.

Paul has not neglected his first and main love, however, nor has it neglected him. Peter Hall still has scripts from the National rotating on his doorstep. Paul follows *Othello* with what should have been a triumphant role, that of Don Quixote, but Cervantes' book does not hold an engrossing plot, nor develops a dramatic character; it is a repetitive epic whose visionary episodes contain a whole philosophy of perception. The way of seeing things did not provide enough fuel for Keith Dewhurst's adaptation to electrify the Olivier stage and somehow, it seemed, the teeth of the biting humour at Quixote's expense were drawn. Everybody is too kind.

> Paul Scofield's Don first appears out of the darkness as a legendary archetype, an immensely tall figure with erect lance, and it is only as he moves downstage that you perceive his mount to be an ancient penny-farthing bicycle. Tony Haygarth's Sancho rides a small-scale version of the same thing: and the silent first image of these two, one diminutive and submissive, the other regal and wrapped in lofty dreams, tells you much of what is to come. For a start, it is not meant to be a great comic double-act.

Clearly this is what it should have been but wasn't, although of course

Paul made as much of the comedy as he could, and the interplay between the two leads was one of the rewarding features of Bill Bryden's production, which lapsed in the end into bucolic predictability. Martin Esslin, a former head of BBC drama, while noting Paul was an ideal Don Quixote, and his performance as "truly heroic," found the script misguided, three hours of "pretty tedious traffic." Irving Wardle picked on Paul's rebuke of a clerical critic, "Is it a vainness to range through the world seeking not its sweets but the bitterness thereof?"

> The line suggests the combined immediacy and archaic flavour of the text: and also Scofield's power to spring surprises. You are prepared for his extraordinary vocal swoops from hollow chest resonance to senile falsetto. This is matched by an equally fantastic range of gothic gesture, always proving robust when you expect him to collapse, and vice versa. The performance moves on an oblique course between folly and moral authority; but, like all this actor's work, it proclaims character to be an organic secret not to be wrenched out by cold analysis.

Another lengthy stage role of the 1980s, a purely comic one, was as an octogenarian spinner of dreams (perhaps more quixotic than his own Quixote), the Lithuanian Jew Nat, in Herb Gardner's *I'm Not Rappaport*. It was, or so Paul said, a role bigger than any of the classic Shakespeare Four. He is on stage all the time (as he was as Salieri) and "I also talk more in this play than I've ever talked in any play."

The script of *I'm Not Rappaport* instantly recalled Central Park for him: "Those terrible corners with seats and a bridge that are meant to be little sanctuaries, and that are so *alarming*." He felt that "the fragility of the old men, in a setting charged with the menace of violence, made for an intensely dramatic situation." It also reminded him that after three "heady-making" months into his Broadway run as Thomas More, "I just wanted to go home." Fortunately, however, there would be no request for him to do it in New York, where it had already opened (and had collected, in June 1986, three Tony awards).

The full scenario, in fact, embraces a sinister stone bridge that carries the transverse bridge over Park pathways, while the flutter of russet leaves proclaims it is autumn. Nat's partner in codgerdom is Midge (Howard Rollins), black, ex-boxer, now janitor of a nearby apartment block, whose long service is jeopardized by enfeebled eyesight. Paul, disguised by beret, goatee beard, wide-framed spectacles and equipped with a walking stick, creates minor havoc as a do-gooder knight errant, convinced that American society is rotten to the core. As the naughty prankster he employs his disguises in the service of others. When the jogging yuppy who is head of the tenants' committee in Midge's block arrives to spell out the janitor's forthcoming enforced retirement, Nat poses as the latter's lawyer and threatens the former with the full panoply of unionized wrath. When the dreamy blonde who comes every evening to the bridge to sketch is assaulted by the twilight cowboy to whom she owes a swingeing drug debt, Nat dresses up as a Mafioso in an attempt to scare the dealer off. Against the menace of a knife-wielding young thug whose business it is to walk old people home in return for a consideration, he has, however, no answer.

"Many things," Francis King summed up the response of how Paul transforms *I'm Not Rappaport,* "can be said of Paul Scofield's performance . . . that it is exhilaratingly funny, that it is achingly sad, that it provides an enthralling lesson in dramatic technique — but the most important is that it has this ability to astonish." (Paul adds that he was very taken in the BBC radio performance of Nijinski's *Diary of a Madman* by Nijinsky's line, "I know how to astonish an audience." "So this comment is very pleasing. Though I'm not sure I know *how*.") King concluded that "it should run as long as he wishes." "Not for many years has he lighted on a role so miraculously tailored to harness his strange mercurial talents," wrote Jack Tinker. It ran, after a lengthy pre-London tour, at the Apollo, for six months until early 1987.

47

Fleet Street Napoleon — Other Worlds Elsewhere

Paul's next ambitious theatrical project was *Exclusive,* by Jeffrey Archer. It was announced in January 1989 in the *Daily Mail* that the play featured an upmarket Fleet Street tabloid, "rumoured to be based on this newspaper," and that Paul and Michael Rudman, the director, had recently visited the *Mail's* offices, where they were shown round by Sir David English, the editor. Archer himself, then in Los Angeles, declared, "I'm absolutely delighted that Paul wants to appear in my play."

Archer knew how to woo actors. He had just acquired his "Playhouse," the 780-seater theatre in Northumberland Avenue where, when used as a BBC studio, *The Goon Show* and *Hancock's Half Hour* had been recorded. For the board of his theatre he had recruited Alec McCowen, among other distinguished names. McCowen recalls Archer's first overture to him, made through his local vicar of The Bolton's church in Kensington, who told the non-churchgoing actor, "A friend of mine wants to meet you — Jeffrey Archer, you're his favourite actor — may I fix up a lunch?"

Archer duly took both out to lunch at the Ritz and at the end produced "a dreaded brown envelope," so described by McCowen — who was then asked, "Will you read a play?" McCowen politely took the script, while Archer said, "You've got to tell me exactly what you think of it." McCowen duly read it, telephoned Archer, and gave his verdict. "It's very bad, and I would not like to be in it." Archer, not at all shattered, responded with good humour, "Oh thank you — that's exactly what I wanted."

This was not *Exclusive*, nor *Beyond Reasonable Doubt*, Archer's court-room drama, which had run recently for twenty months at the Queen's Theatre, and which even now, in 1989, was touring the provinces, but an earlier work. When Paul had been sent *Exclusive* he found an "extraordinary form of vitality, an energy in the writing," and he was intrigued by the challenge, the risk, of playing the role of Nicholas Brittain, the powerful editor:

> There is a ruthlessness about him, an apparent lack of scruples, but always for the good of the paper. He can behave with extreme self-ishness, but in the end what matters is that the paper has to come out the next morning and be the best.
>
> Playing good men is very limiting. So if you play a bit of a bas-tard, which is what this editor is, you have to find something good. If you play an entirely good man, you have to find something fal-lible, just as with a tragic part you must find a bit of comedy.

John Stride also read the script of *Exclusive* and agreed to be in it. So did Eileen Atkins, who had just performed her solo show, *A Room of One's Own*, based on the writings of Virginia Woolf, which Patrick Garland directed at the Archer Playhouse after playing it all round the world. Archer made a good impression on all these actors: said Garland, "I think of him as the 'Tigger' of our troubled age," noting how, unlike many the-atre owners, he greeted them in a very friendly and welcoming way. Atkins found *Exclusive* very straightforward, with a good story, an ordi-nary play and something very different, as she said of herself, from her usual classical fare. "I wanted to do something that my Auntie May could see." Lee Menzies, the impresario who presented *Exclusive*, also thought highly of the script, and considered it much superior to *Beyond Reasonable Doubt*: "Very well written, a beautifully constructed play," although a fairly humming and accurate documentary of newspaper life.

But it seems that Archer, with or without the advice of Michael Rudman, became overexcited at having such a strong cast and wanted to make the piece more prestigious and, in one sense, artistically ambitious. Instead of being an ordinary little play, he saw himself rivalling such effective workplace drama as Arthur Miller's *A Memory of Two Mondays*, Hecht and MacArthur's *The Front Page*, and Arnold Wesker's *The Kitchen*. He and the director thus introduced fancy staging, broke up the text into an inconsequential, fragmented narrative (which weakened if not entirely lost the mundane plot; as McCowen called it, "a bit like a soap opera"). The actors wanted solid West End audience fodder, the fantasist Archer suddenly had a vision of his play as "Higher Art."

It foundered before it began. They rehearsed in a hall in Chelsea, by the river, near the statue of Sir Thomas More. One day when Paul arrived there by taxi from the station he told McCowen, "I've had a very talkative taxi driver. As we passed the statue he said, 'You're at home now.'" Having agreed to do it, as good troupers, the cast grimly set out to do their best and hoped that audiences would like the play. The text, with very short speeches and intricate ever-changing demands as the focus shifted from one part of the set to another, demanded considerable concentration and was very hard to learn. They communicated little, encumbered as they were with the two revolving levels to handle, and supplied with computers, their screens and terminals and all the hi-tech detritus of modern newspaper life.

"We never spoke," said McCowen, "the technical complications took your mind off it. We were all frightened. Paul never said anything to the director. Rudman used to say, 'I wish you'd ask me something.'"

As one rehearsal came to its close, Paul put up his hand: "I have a question, Michael."

"Yes, Paul. Anything wrong?"

"May I go home now?"

Eileen also considered Rudman not easy to work with; according to her, after they opened on the pre-London tour in Bath, when the audiences were finding the play too complex to follow and were rather dismayed and did not know what to make of it, the director and author said, "Why don't we go back to the old script?"

Paul firmly put his foot down. "No, I can't. It's too late."

The set did not work, either. Before *Exclusive*'s opening night at the Strand the cast were called in for a press photo at 3 or 4 P.M. Then they went off to Joe Allen's, but without Paul, who had his sandwiches ("Joy always," said McCowen, "made him sandwiches"). When they came back McCowen found him looking rather distraught: "Where were you, where were you?" asked Paul. McCowen told him at Joe Allen's. "Oh," he said, "I've heard of that. I must come there sometime with you."

Paul's learning feat, for he was now aged sixty-seven, was extraordinary. He was on stage for virtually the whole play and hardly a page passes without him speaking, sometimes at considerable length. He brought to *Exclusive*, said McCowen, his "extraordinary authority and integrity. I don't now how he managed it." He never said anything derogatory about the play, Archer, or the audiences. Nor did he show any unhappiness: he was, said Eileen Atkins, "amazingly good-tempered," and he and she (as the editor's secretary) played jokes on each other to keep them going, such as placing eccentric photos in the files, or him using his eyebrow trick. He was, she said, "hugely funny."

While she found average audiences enjoyed *Exclusive* (and how could they not, with such an array of talented actors playing off one another?), the London critics savaged it. "Mr. Scofield has never looked less comfortable on any stage," wrote Jack Tinker in *Exclusive*'s real-life model. "By the end of the first half, it would have taken a Molotov cocktail to wake up the audience"; "crashingly banal dialogue"; "embarrassingly bad"; "asinine humour" — these were general comments. Specifically, Paul was berated for his "ridiculous nasal whine" and compared to a "tetchy proprietor of a minicab firm in Clapham."

Examining the script, as I have now, it seems it was mainly the complexity of the staging that exposed the play to such charges, for it ruined the actors' first need on a stage: to build an *illusion* of reality. They were forced into trying to be the real thing, so the story never took over. As one newspaper editor commented, "Fleet Street is a little more complicated than this play."

Paul did not attend the first night party, thereby avoiding Archer's adherent glue of show business celebrities, Tory ministers, and media moguls. Archer dressed up as a paper boy and distributed specially printed mock copies of his fictional newspaper, *The Chronicle*. He rigged a *This Is Your Life* for Paul, to create further publicity, but according to McCowen Joy said no. (Paul says Joy was never approached, and he was sure it was Alec they wanted.) McCowen said that "Jeffrey was very shattered by the reaction, nevertheless he retained his extraordinary optimism." He himself was a bit cross when the shadow of Paul's rejected *This Is Your Life* then fell on him, especially as personally he was not going through a good time. Although Michael Aspel lined up with the curtain call after one performance of *Exclusive* and McCowen joined in with the artifice of public exposure, he felt he was being used by Archer for publicity. Later he refused to let the recording go out.

The advance booking for *Exclusive* had been heavy, but after two months audiences dwindled and it closed on the completion of the third month. Paul had no regrets, however, and it struck Eileen Atkins vividly how he never, unlike most actors, commented adversely on any audiences — or even commented on them at all. He seemed to bear it all, she said, as Marcus Aurelius would have done.

Subsequently, Paul did have this to say about *Exclusive* when questioned over the "unfathomable mystery" as to how he ever became involved as the editor:

> It was a very odd experience. It was very much changed from the time of first reading. It was rewritten quite considerably. I think the first script was better. In a strange sense we got stuck with something that was not as good as it had been in the first place. Not that it was that good but I did think it would work as a piece of entertainment. In performance I found that myself and everyone in the play really enjoyed it but we were aware that it did not work. When it folded, which it did rather quickly, we knew that was the right thing to happen.

The first film to be produced by Sir James Goldsmith, an ecological fable called *When the Whales Come*, from the story by Michael Morpurgo, directed by Clive Rees, gave Paul the opportunity to spend six magical weeks in early summer on the Scilly Isles. This was before the Archer debacle. Paul played the Birdman, Woodcock, who, as the last inhabitant of the Scilly island Samson, was driven off as a young boy seventy years before the story begins. He resettled as a hermit on a hill overlooking the sea on the nearby island of Bryher, and the action begins in 1914, on the eve of the First World War.

The curse that drove everyone to their deaths, or off the isle, was the arrival on the seashore of the narwhal whales, with their unicorn horns, which beached themselves and then were mercilessly butchered for profit by the islanders. As the only survivor Woodcock is worried lest this might happen again, and in the heightened atmosphere of war, mooted adultery, and poverty the two children, who are the film's heroes, become friends with Woodcock. He teaches the boy Daniel to make carvings of the seabirds, and supplies the girl's mother (Helen Mirren), whose fisherman husband has joined the navy, with fresh eggs and potatoes. The children visit the forbidden island to catch fish.

The touching relationship with Woodcock provides the best scenes. Woodcock is deaf, and while Daniel's father beats him for being lazy, Clemmie, the girl's mother, believes he did the carvings given them by the Birdman. The impact of war deepens as the local schoolmaster inculcates jingoism, the fisherman is reported missing at sea, and local boys burn Woodcock's house claiming he is a German spy sending messages to ships. The climax is when he finds a narwhal whale has beached itself and the whole island turns up to ritually slaughter the beast, expecting huge profits from the horn and meat.

Woodcock (Paul, looking remarkably like the Lear of twenty years earlier) confronts them and delivers a passionate speech: "It happened before on Samson . . . The whales came . . . then came the hunger . . . the disease . . . the curse of Samson drove us off . . . " and convincingly (but surprisingly) the hostile islanders are turned into saviours who truss up the helpless whale in a huge expanse of blanket, and return it to its rightful domain. The other whales, drawn also to beach themselves suicidally, are driven off with fire. The island is redeemed.

It is a movingly rendered fable about reverence for life and again Scofield, acting the good but impaired man, with an entirely convincing Scilly accent, is the prophet-like centre of the tale. The range and depth he shows is remarkable. He should have played all of Victor Hugo's old men. As Helen Mirren commented to me, "He aspires to the soul rather than the character. He has no sense of personal ambition. He's one of our great, great actors. We're lucky to have him."

48

Interlude: If You Want a Title,
What's Wrong with Mr?

Scofield's seventieth birthday, wrote Benedict Nightingale, the *Times* critic, passed almost unnoticed by the public at large: Nightingale lamented that, with "equal lack of public ado," he had rejected the "inevitable" offer of a knighthood. A pity, he said, regretting his "thin" last decade for an actor of his greatness. To be fair to Nightingale, he listed the qualities:

> Name another actor who combines such power with such depth, and such depth with such variety and concentrated attention to detail. Beside him, Gielgud lacks physical energy. Olivier was wanting in soul, and even Richardson had less versatility. Name another actor who could have made successes of Hamlet, Othello, a homosexual barber in Charles Dyer's *Staircase*, Volpone, Mercutio, Thomas More in Bolt's *A Man for All Seasons*, Don Armado in *Love's Labour's Lost*, Aguecheek and Lear.

He might have listed another dozen roles, but he ended, "Am I alone in feeling that Paul Scofield is a major national resource, and is currently going to waste?"

On the other hand we have Paul, who might have agreed with Byron's great (though neglected) lines that no one goes to waste.

"Birthdays are a bore, really," Paul said of his seventieth: and "It's true, I do like my fallow times . . . I hate missing anything that might be happening outside on a summer evening, something in the garden." Yet even here he is tactfully evading the truth: it is his diligence that makes him pick carefully and creates his fallow times, his attachment to high standards. His unproductiveness has quality in itself, and makes its own statement.

Make a list of those playwrights in whose plays he has tactfully declined to appear and ask yourself why. A comment, perhaps, on our culture and its playwrights.

Paul began the next decade, the 1990s with two short but impressive Shakespearian film performances, both of which, in the plethora of the supermarket era, with unlimited choice and unlimited supply, have tended to drown in a sea, or thick soup, of undifferentiated highbrow drama. These were Kenneth Branagh's film of *Henry V* and Franco Zeffirelli's *Hamlet*, with Mel Gibson. Rightly he remarked that in Branagh's film, "The battle scenes were quite extraordinary," while Mel Gibson: "Not the sort of actor you'd think would make an ideal Hamlet, but he had enormous integrity and intelligence."

Both films were enriched, their principals apart, by superb locations and immaculate supporting actors. But the two scenes in which Paul dominates have an eminence all of their own. In *Henry V* he plays the King of France and when, on the eve of battle, the herald Mountjoy (a surly Brian Blessed) comes to deliver his belligerent reply the tension, the interchange of challenge, is riveting.

Even more impressive is the long and Byzantine pursuit of the Ghost (Paul) by Hamlet. With the lurid display of Claudius' feasting in the background (glimpsed through an iron grille), Gibson harrowingly pursues the quarry of his father, cornering him at last in the topmost battlement.

This weak and broken testament of his father's murder by his uncle is then most movingly released from the spirit of Paul's compassionate ghost — a reluctant and unhappy victim, the perfect incitement for Hamlet's revenge. Although I regretted losing the first scene of the play in this film version (itself a script of perfect camera directives), to make the ghost more sinned against than sinning, more pursued himself than cornering and invading Hamlet, is a master touch. Paul's tortured face and those great lines of harrowing description of his own murder by his sibling are impossible to forget. As Imogen Stubbs says, "You'd care about someone like that."

These are two talismanic performances, full of echoes down the corridors of time. Paul does not repeat himself, nor does he repeat others. In the next and final decade we cannot look forward to him playing Lear again, or embracing every film role or television commercial that comes along. He does, however, amid quite a volume of no less distinguished work, nor of less taxing demand, again scale the heights of dramatists he has hitherto quite overlooked, or been too busy to undertake; he also wins an Oscar nomination for a film role, and acts not one but two major and leading roles in an outstanding television dramatization of Dickens.

But we are declining into lists; for this reason, "I don't like theatre biographies," Paul tells me with justification.

49

Who Is the Hero? Who Is the Villain

The 1990s begin with the winding up, disappointingly, of the film project of Joseph Conrad's *Nostromo*, which David Lean was due to direct. More than twenty years before Lean had asked Paul to play one of the leading roles in *Ryan's Daughter* — Charles O'Shaughnessy, the village teacher who, although created by David Lean and Robert Bolt, was based on Flaubert's Charles Bovary. They changed him from a doctor into a teacher. Paul was their first choice; Robert Mitchum in the end played O'Shaughnessy (he was paid $870,000), after Gregory Peck and George C. Scott were considered.

Perhaps characteristically of David Lean, the story of how *Nostromo* never quite came to be made is itself a bit of an epic. Christopher Hampton began work on a screen adaptation of *Nostromo* as far back as 1985; from the very beginning Paul was "cast" as Dr. Monygham — as Hampton says, "I'd written Monygham with him in my mind, and his voice very much in my ear."

And, of course, one can see and hear Paul in Hampton's script: Monygham's feet are seen first: protruding from behind a screen on a consulting couch:

GOULD: Mr. Monygham?
> [*The owner of the feet grunts interrogatively by way of response.*
> *Gould peers round the screen.*]
My name is Gould.
> [*Dr. Monygham is a man of 50, with iron-grey hair and a*
> *habitually sardonic expression made fiercer by two deep and*

irregular scars, one on each cheek. He wears an old flannel shirt with a large check, outside his trousers. He looks up at Gould with profound suspicion.]

MONYGHAM: I know who you are.

[*Mrs. Gould's face appears around the screen.*]

GOULD: And this is my wife.

[*Monygham is dreadfully disconcerted by the appearance of a woman; he rises abruptly from the couch.*]

And later, when declining the offer of becoming the new medical director, the impression continues:

MONYGHAM: If you spend long enough failing to help people at their hour of greatest need, you'll find that interest hardly comes into the matter. I can't imagine why you thought of me in the first place.

GOULD: My father spoke of you in his letters.

MONYGHAM: And did he tell you that I am distrusted and cordially disliked by the entire population of Sulaco?

GOULD: He did.

MRS. GOULD: But he also said you were an extremely good doctor.

[*She's succeeded in disconcerting him again. He looks at her fully aware, for the first time, of her forcefulness and charm.*]

And we've discovered it's your practice to treat the poorer families in the town free. So you can't be entirely indifferent to the welfare of your patients.

[*She looks at him, half-stern, half-candid. And he looks away, troubled, unable to hold her clear gaze.*]

Hampton and Lean worked intensively on the screenplay until Hampton accumulated over a thousand pages of manuscript. He began to formulate a distressing theory: "Namely, that for some reason David was more interested in continuing to work on the screenplay than in actually making the film. This was for the first nine months or so when, in my opinion, the script continued to improve, but now we seemed to be going round in circles."

But Steven Spielberg, the film's producer for Warner Bros., made constructive suggestions or improvements. These unfortunately angered Lean and he felt insulted. Not wanting to become antagonistically entangled with the prickly Lean, Spielberg withdrew. Hampton gave his notice. Robert Bolt had now joined Lean to work on the script and, although Bolt had become victim of a stroke, with a severe speech defect, they continued reworking Hampton's script until February 1990, by which time Serge Silberman had assumed the role of the film's producer.

At first they argued about casting. Because Paul Scofield had decided to do a play, David had offered his part to Eric Porter, and when Scofield's play ended its run, David felt unable to re-offer Scofield the part because of his commitment to Porter. But Silberman, making a commercial judgement, wanted Scofield. Lean said, "And he started pressuring me; it became pretty nasty. In fact, nobody's talked to me like that, I don't think, ever. He said, 'I'm going to tell you something that'll probably shock you. Warner Bros. dislike you, don't want you, and don't want to have anything to do with a film that you've got anything to do with.' You know, rough stuff."

By the time the film was ready for shooting Bolt had gone the way of Hampton. The last draft was by Lean on his own. "It was so concentrated an essence, so abstract a succession of vividly imagined tableaux, that he must at some point have stopped worrying about how much the audience would understand."

Some $45 million had been raised, locations agreed on in Spain, the Victorine Studio booked in Nice, and the cast assembled — with a stand-by director, Kevin Kostner, on hand. George Correface (from Peter Brook's production of *The Mahabharata*) was to play Nostromo. But Lean already had advanced cancer, and he died on 16 April 1991.

Perhaps the stalling, the spinning out of the painful creative process was a symptom of some deeper frustration; as Thomas Mann, almost in words Conrad might have used himself, said, cancer is "like a hidden assassin, waiting to strike at you . . . as if there had to be some outlet for foiled creative fire."

What a shame we were never to see Paul playing Hampton's script, especially as Hampton had him so clearly in his sights. (As he also did for Thomas Mann's brother Heinrich in *Tales from Hollywood*, who was played instead by Alec Guinness.)

At the end of the unmade script Monygham tells Mrs. Gould that Nostromo has turned into a tycoon and become principal financier of groups stirring up trouble. Mrs. Gould asks what's wrong with that:

MONYGHAM: You should know by now, there is no peace and no rest in the development of material interests.

MRS. GOULD: What do you mean?

MONYGHAM: Their demands have never been compatible with moral principles. Eventually, the Gould Concession will weigh as heavily on the people as any of the barbarities of the Civil War. [*Mrs. Gould shakes her head, genuinely appalled by his suggestion.*]

MRS. GOULD: How can you say that?

MONYGHAM: I can say it because it's true.

MRS. GOULD: But it's been the most colossal success. And surely, to create something lasting, what could be more important than that?

MONYGHAM: Love, perhaps?

MRS. GOULD: No. Love is only a moment of intoxication. Something you remember with sadness, like a bereavement. [*She breaks off, conscious of having revealed too much; and looks away, her eyes liquid. She makes a great effort and turns back to him, speaking in her normal balanced tones.*]
Do you still dream about the priest?

MONYGHAM: No, I'm a changed man. [*He makes a gesture, indicating the silk handkerchief in his breast pocket and his impeccable dress coat. Then he adds, in a scarcely audible murmur*]
Thanks to you, Emilia.
[*Mrs. Gould looks at him, her expression tender. He scarcely*]

dares to ask the next question.]
What are you thinking?
[*She looks at him for a moment, moved.*]

Echoes of Vanya?

There is perhaps some mild compensation for the loss of *Nostromo* in *Utz*. Originally based on the novel by Bruce Chatwin, and dramatized for television by Hugh Whitemore, in *Utz* Paul plays the white-haired friend of the protagonist, a Prague collector of Meissen porcelain, whose life is investigated in a series of flashbacks to pre-Nazi days through to Eastern bloc philistinism. Shown, or at least just about made before the independence gained by Czechoslovakia in the early 1990s, it moves lugubriously through this former aristocrat's life — he used to be Baron Utz — and his mania for collecting, proposed as an alternative for possessing the beautiful high-society women of his dreams. He collects a whole orchestra of china figures, but porcelain women do not compensate much for the loss of the real thing. As Utz's old friend, Orlik, Scofield, towering and white-haired, looks splendid, but really ought to be playing, in his shabby garb, convict Jean Valjean (even in the musical). He seems, now aged seventy, full of loping, unchannelled energy.

Hugh Whitemore recounts to me an incident during the filming: he and Paul are staying, during filming, in the same rather grand hotel in Prague. They are sitting opposite one another at breakfast. Whitemore, reading his paper, says to Paul, "Bad news — Peggy's died." "Recently," he adds, "someone set fire to her office, and since then she hasn't been the same."

Paul, after a silence answers, "It wasn't entirely unexpected." They continue eating their eggs for some time but then Paul, who has assumed the deceased lady is Peggy Ashcroft, asks, "What did she do in her office? I didn't know she had an office."

They have talked at complete cross-purposes. The "Peggy" is Margaret Ramsay, Whitemore's play agent. Whitemore also recalls how, one day, Armin Müller-Stahl, the distinguished German actor best known as the pianist's father in *Shine*, who plays Utz, was visited by his son on the set. Christian, the son, had been waiting outside the Church Hall for them to finish, and Müller-Stahl came out with Paul. He introduced Paul to Christian. "I want you to met Paul Scofield, the greatest actor in the world." Paul, says Whitemore, didn't know where to put himself.

50

You Will Never Find an
Englishman in the Wrong

"This is the moment to do it," says Paul.

The first of his great roles in this last decade was Captain Shotover in Shaw's *Heartbreak House*. This was the first time he was directed by Trevor Nunn who, as Peter Hall's assistant on *The Government Inspector* in 1966, was often to be found in the wings during performances "marvelling at everything he did":

> I have asked him to do things many times since. I tried hard to get him to play Antony and I even asked him to do one of the musicals. [This was Andrew Lloyd Webber's *Aspects of Love*.] I think Paul is very idealistic and needs to feel a special enthusiasm before he commits himself. I get the sense he enjoys his life a lot and needs to feel he will enjoy his work as much.
>
> I think I caught him this time just as he was getting the appetite for wanting to do a play, though he did say no at first. Then he thought about it and, to my joy, agreed.

There are, as Nunn points out, parallels with Lear, for Shaw wrote the play, in part, as a response to *King Lear*. But, he says, Shotover is also mischievous, wily and eccentric; eccentric rather than mad. It needed a natural comic actor.

Paul acknowledged the comparison with Lear: "This is an ensemble play, we all share it, so it is not like *Lear* in that respect but there are parallels. Shotover is an old man with two daughters who feels a sense of disappointment about them. He has his own set of values against those of a younger generation around him."

Desmond MacCarthy pointed out at the play's first production that the breaking of hearts is not something that Shaw knew much about. Ellie's so-called "heartbreak" — that her romantic acquaintance is Mrs. Hushabye's posturing husband — Emrys Jones wrote later on reviewing the Nunn production, "seems merely notional and perfunctory. The play is really about the spiritual sleep of a nation and its rude awakening."

Shotover is one of the best, if not altogether the best, of Shaw's characters, and therefore it is no surprise that Paul should elect to play him. In himself, Shotover is not only a fascinating dramatic character: as a self-portrait Shaw shows us a mind made up and dead, because finished (Shaw, unconsciously perhaps, revealing why he was a great admirer of Stalin); but also a mind self-mocking, comically self-absorbed and eccentric — a self-portrait which, like the proverbial cake, has its vanity and eats it.

But theatrically, Shotover is also a cunning artifice because he holds the play together, gives it a political context and wider significance: very much, therefore, a play which, in spite of its meandering and its verbosity, appeals to anyone with a prophetic or poetic turn of mind.

Appropriately for Paul, *Heartbreak House* is very much a writer's play, in many ways Shaw's best, because he, as Shotover, is so firmly at its centre. Paul must again feel echoes of the younger Shaw he acted, years before, as Jack Tanner in *Man and Superman,* which, in Peter Brook's unlikely production, was the only other major Shaw role he ever played. Instinctively, unerringly, he has over a lifetime picked Shaw's two best, most tempting plays.

The cast was "a dream team." Vanessa Redgrave was Hesione, "an indolent tigress, sleek but slightly fretful," and Felicity Kendall was Ariadne, "a brittle, dangerous hunter who does not like to eat but only to capture" — both Shotover's daughters. Imogen Stubbs was Ellie Dunn, Daniel Massey played Hector, and otherwise "solid support" was found in Oliver Ford Davies and David Calder. Joe Melia "climbed on board for one scene as the burglar." All of them have joined because of Paul: as Vanessa said, "I just wanted to be in the vicinity to hear that voice when Paul opened his mouth."

They began rehearsals in early 1992 and opened at the Haymarket on 22 March 1992: "Actors and actresses speculate," says Paul, "on how they would direct a play, and I am one of them. As an actor I aim the work of rehearsal and preparation at the director as a temporary substitute for an audience, and as a source of advice and interpretative discussion; but I wouldn't wish to be in his shoes, to search for the best way to use the talents of others. I want to use myself."

Shotover's closest relationship in *Heartbreak House* is with Ellie, and they have considerable, lengthy scenes together. Imogen Stubbs considered it hard to describe how "wickedly twinkly" Paul was "the more serious the script gets." He can transfix you "just by a little quaver of the voice," he is "wickedly unpredictable." She had worked with him, over a short distance, not long before on the radio production of Ibsen's *When We Dead Awaken*, and his "mischief" was such that she could hardly keep a straight face, especially when, as Maria, she had the poem to recite expressing her awakening:

> I am free! I am free! I am free!
> No more life in prison for me!
> I am free as a bird! I am free!

Stubbs described it to me as "heaven to be among such a galaxy of incredible people." While she was at RADA, Paul was for her, as for many other students in the mid-seventies, a powerful influence. "Everyone wanted to sound like Paul": she named in particular Ralph Fiennes.

She values how little Paul flaunted himself: he was "a team player." Actors today, Imogen laments, are used by the publicity machine: "You're asked to de-mystify yourself, with the result you arrive at each new part with 'your baggage' — it goes before everything you are." She believes the actor, no longer enigmatic and surrounded by mystery, has lost much of his or her appeal.

The experience of being in *Heartbreak House* transformed itself for her from an inauspicious beginning. "At first I thought 'God! All this simpering, *faux*-romantic rubbish, just to get to one single punchline.' But then I realized that Ellie gets to say some wonderful things. I've played a lot of *ingénues* and victims who cry a lot, and this is someone who's articulate and intelligent. There's a wonderful arc to her character, from a naive young girl who develops, and then develops again. In each phase she has a different tone." It was the relationship with Paul that brought this out of her.

Yet who'd heard of Paul? "They'll ask if he's a relation of Philip Schofield, the children's television presenter!"

For Imogen every performance was a treat: "Totally the most attractive person I've played off. His lightness of touch is so at odds with the resonant voice." Every night something funny would happen; at one, extended part of the play they sit together — a father-daughter relationship in which Ellie develops a passion for Shotover ("I'd like to marry you") — on an uncomfortable park bench, and only occasionally have lines to utter. "It was a true Shaw world," says Imogen, "a world of make-believe."

And the acclaim continued to grow as the number of stage appearances diminished. "Critics agree," wrote John Peter, "his Shotover is one of his greatest and most cunning performances . . . Both rocklike and delicate: a warm portrayal of someone gripped by the lure of the impersonal." John Gross commented that the two absolute necessities, if the play was to work on stage, were a convincing Shotover and a convincing Ellie. On both counts Trevor Nunn's production was an unqualified success. Paul was much more than just convincing: "You feel while you are watching him that it would be wrong to play Shotover any other way. He uses his magnificent voice to full effect, so that every tremor registers; he has the look of a time-worn Victorian sage; he makes the seemingly disparate aspects of the play hang together — the strength, the pathos, the farcical memory lapses, the gruff detachment, the bitter passion."

Gross also complimented Imogen on her Ellie: never overwhelmed. She was "innocent, flustered, determined, prematurely cynical, innocent all over again, and at every stage thoroughly winning, with none of the friskiness which can be so tiresome in Shavian young women."

Is any more proof needed that Scofield is our greatest actor in relating to opposites, female or male roles?

There has not been much of Paul seen on stage after *Heartbreak House* closed in 1992. But he was still continually heard: he recorded *Don Quixote* in a different, better version than the National Theatre production; then *Amadeus, The Three Sisters* (Vershinin), and another new play by John Harrison, *Rediscovering Leo*, a light-hearted exploration of artistic failure (Leo is an old, neglected composer) and youthful death wish (in the form of the young woman sent to interview him). Variations, one might say, on the Shotover enigma — and highly entertaining too — with a shadow of John Whiting's remoteness and sense of alienation cast across it. Most recently of all he played a jovial and rightly self-forgiving Ibsen, who nevertheless wishes to keep the existence of his illegitimate son a secret, in *Dr. Ibsen's Ghosts*.

But the barbarians were at the gates of Rome. Culture, as disseminated by a public broadcasting system, and standards other than that of the lowest common denominator and highest audience ratings, were continuing to fall drastically. It is typical of BBC Television of its day that having set up, and commissioned and filmed, a whole team to make Dickens's great sprawling epic of *Martin Chuzzlewit* — in many ways his most dramatic fiction — into a prestigious five-part serial, it should then, when it came to the actual broadcasting, sideline it.

At least it was made and shown, although the impact on Benedict Nightingale, theatre critic of *The Times*, was such that he exploded with anger over a full page. "I have come near to throwing my telly out of the window in an agony of frustration. When will we see the man where he really belongs, on the stage?"

Well, no one really "belongs" on the telly, except perhaps the weatherman. A TV serialization such as *Chuzzlewit* is a mammoth enterprise involving "writing, casting, designing, costume, design, location-finding, studio set construction, make-up, acting, directing, cinematography, stunt arranging, lighting, sound recording, editing, and musical composition, not to mention the provision of horses and horse-drawn vehicles of various kinds, and practical matters like arranging catering, transportation and accommodation for the unit on location."

The rich gallery in *Chuzzlewit* includes Pecksniff, the epitome of comic hypocrisy and self-delusion (and not without a streak of sinister malevolence), Mrs. Gamp, Montague Tigg, Moddle, Anthony Chuzzlewit and son Jonas, the list is long. Old Martin, the main brother Paul was to play together with Anthony, not only provides the dramatic framework within which the whole plot unfolds, but he is also the Prospero figure in the story, or perhaps, more accurately, the "Duke of dark corners" from *Measure for Measure*. It is more than a coincidence that Dickens, having drunk deep of a pocket edition of Shakespeare's plays just before he sat down to write this novel, should saturate it "more densely with Shakespearean quotations and allusions than any other."

The setting is mainly rural, and for much of the five months of filming they commuted to, or lived near, the village in Warwickshire noted for being the real-life setting for David Rudkin's gruesome *Afore Night Come*. Paul had already read aloud at home with Joy the whole of *Chuzzlewit*, an enterprise that David Lodge, the adapter, tells us takes some forty-eight hours. The adaptation, satisfactorily from Paul's point of view, concentrates on character and the novel's richly comic vein, and not on lavish sets or sex scenes (there are none).

What persuaded Paul to do it is because Chuzzlewit is "such a curious personality, somebody unable to trust other people. I suppose that's like many self-made rich men — they find it very easy to imagine that people are just after their money. Martin says there's a kind of selfishness which is always on the watch for selfishness in others, and he keeps others at a distance and then wonders why they don't approach and confide — and that is the centre of the character."

It is, too, the centre of Dickens's intention, for he calls it a novel about selfishness, claiming "the greater part of my observation of parents and children has shewn selfishness in the first, almost invariably."

Chuzzlewit abounds with monsters of selfishness minted with comic precision in the heat of Dickens's teeming mind. "Gamp is my name, and Gamp my nater," is the best known, with her rallying cry, "Drink fair, wotever you do." She is played by the fierce and formidable Elizabeth Spriggs, and becomes an unforgettable creation. But if the casting of Paul as Chuzzlewit is a natural choice, the way Tom Wilkinson breathes reality and conviction into the theatricality and false feeling of Pecksniff is surely screen acting, alongside that of Paul and Peter Postlethwaite as Tigg, of a standard rarely witnessed. The extraordinary element in Wilkinson's performance is that you like him, he entrances, mesmerizes even, with his specious good humour and infectious self-belief. And he is entirely credible.

Paul is entirely credible, too, in both roles. To the role of the elder Chuzzlewit he brings his by now enormous and unchallengeable authority, to the miserly sibling Anthony an odiousness and irascibility from a master hand deep dyed in venom. The coincidence that misanthropy and anti-Americanism should be joined together when Dickens wrote *Martin Chuzzlewit* makes it possibly a particularly apt venture for Paul to undertake, but although he keeps Martin Senior at a distance from the others he never loses that sense of ambiguity about his moral nature, and the suggestion or potentiality of humour. It is sometimes like Salieri in reverse, but one finds oneself asking, "Is he really having the family on?" and "What if he turns out to be as cruel a monster as his nephew, the evil murderer Jonas (played by Keith Allen, a part that should have emerged as more self-tortured and not just reduced to brutal tabloid thuggery)?"

When the series was shown, in mid-November 1994, it was marginalized by *Pride and Prejudice*, for, as one of the Chuzzlewit cast says, "Everyone ogled Colin Firth in a wet T-shirt." It was not given a prestigious Sunday-night slot, but "set up" to fight a ratings battle against the formidable and easily digested (to use a polite phrase) *Cracker* on ITV.

Subsequently, in the year's BAFTA awards three of the four nominations for Best Actor were from the cast of *Chuzzlewit* — Paul, Peter Postlethwaite, and Tom Wilkinson. Predictably, perhaps, in view of the current predilection, the fourth nominee, *Cracker*'s Robbie Coltrane, with the members' vote behind him, scooped the award.

The Royal Television Society's award a few months later was, with more justice, given to Wilkinson; but as David Lodge (who should also have gained more kudos for his outstanding adaptation) observed several other actors were unlucky not to gain nominations or prizes. I would pick out Philip Franks in the expanded role of Tom Pinch (in spite of an unfortunate wig which made him look as if he'd just come out of the circus ring); and of course Elizabeth Spriggs who appears so very scary as Mrs. Gamp, with an extraordinarily heavy face as if moulded from clay. She famously remarked to Scofield (he has recounted this gossip with relish to others), during the tour of the ill-fated Scottish play in which she played one of the witches, that she came into his dressing room one night, and threw her arms around him — "Paul darling, darling Paul, you used to be such a wonderful actor! Where has it all gone?"

51

And the Other Giant

"You can call Paul Scofield great because his life has proved consistently that that's true," said Imogen Stubbs. "It is hardly his fault if hagiography, like church imagery, waits on every corner," recently wrote a columnist for the *Daily Telegraph*. People are upset by transparent goodness, but one film star turned director, and perhaps even more than that, social missionary, remembers seeing Scofield way back in New York in 1964 while he himself was also appearing on Broadway, in *Barefoot in the Park*. It was the actor's night off, a Monday, and the performance he saw was for an actor's benefit.

"I am very critical by nature," Robert Redford recalls, "but here [Paul as Thomas More] was a consummate actor." Thirty years later Redford was casting his film of *Quiz Show*, the true 1950s story exposing a national TV quiz show as a fraud, which he intended to use as a metaphor for the moral decline of America. "I'm taking a hard look," he tells me, "at a moment in society, an acceleration of the downturn, we are watching morality erode."

The main character, Van Doren, was to be played by Ralph Fiennes: it is Van Doren's on-air corruption that violates his own family's cherished ethical code. His father, Mark Van Doren, is a Pulitzer Prize-winning poet and academic, a character of absolute integrity, the upright New England intellectual who stands for all that is best in American life. For the father, Paul, from thirty years earlier, immediately came into Redford's mind. He further says, "I inquired of casting directors: I was immediately told he was not available, he had returned, he did not come to collect his Oscar because he disliked America, he'd declined a knighthood and so on."

Redford tried another casting director, and then decided to take control of the quest himself, finally tracking down Paul in Mull, where he was on holiday. But Mark Van Doren's character did not exist in the script. "It was symbolic, off-stage. I'm imagining four to five scenes." When he "phoned and told me what the film and my character involved, he was very eloquent, but he didn't try to persuade me," related Paul. Redford wrote the script and sent it: "As soon as I read it I saw what a good story it was, and how relevant too." Paul says the role would have amused his father.

When they came to film in New York for six weeks in 1993 Redford found him special — wonderful. "He had no problem in accents, and was convincing New England — very American." The qualities he showed to perfection in the role were, for Redford, "dignity, static intelligence, and grace. He was deep in confidence; he sat on himself. Above all he had fun doing it — a complete joy in acting." As for Paul himself, it was "a happy experience," proving to him "that it was not the city itself that disturbed me, but the long absence from home."

Redford was "incredibly sympathetic and incredibly intuitive and very disciplined. He's a man of few words but with a kind of easy, open quality which is not inhibiting at all. He makes you open up, just because of the kind of man he is. Redford had something to say about America and he said it." Indeed, *Quiz Show*, for which Paul won an Oscar nomination, stands as an isolated outcry against the debasement, the mass dumbing down by television, of contemporary culture: as such, Redford noted, it has become something of a cult film.

"All the pride he has is channelled through the things he does brilliantly," declares Richard Eyre to me. Eyre, as director of the National, now Royal National Theatre, cajoled him into Ibsen's great role of John Gabriel Borkman. "He has a very powerful personality, but it is not there as a parallel idiosyncrasy," Eyre goes on to say. So now, the "unclubbable purist in a lounge of chancer," is to attempt Ibsen's self-isolated demon.

The Establishment, at this time, set out again to slap a knighthood on Paul, but even his well-known refusals to speak about it was one of false warnings, although we can see, by now, his fellow professionals would canonize him if they could: "I have every respect for people who are offered it [a knighthood]," he says, "and accept it gratefully. It is just not an aspect of life that I would want."

A *Times* reporter in 1996 questioned if such an honour would be tantamount to a writ, in that it would threaten to take something from him. "Not money or property, but identity itself." Since acting means borrowing the identity of others, could it be that he is "all the more determined to hang on to his own?"

"Yes, I think that is true," answered Paul. "Your identity is vital to your sense of balance. I have had to inhabit other people. I have spent enormous amounts of time in this activity. It's not that it's a problem to return to being yourself. It isn't difficult to leave Lear, or Macbeth, or this fellow Borkman. But once you have gone back to yourself, you want it to be the same self you have always been."

The *Times* man diligently pursued his quarry next by querying if turning into a real-life knight would be an act of alienation: Paul answered, "Well, I think the word 'title' is very important in all this. If you want a title, what's wrong with Mr.? If you have always been that, then why lose your title? I have a title, which is the same one I have always had."

Ah, riposted the interrogator (shades here of Thomas Cromwell?), "It smacks of principle" (intimating that this was a late-20th-century treasonable word).

"It does," Paul deftly parried, "But it's not political. I have a CBE, which I accepted very gratefully. My wife feels the same way. 'Oh, don't let me be called Lady,' she says. My son felt the same, and my daughter said I should do as I wanted to do."

"You just want to sit near him," Eileen Atkins tells me, to absorb something of that presence. This echoes or repeats so many expressions of possessive warmth that by now I am hesitating over recording any more. "You want to take him home," Imogen Stubbs sums up Scofield worship, while that earlier encomiast went to the heart of the problem. "He has all the virtues which everyone wants to meet, but few want to read about. Baddies make great reading."

"I'm always nervous before a new part," Paul said of the giant he was about to tackle. "As one goes on it gets worse — oh, it does! But one's fatalism also increases. When you're very young, if you fail it's the end of the world. Not that you don't care as much as you did, but you do achieve a sense of proportion about what is important. What is important is to do your best. If it's your best, and they don't like it, that's too bad."

Why did he agree to Borkman when resisting so much else? Peter Brook told Eyre, so the latter reported, "There is a Borkman inside Paul — answerable only to himself." In rehearsal Eyre found Paul was much more flexible, sensitive, open to suggestions, than he expected. Just his presence at rehearsal was "like an epiphany" and "placed a benediction" on the enterprise. But Paul "likes a dialectic," and he likes corroboration. He really despises "ego." "He didn't like Olivier, he wasn't keen on Ralph Richardson," claims Eyre. "He would never say it, but I believe he thought they were rather cruel — which they were."

For Borkman Paul adopted a unique strutting and jerky walk; with his crest of white hair he resembled a cockatoo, and wearing a frock coat and white spats only enlarged the bird image — the cagey carefulness of the walk suggested an oversized fighting cock. But now there were no combatants, and the cage was self-imposed. Borkman might be a murderer of the hearts of his two women, Gunhild, his wife, and her sister Ella, both superbly played by Atkins and Redgrave, but his Olympian irony has been subdued by the demon of the vision that bewitches him.

In his last big speech, as he looks down on his dream kingdom, expanding the legend he has created of himself in his own mind — factories humming, wheels turning — Paul as Borkman came close to entrapping you in his own belief. He is a swindler, yes, on a Robert Maxwell scale, but there is an imprisoned soul there, the "Gabriel" that Paul so lovingly nurtured and imbued with touches of gaiety and humour. Gradually his need for something other — Truth? Redemption? Atonement? — drives him to self-destruction.

> The revelation of his character both developed and stood still at the same time [records Paul], he began as a man frozen and trapped by the past, recaptured for a moment his knowledge of passionate human love; after which encounter with Ella he seemed to again embrace his own obsessive drive towards an anarchical climax, proclaiming his mad preoccupation with the forces and spirits of the earth, until his brain and body simply cracked under the force of his avid desire to dominate his own small kingdom.
>
> Any rational progression of development, from the actor's point of view, was out of the question — the emotions only could be followed, and in whatever direction they demanded. So a retrospective examination or analysis is not possible. Just as one can't remember the details of a long and hellish journey.

Once they opened, again in Paul's words, "its power took over in performance." And, says Eyre, "when he was flying he was sublime." Eyre singled out the moment when, on the edge of the mountain, Borkman is looking out over the valley and the bottomless drop below him. In the stalls Eyre is sitting only three feet away. "Every time I heard it, it made the hairs stand upon the back of my neck. It was the most beautiful thing I've ever heard. Distilled. Savagely beautiful; and he looks so extraordinary."

Hugh Whitemore had the same experience watching Paul as Borkman. When he had his back to the audience it was overwhelming: "he grew, he became immense." It reminded Whitemore of Sacha Guitry. For Atkins the play came as a salvation. In 1995 she had breast cancer, and knowing she was due to perform the play in nine months' time was a great aid to recovery while she underwent chemotherapy — "a wonderful boost." The scenes with Redgrave ("Paul feels utterly safe with her") and Atkins are a continual revelation. Finally, lost for words, Atkins tells me, "His acting is of another order," and that, as a person, "He's simply one of the most beautiful men I've ever set eyes on."

The critics, the distant strangers, were unanimous in their praise. "Combines emotional integrity with rare wit"; "total enthralment"; "perfectly pitched"; "absolutely serious, searchingly intelligent, and wholly riveting"; finally, "his greatest performance since King Lear."

52

L'Oreille Est le Chemin du Coeur

Biographers often finish by attempting to sum up the greatness, or short-comings, of their victim. Is this obligatory in Scofield's case? To actors, many biographers have applied what by now may seem clichéd yard-sticks, such as the powerful voice, the large eyes, the towering personali-ty, the retentive memory, and so on. Much has been said along these lines about Scofield already. An actor's work also too often tends "to wither away in discussion, and become emptily theoretical and insubstantial," as Scofield himself observes, although none has been more generous and careful in his contributions in interviews and letters to the lives of his col-leagues and peers (it is on these I have frequently drawn, as well as the many interviews he has given to newspapers and radio, for he is not at all reclusive).

Paul quotes Metternich: "In some ways we devalue things as soon as we give utterance to them." I hope this has not been the case with Paul. Instead of trying to analyse his work I would suggest a final image of alchemy to describe it.

Richard Eyre considers Scofield not only the best there is, but "the best there has ever been," without hesitation placing him higher than Olivier, Richardson, and the rest. Yet Scofield is strong, without that self-torturing, dark element. He is manifestly decent, humane, and quietly authoritative, so why is it he can hold our (or my) attention when evi-dently without that "flaw" in personality that is opened or reactivated in many actors approaching a new role, and when only crime, sexual scan-dal, distortion, and other forms of self-publicity are all that would seem ultimately to catch the eye?

The answer: because he is also, or has the potential of being, all that he is not, but he holds it back, he has not acted upon it. He has preserved his integrity and resisted temptation — "They that have the power to hurt and will do none." He has kept alive those qualities identified by Kierkegaard as necessary for continuing quality: potentiation and perfectibility. Here, perhaps, is both the clue to, and secret of, his greatness. He remains apart. "The emotions are mine, but they aren't real."

"All the pride is channelled through the thing he does brilliantly," also commented Eyre to me. So his rejection of a knighthood, to take but one example, is an aspect of life that he does not want. I find, yet again, another statement showing his non-intellectuality and his innate wisdom: "It is a snare and delusion to become too well known." I was struck by the reporting, in 2000, of John Gielgud's funeral service in Wootton Underwood when we were told, in words to this effect, "Theatrical knights Sir Alec Guinness, Sir Donald Sinden, and Sir John Mills attended the service" (an aside might be that Mills for all his gentleness and virtue, and while he acted in prewar and wartime plays, and musicals, is best known as a film star— but there you are).

However, the next paragraph begins, "*Actor* [my italics] Paul Scofield gave the address." This would appear to make a distinction between a "theatrical knight" (is this a rapidly expanding profession in itself?) and an actor. Perhaps I am making too much of this.

Well, the actor Scofield may go into his own unlived life, but he does not analyse. To some degree when finding the role he is prepared to descend into chaos and despair, so that his gold-making becomes an inner process. The making of gold, which fascinated the alchemists, could be taken not only as an outer operation leading to frustration but in metaphor as an inner process that depended on the securing of the *prima materia*, the alchemist's unadulterated and authentic experience. This is to use alchemy as an image for Paul's acting.

Throughout rehearsals and continuing still as actively (although to a slightly lesser degree) during the run of a play, Paul is always trying out new tunes, new voices, new inflections, for the voice is the means by which the creative power of his acting works — and it is here he manages to experience the self-hood of the character — usually very different from his own sense of identity that he has always rigorously maintained.

The approach is always empirical; he calls the rehearsal process "very haphazard."

The physical sensation that happens in reading a script is like the first impression of meeting somebody: a bit later you may forget it, but you always come back to what that first impression was. I become thoroughly acquainted with a play by reading, but never go beyond that, because what happens in rehearsal in relation with the other people is the most important thing of all. One can only discover how it can be done by standing up and seeing what is possible and what is impossible. And one should be empty of preconceived notions at the time. Within about two days it becomes clear how you want to do it; and the final result is a concerted impression of people's spontaneous attitudes to what has been written.

This is different from the late Alec Guinness, with whom he has often been compared. Autobiographical search has always been central to the practice of Guinness's art, so much so that in the latter part of his life he had actually simplified himself into a distinguished autobiographer, with three volumes of memoirs and diaries published. For the essential fact about Guinness was that he transmuted his inner drama — that of his life — into acting, although not in an autobiographical sense. Simon Callow has described this as being achieved "by becoming a sort of ontological magician. He was able to release himself into character, or rather, perhaps, he was able to allow himself to be seduced by, to be taken over by, another self." The need to control and release the emotions of rage, the feelings of impotence, other primary experiences of his childhood, "produced the powerful mental instrument that is central to Guinness's work."

There has been no such ontological process in Paul's work, and while Guinness may have embarked as a result on a quest for characters rather than roles, Scofield has definitely, in this huge and expansive stage career, gone for one great role after another. No actor has come so near to complete success with all four of Shakespeare's great tragic roles, as well as the only slightly lesser lights of Timon, Pericles, Coriolanus and Richard II. These have been backed up by a considerable host of secondary and smaller roles. But this is only in Shakespeare. The range of other leading roles is quite awesome.

Choosing the right part Paul also calls a haphazard process, but intrinsically a part of what the actor is: "he can only be interested in a thing when he's asked to do it, he's totally absorbed in what he's doing, and then it's gone . . . it's shifting sands."

No actor places a higher value upon his audience, and the fact that it, and he, is "live." His statement I include in full.

> You know, it is only to an audience that a working actor like myself gives himself completely and at once. The real part in the development of any actor is to satisfy his vision by way of the audience, to involve them because they are tangible evidence of what is true in what you are doing.
>
> It is vitally important for me to know whether they are liking it for the right reasons or the wrong reasons, by which I mean reasons which I never intended. The audience is a feedback and nourishment. You get a subsequent reaction from strangers, from critics say, and I count critics as strangers because they are an anonymous part of the audience; but it is the direct, immediate contact that is important. For me, an audience never laughs in the wrong place. If they do that in the theatre you adjust your calculations about the effect that you are trying to achieve. It is an extraordinary process with an audience. I don't want to sound mystic or pretentious, but there is a kind of ESP; perhaps they can make you look at a play in a new way.

So what finally can be said about the "secret" that lies behind Scofield's acting? I think it is now up to the reader to work this out for him or herself from what has been given or suggested in these pages. Here is a final clue. Paul acted Ibsen in a radio play broadcast in November 2000 called *Dr. Ibsen's Ghosts*, by Robert Fergusson.

Ibsen is an intriguing representation, Paul believes, with a touch of the bully and "an obsessive desire to protect the springs of his work." He successfully evades having to reveal the existence of his illegitimate son, the result of his short affair as an adolescent with a working-class woman, the secret of which he needs to keep. This need to protect his secret emerged especially in his final "secret" speech, in which he defends his refusal to reveal the truth and which "epitomized the need of the creative artist to preserve and conserve that which controls, unknown perhaps even to himself, the essence of his work. To a much *much* lesser degree of creativity I think this applies also to an actor, who perhaps feels he will no longer be able to do it if he knows exactly where it comes from."

Paul continues explaining to me: "Ibsen's wife's startling combination of total honesty and of being completely non-judgemental was very striking — their relationship being both close and separate — I thought this very moving."

Finally, "And having played John Gabriel B., and having in the course of that experience had the sensation of really knowing the man, Ibsen that is, — as often in the act of acting you feel alarmingly close to the mind of the writer, be he alive or gone before, it was therefore a particularly rewarding undertaking."

As for Paul's personality, the qualities he has displayed both in and out of his profession may be summed up as a powerful humility. He is a remarkable human being, fundamentally serious about his work, without envy or jealousy, able to direct on to what he chooses an innate simplicity and directness of purpose. He has been difficult to photograph out of a role because, as he told Cecil Beaton, "He did not know, in front of the camera, which role he was playing. His face can express many moods and qualities. Some aspects of his features — the hard, downward line of the mouth, the snarl around the pointed nostrils, the brilliant, black, sharp points of his eyes belying the tired-out declivities below — most probably deny his innermost character, for he seems to be a man without bitterness, regret, disappointment, or undue sadness."

True virtue, or true talent, never needs to advertise itself. The aggressive packaging of personality, some of which (in the form of others) I have included in this book by way of contrast to Scofield, is ultimately sad, speaking, or declaring as it does, the profound loneliness of a world without relationships of fidelity or trust.

There is no grandeur in the manner of Scofield, and I would point to that lightness that he perceives in the heaviest and darkest of roles he has played. I counted nearly a dozen laughs from the audience during his performance as Borkman, even in this monolithically egotistic monster, to show his weakness and shortcomings with humour. As described in the last chapter Paul evaluates Borkman, together with Timon of Athens, as "perhaps the profoundest work I've attempted, and full of surprises in its execution which were quite unforeseen in the initial study of it, or in early rehearsal. The confused humanity of the man, where one at first perceived only a rigid obsession — the passion and overwhelming capacity for love within what appeared to be a deep coldness."

Humility, such as is and has been shown by Scofield, is more than just a virtue, and certainly more than the superficial virtue shown by celebrities who embrace victims of illness or famine, or noisily and visibly contribute to charities. It is a form of perception, a language in which the "I" is silent so that the other is allowed the voice. In a tribute that Scofield wrote to John Gielgud, after his death, he never once mentions himself. This is the kind of humility that opens us to the world and to others, just as, in his acting, this humility opens us to a full and compassionate understanding of the role he is playing.

We, the audience, the public, feel affirmed, enlarged, and with good reason. For he has displayed, revealed himself in his attitude towards his work, the craft he loves, of acting. We have met the person, and shared in the life and work of someone who, we conclude, not taking himself seriously at all, has shown us what it is to take with utmost seriousness that which is not I.

Appendix:
Irene Worth on Scofield's King Lear

His entrance held both Court and audience in awe. He was a man of power and he was wilful, insulated, ran his Kingdom with autocracy and fear, lacked curiosity, was shrewd and unused to opposition. He barely raised his beautiful, resonant, deep voice when, after a pause, he spoke his first sentence: "Attend the Lords of France and Burgundy, Gloucester." Alan Webb was the superb Earl of Gloucester, relaxed, graceful, a true courtier. Little do we then know that the Earl's life will be an echo of Lear's.

Paul continued in a contained, quiet way until he said the words "our darker purpose," which filled us with terror. Paul had not changed intonation or emotion. He spoke the words with their true meaning and that has been the genius of Paul's talent: he respects words.

Through the speech he had explained the purpose of the meeting. One saw a very reasonable and farsighted father except for a cheeky flash in his eyes when he spoke, "Which shall we say doth *love us most?*" The fealty of the daughter which he took for granted was turned to ice in him when he heard Cordelia say, "Nothing." The first time he became domestic was when he said, "Mend your speech a little." He was querulous and cross, so was his voice. The vindictive curse on the daughter whom he said he loved most was his hurt pride and at his exit one had the feeling he was already lost. The stability of the Kingdom was unsteady.

It righted itself for a moment when he came to Goneril's castle, quarrelled with her, and like a naughty boy, overturned the large table where his Knights had been dining and drinking and then (I was Goneril) looked me straight in the eye as if to say, "How do you like that? And I'll do more!"

Paul is musical and has an absolutely true sense of rhythm in a scene so it often seemed as if we were improvising. His eyes always spoke more than his words and our fury and hurt against each other was fierce. It was Lear's own great temper which began to unsettle him. In the scene following, with his Fool, he said one thing and was thinking another. It diminished into quietly saying, "I did her wrong." His Fool had invaded the insularity. Then he said to himself, inwardly, "O, let me not be mad . . . Keep me in temper; I would not be mad." He had lost temper in his walk. His walk became heavy and he began to stoop. He spoke almost as if he were frightened of being alone. "Come, boy."

Now he goes to see his daughter Regan and on the way encounters Kent in the stocks. Tom Fleming was Kent. Here Paul gave Lear a grave innocence. It was as though he had never seen a man in stocks. Being with his knights had freed him. He began to feel "one of the boys." The rather rough life enlivened him and he began to pay attention. When the Earl of Gloucester tells King Lear that the Duchess Regan has been informed of his arrival Lear's anger was moderated by mockery and an attempt at patience. He got down on his knees when Regan says she cannot accommodate him. He says, "Dear daughter . . . Age is unnecessary, on my knees I beg That you'll vouchsafe me raiment, bed and food." Paul's anger grew into a cracking inner turbulence, spouting a curse on his two daughters who had thrown him out and literally left him to the rising wind and storm. And now they are *in* the storm. Mind and weather.

Peter created the scene for this mighty storm with nothing but a large piece of rusted metal that trembled, hanging over an empty stage. Paul and Alec McCowen the Fool, orchestrated the storm with their movements of being blown back and sideways, lurching, losing balance, as one entity. Two together. It was touching to see Lear protect his Fool. I can't forget the voice and timing when they sat on a bench and Lear said, "How dost, my boy? Art cold?," pause, "I am cold myself," or the chill with which he said, "my wits begin to turn." He managed to say every-thing quite reasonably. There was no pity, least of all for himself. He was beginning to see life raw, the protections were being washed and blown away. It was moving to watch him say, as a new way of thinking, "I'll pray and then I'll sleep." He says, apropos a new contrition: "O, I have ta'en Too little care of this." The tempest in his mind has begun. He is mad.

Then proceeded a scene I can never forget. Alan was very quiet, inert, after the desolation of the blinding scene and his attempt at suicide. Paul's Lear was alert and as relentless as a five-year-old child who speaks open-ly, without tact. He was playful. Oh, the happiness he had when he thought he was hawking. He was very diligent: Lear, "Give the word"; Edgar, "Sweet marjoram," Lear: "Pass." This was spoken with great musi-cal rhythm.

When he came upon the blind Gloucester he was matter-of-fact. Prefaced by a chuckle he said, "Are you there with me? — No eyes in your head, nor no money in your purse?" Alan said, "I see it feelingly." Paul said, "What, art mad? A man may see how this world goes with no eyes." More dialogue and suddenly Paul said, "Pull off my boots. Harder, harder."

These two ruined men, helpless, fussing over the boots, was heartrend-ing. Peter Brook had drawn inspiration from Beckett, as suggested by Jan Kott's book. I had to go off to a corner because I was weeping so much. I believe these two actors reached a dead centre of truth in that rehearsal, *that day*, which perhaps they never found again. It often happens during one stage in rehearsal. There's no audience or distance involved, the space is compact and the world is of your own making so no projection is need-ed, words have become instinctive, the mind is strong.

Paul then stood in his imaginary pulpit like John Donne, his voice intoning, the words spaced, and he began to preach: "When we are born, we cry that we are come To this great stage of fools." He did the succes-sive line with the speed of a whizzing mind, thought in an electric blender. "It were a delicate stratagem to shoe a troup of horse with felt . . . And when I have stol'n upon these sons-in-law, Then kill . . . " There are six "kills" and every one was spoken like a stab. At this moment Lear suspects danger. A newcomer, a servant from Cordelia, has arrived to rescue her father. Lear is a boy again, tricks them by dodging, in ancient play: "Nay, an you get it . . . Sa, sa, sa, sa." Paul's run was the swift run of an old man who was mad who thought he was a boy. He had a great triumphant grin on his face, and airy freedom, as he ran off stage. Tragedy had transformed itself.

The next time we saw Lear was when he had been caught, rescued, given balm, and cradled. He was asleep. When he woke Paul's transformation was nearly unbearable because his true repentance was so profound but yet so painful: "I am bound upon a wheel of fire." Then he said, "I am a very foolish fond old man," not as a dismissal if his former self and actions but in the deepest humility. It made one understand Pardon and Forgiveness. The arc of Paul's progress through the play had been that of a man whose life was protected against Life itself. Now the "great rage" he had carried with him into madness had burned out and left a hunger for the "mystery of things." His reconciliation with Cordelia, played by Diana Rigg, reconciled him to man's condition. The King had become a man. When Cordelia died, Paul's howl was so truly a howl that I marvel he could create this time after time. Of course he rested a great deal and Joy devised a programme of foods and vitamins for high energy. But a man with great talent makes these miracles.

When we arrived in Moscow Paul was treated with the greatest love. He very generously invited me to come with him to the house of a great acting family, the Kachalov's where all the guests were leaders in the arts, dance, poetry, and so on, and we had a wonderful evening and stayed for hours, talking and laughing. A strange gibberish develops which actors always find with each other when sheer goodwill and sympathy makes them understand each other's language even though they don't speak it.

Our host, Vadim Shverubouitch, could speak a little English and after our delicious dinner he rose and said: "Paul! We Russians love acting. We consider that we are the greatest actors in the world. Now we must say, Paul! You are Russian."

CHRONOLOGY

Plays

ALL THEATRES ARE IN LONDON UNLESS OTHERWISE INDICATED.

d = director

1940

January   Walked on in *Desire Under the Elms* by Eugene O'Neill, d. Henry Cass, Westminster Theatre.

April   Third clerk and first soldier in *Abraham Lincoln* by John Drinkwater, d. Henry Cass, Westminster Theatre,

August   Walked on in *Cornelius* by J.B. Priestly, d. Henry Cass, Westminster Theatre,

1941

Spring and Summer   Petruchio in *The Taming of the Shrew* and King Lear, Macbeth, programme of Shakespearean extracts.

— Dan in *Night Must Fall* by Emlyn Williams.

— Tom Pettigrew in *Berkeley Square* by John L, Balderston in collaboration with J. C. Squire.

— Albert Feather in *Ladies in Retirement* by Edward Percy and Reginald Denham.

— Prosper in *Granite* by Clemence Dane.

— Richard Greatham in *Hay Fever* by Noël Coward.

— George Pepper in *Red Peppers*, Alec Harvey in *Still Life*, Henry Gow in *Fumed Oak*, three one-act plays by Noël Coward, forming a "Tonight at Eight Thirty" programme, ds Eileen Thorndike and Herbert Scott, Bideford Repertory Theatre, North Devon.

Summer and Autumn   Noah in *Noah* by André Obey, translated by Arthur Wilmurt, d. Eileen Thorndike, in Eileen Thorndike and Herbert Scott's company, Houghton Hall, Cambridge.

Autumn and winter   Vincentio, and later Tranio, in *The Taming of the Shrew* by William Shakespeare, d. Robert Atkins, E.N.S.A. tour.

1942

Spring   Rehearses Messenger in the *Medea* of Euripides, d. Lewis Casson, C.E.M.A. tour in Wales.

March   Hotel clerk in *Jeannie* by Aimée Stuart, d. Noël Plant, tour,

June   Ainger in *Young Woodley* by Jon van Druten, d. Kathleen O'Regan, tour.

August   Algy in *The Importance of Being Earnest* by Oscar Wilde, C.E.M.A. tour.

September   Stephen Undershaft in *Major Barbara* by George Bernard Shaw, d. John Moody, Travelling Repertory Theatre, Repertory Theatre, Birmingham.

October   Horatio in *Hamlet, Prince of Denmark* by William Shakespeare, Ophelia played by Joy Parker, d. Basil C. Langton, Repertory Theatre, Birmingham,

1943

Winter 1942 – Spring 1943   Major Sergius Saranoff in *Arms and the Man* by George Bernard Shaw, d. Basil C. Langton, Travelling Repertory Theatre, C.E.M.A. tour of munitions hostels.

June   Alex Morden in *The Moon Is Down* by John Steinbeck, d. Basil C. Langton, Whitehall Theatre.

Autumn   Donald in *Three-Cornered Moon* by Gertrude Tonkonogy, d. Basil C. Langton, Travelling Repertory Theatre and Bristol Theatre Royal, C.E.M.A. tour of munitions hostels.

1944

December 1943 – January 1944   The stranger in *The Cricket on the Hearth* adapted by Sir Barry Jackson from the November by Charles Dickens.

— Donald in *Three-Cornered Moon* by Gertrude Tonkology.

— Tybalt in *Romeo and Juliet* by William Shakespeare, d. Basil C. Langton, Travelling Repertory Company, Theatre Royal, Bristol.

Spring   Oliver Farrant in *I Have Been Here Before* by J. B. Priestly, d.

Robert Newton, C.E.M.A. tour of munitions hostels.

1945

Autumn 1944 – Summer 1945   Birmingham Repertory Theatre Company.

— Prince Po and the First Coolie in *The Circle of Chalk* adapted by Klabund from the Chinese, English version by James Laver, d. John Moody.

— Reginald Bridgnorth in *Getting Married* by George Bernard Shaw, d. John Moody.

— The clown in *The Winter's Tale* by William Shakespeare, d. H. K. Ayliff.

— William D'Albini in *The Empress Maud* by Andrew Leigh, d. H. K. Ayliff.

— Toad in *Toad of Toad Hall* by A. A. Milne adapted from *The Wind in the Willows* by Kenneth Grahame, d. John Moody.

— Valentine in *The Doctor's Delight* adapted by Sir Barry Jackson from *Le Malade Imaginaire* by Molière, d. John Moody.

— A fisherman in *Land's End* by F. L. Lucas, d. John Moody.

— Young Marlow in *She Stoops to Conquer* by Oliver Goldsmith, d. John Moody.

— Jerry Devine in *Juno and the Paycock* by Sean O'Casey, d. John Moody.

Autumn   John Tanner in *Man and Superman* by George Bernard Shaw, d. Peter Brook.

— Philip Faulconbridge, the Bastard, in *King John* by William Shakespeare, d. Peter Brook.

— Dr. Wengel in *The Lady from the Sea* by Henrik Ibsen, d. Peter Brook.

— St. Patrick, a crusader, Colonel Bygadsby, etc., in *1066 And All That* adapted by Reginald Arkell, from the November by ?, d, Birmingham Repertory Theatre.

1946

20 April – 28 September   Festival Company, Shakespeare Memorial

Theatre, Stratford-upon-Avon.

— Cloten in *Cymbeline* by William Shakespeare, d. Nugent Monck.

— Don Adriano de Armado in *Love's Labour's Lost* by William Shakespeare, d. Peter Brook.

— King Henry V in *King Henry the Fifth* by William Shakespeare, d. Dorothy Green.

— Oliver in *As You Like It* by William Shakespeare, d. H. M. Prentice.

— Malcolm in *Macbeth* by William Shakespeare, d. Michael MacOwan.

— Lucio in *Measure for Measure* by William Shakespeare, d. Frank McMullan.

November Tegeus–Chromis in *A Pheonix Too Frequent* by Christopher Fry, d. Noël Willmann, Arts Theatre Club.

1947

April – September Shakespeare Memorial Theatre, Stratford-upon-Avon.

— Mercutio in *Romeo and Juliet* by William Shakespeare, d. Peter Brook.

— Mephistophilis in *The Tragical History of Dr. Faustus* by Christopher Marlowe, d. Walter Hudd.

— Lucio in *Measure for Measure* by William Shakespeare, Frank McMullan's production re-staged by Ronald Giffen.

— Don Armado in *Love's Labour's Lost* by William Shakespeare, d. Peter Brook.

— Sir Andrew Aguecheek in *Twelfth Night* by William Shakespeare, d. Walter Hudd.

— Pericles in *Pericles, Prince of Tyre* by William Shakespeare, d. Nugent Monck.

October Mercutio in *Romeo and Juliet* by William Shakespeare, Stratford-upon-Avon Company.

— Sir Andrew in *Twelfth Night* by William Shakespeare, short season at His Majesty's Theatre,

December Young Fashion in *The Relapse or Virtue in Danger* by Sir

John Vanbrugh, d. Anthony Quayle, Lyric Theatre, Hammersmith.

1948

January   *The Relapse or Virtue in Danger* transferred to the Phoenix Theatre.

April – October   Shakespeare Memorial Theatre, Stratford-upon-Avon.

— Philip, King of France in *King John* by William Shakespeare, d. Michael Benthall.

— Bassanio in *The Merchant of Venice* by William Shakespeare, d. Michael Benthall.

— Hamlet in *Hamlet, Prince of Denmark* by William Shakespeare, d. Michael Benthall.

— The clown in *The Winter's Tale* by William Shakespeare, d. Anthony Quayle.

— Troilus in *Troilus and Cressida* by William Shakespeare, d. Anthony Quayle.

— Roderigo in *Othello, the Moor of Venice* by William Shakespeare, ds Godfrey Tearle and Anthony Quayle.

1949

March   Alexander the Great in *Adventure Story* by Terence Rattigan, d. Peter Glenville, extensive tour and St. James's Theatre.

October – November Constantin Trepleff in *The Seagull* by Anton Chekhov, d. Irene Hentschel, Lyric Theatre, Hammersmith, then St. James's Theatre.

November   Romeo in the balcony scene in *Romeo and Juliet*, with Peggy Ashcroft as Juliet, in, . . . *Merely Players*, London Coliseum.

1950

January – December 1951   Hugo and Frédéric in *Ring Round the Moon* by Jean Anouilh, adapted by Christopher Fry, d. Peter Brook, Globe Theatre.

July, Sunday   Pericles in *Pericles, Prince of Tyre* by William Shakespeare, d. John Harrison,

performance   Rudolf Steiner Hall.

November   Pryce Ridgeley in the second act of *His House in Order* by Sir Arthur Pinero, Irene Vanbrugh Memorial Performance, Theatre Royal, Drury Lane.

1952

January   Don Pedro in *Much Ado About Nothing* by William Shakespeare, d. John Gielgud. Phoenix Theatre.

August   Philip Sturgess in *The River Line* by Charles Morgan, d. Michael MacOwen, Edinburgh Festival, Lyceum Theatre, Edinburgh, transferred to Lyric Theatre, Hammersmith, transferred to Strand Theatre.

December   Richard the Second in *King Richard The Second* by William Shakespeare, d. John Gielgud, Lyric Theatre, Hammersmith.

1953

February   Witwoud in *The Way of the World* by William Congreve, d. John Gielgud. Lyric Theatre, Hammersmith.

— Pierre in *Venice Preserved*, d. Peter Brook, Lyric Theatre, Hammersmith.

December   Paul Gardiner in *A Question of Fact* by Wynyard Browne, d. Frith Banbury, Piccadilly Theatre.

1954

May   Charles Surface, in Screen Scene, *The School for Scandal* by R. B. Sheridan, with Vivien Leigh and Alec Guinness, Sybil Thorndike Jubilee matinee, Her Majesty's Theatre.

December Prince Albert Troubiscoi in *Time Remembered*. William Chappell, Lyric Theatre, Hammersmith, later transferred to New Theatre and long tour.

1955

October – November   Phoenix Theatre, Hamlet in *Hamlet, Prince of Denmark* by William Shakespeare, d. Peter Brook, toured prior to Art Theatre Moscow.

December   Hamlet .

1956

April A priest in *The Power and the Glory* adapted by Denis Canton and Pierre Bost from the novel by Graham Greene, d. Peter Brook, Phoenix Theatre.

June Harry, Lord Muncheshayen in *The Family Reunion* by T. S. Eliot, d. Peter Brook, Pheonix Theatre.

1957

May Fred Dyson in *A Dead Secret* by Rodney Ackland, d. Frith Banbury, Piccadilly Theatre.

1958

April Me in *Expresso Bongo* by Wolf Mankowitz and Julian More, David Heneker, Monty Norman, Saville Theatre.

1959

June Clive Root in *The Complaisant Lover* by Graham Greene, d. John Gielgud, Globe Theatre.

1960

July Sir Thomas More in *A Man for All Seasons* by Robert Bolt, d. Noël Willmann, Globe Theatre.

1961

June – September Coriolanus in *Coriolanus* by William Shakespeare, d. Michael Langham, Shakespearean Festival, Stratford. Ontario.

— Don Armado in *Love's Labours Lost* by William Shakespeare, d.

1962

November 1961 – June 1962 Sir Thomas More in *A Man for All Seasons* by Robert Bolt, d. Noel Willman, Anta Theatre, New York.

November King Lear in *King Lear* by William Shakespeare, d. Peter Brook, Royal Shakespeare Theatre, Stratford-upon-Avon, transferred to Aldwych Theatre.

1963

May King Lear in *King Lear* by William Shakespeare, d. Peter Brook, tenth season of the Theatre des Nations Théâtre Sarah-Bernhardt, Paris.

1964

February – May King Lear in *King Lear* by William Shakespeare, tour: Berlin, Prague, Budapest, Belgrade, Bucharest, Warsaw, Helsinki, Leningrad and Moscow.

May King Lear in *King Lear* by William Shakespeare at Lincoln Center, New York,

1965

July Timon in *Timon of Athens* by William Shakespeare, d. John Schlesinger, Shakespeare Memorial Theatre, Stratford-upon-Avon.

1966

January Khlestakov in *The Government Inspector* by Nicolai Gogol, d. Peter Hall, Aldwych Theatre.

November In *Staircase* by Charlie Dyer, d. Peter Hall, Aldwych Theatre.

December The dragon, recorded voice only, in *The Thwarting of Baron Bolligrow* by Robert Bolt, d. Trevor Nunn, Royal Shakespeare Company, Aldwych Theatre.

1967

August Macbeth in *Macbeth* by William Shakespeare, d. Peter Hall, Royal Shakespeare Company, Stratford-upon-Avon.

1968

January *Macbeth* toured Finland and Russia.

— *Macbeth* run at Aldwych Theatre.

July Laurie in *The Hotel in Amsterdam* by John Osborne, d. Anthony Page, Royal Court Theatre.

September Transferred to New Theatre.

December Transferred to Duke of York's Theatre.

1970

February   Uncle Vanya in *Uncle Vanya* by Anton Chekhov, d. Anthony Page, Royal Court Theatre.

1971

March   Wilhelm Voigt in *The Captain of Köpenick* by Paul Zuckmayer, adapted by John Mortimer, d. Frank Dunlop, National Theatre Company, Old Vic.

May   Leone in *The Rules of the Game* by Luigi Pirandello, d. Anthony Page, National Theatre, New Theatre.

1973

April   Alan West in *Savages* by Christopher Hampton, d. Robert Kidd. Royal Court Theatre, transferred to the Comedy Theatre.

1974

November   Prospero in *The Tempest* by William Shakespeare, d. John Harrison, Leeds Playhouse, transferred to Wyndham's Theatre.

1976

April   Dimetos in *Dimetos* by Athol Fugard, d. Athol Fugard, Nottingham Playhouse, transferred to the Comedy Theatre.

1977

April   Volpone in *Volpone* by Ben Johnson, d. Peter Hall, National Theatre, Olivier.

June   Constantine Madras in *The Madras House* by Harley Granville Baker, d. William Gaskill, National Theatre, Olivier.

1978

May   Reddie Kilner in *A Family* by Ronald Harwood, d. Caspar Wrede, Royal Exchange Theatre, Manchester, transferred to Haymarket Theatre.

1979

November   Salieri in *Amadeus* by Peter Shaffer, d. Peter Hall, National Theatre, Olivier.

1980

March Othello in *Othello, the Moor of Venice* by William Shakespeare, d. Peter Hall, National Theatre, Olivier.

1982

June Don Quixote in *Don Quixote* adapted by Keith Dewhurst from the novel by Cervantes, d. Bill Bryden, National Theatre, Olivier.

1983

June Oberon in *A Midsummer Night's Dream* by William Shakespeare, d. Bill Bryden, National Theatre, Olivier.

1986

May Nat in *I'm Not Rappaport* by Herb Gardener, d. Daniel Sullivan, Apollo Theatre.

1989

July Nicholas Britain in *Exclusive* by Jeffrey Archer, d. Michael Rudman, Strand Theatre.

1992

Captain Shotover in *Heartbreak House* by George Bernard Shaw, d. Trevor Nunn, Theatre Royal, Haymarket.

1996

July John Gabriel Borkman in *John Gabriel Borkman* by Henrik Ibsen, d. Richard Fyre, National Theatre, Lyttleton.

Feature Films

1955
Philip of Spain in *That Lady*, d. Terence Young.

1958
Tony Frazer in *Carve Her Name With Pride*, d. Louis Gilbert.

1963
Colonel von Valdheim in *The Train*, d. John Frankenheimer, with Burt Lancaster, Jeanne Moreau.

1966
Thomas More in *A Man for All Seasons*, d. Fred Zinnemann.

1969
King Lear in *King Lear*, d. Peter Brook.

1970
The accountant in *Bartleby*, d. Michael Friedman.

1973
Tobias in *A Delicate Balance*, d. Tony Richardson.

1974
Zharkov in *Scorpio*, d. Michael Winner.

1975
Nicholas Fennick in *When Greek Meets Greek*, d. Simon Langton.

1977
Lambert Strether in *The Ambassadors*, d. James Cellan-Jones.

1984
Alexander in *Nineteen Nineteen*, d. Hugh Brody.

1986

Mr. Corbett in *Mr. Corbett's Ghost*, d. Daniel Houston.

1988

The Birdman in *When the Whales Came*, d. Clive Rees.

— The King of France in *Henry V* by William Shakespeare, d. Kenneth Branagh.

1990

The Ghost in *Hamlet*, d. Franco Zefferelli.

1991

Utz's friend in *Utz*, d. George Spuizer.

1994

Professor Mark Van Doren in *Quiz Show*, d. Robert Redford.

1997

Danforth in *The Crucible*, d. Nicholas Hytner.

Television

1959 – 60
Henry IV in *Henry IV* by Pirandello, d. John Harrison, BBC.
— *Windmill Near a Frontier*, BBC.

1965
The Captain in *The Dance of Death*, Associated TV.

1966
March   *Hydrogen Bom*, dubbing/reading, BBC.

1967
January   The solicitor in *Accolade*, Rediffusion TV.

1970
The Male of the Species by Alun Owen, d. Anthony Page, CBS.

1971
November   *The World About Us*: "Surrender to Everest," narration, BBC.

1974
June   Fennick in *Shades of Greene: When Greek Meets Greek*, d. Alan Green, Thames TV.

1976
February   *Closedown,* read out-of-vision poem, BBC.
November   *Closedown*, seven programmes, BBC.

1977
February   Lambert Strether in *The Ambassadors*, d. James Cellan Jones, BBC.
October   *Hammer & Sickle*, commentary, Thames TV.

1979

March   *K2: The Savage Mountain,* narration, Yorkshire TV.

June – July   James Callifer in *The Potting Shed,* d. David Cunliffe, Yorkshire TV.

1980

April   *The Curse of King Tut's Tomb,* narration, HTV.

December   *Night of 100 Stars,* LWT.

1981

March   *Royal Gala: The Palace Reborn,* Granada TV.

October   Moroi in *If Winter Comes,* d. Peter Sasdy, BBC.

November   *Playhouse,* "Noël Coward."

— Hugo Latymer in *Song at Twilight.*

— Verner Conklin in *Come Into the Garden Maud,* d. Cedric Messina, BBC.

1984

February   *Arena,* "The Life and Times of Don Luis Brunel," d. Alan Yentob, BBC.

June   Hornby in *A Kind of Alaska,* d. Kenneth Ives, Central TV.

1985

March   Karenin in *Anna Karenina,* d. Simon Langton, CBS.

May   Sir Robert Clarke in *Summer Lightning,* d. Paul Joyce, R.T.E.

1986

Oliver in *Only Yesterday,* d. Robin Slater, BBC,

February   In *Darley's Folly,* BBC Scotland.

1987

February   *Variety Club Awards,* BBC.

April   Documentary, CTVC.

August   *Man on the Hill,* Narration, HTV.

October   Otto Frank in *The Attic,* d. John Erman, Yorkshire TV.

1990

May   *Timewatch Dunkirk 1940*, narration, BBC.
June   *Joseph Campbell and the Power of Myth*, narration, BBC.

1994

November   Martin Chuzzlewit in *Martin Chuzzlewit* adapted by David
Lodge from the novel by Dickens, d. Pedr James, BBC.

Selected Radio Drama BBC Home Service or
Third Programme 1946-67

WRITER FOLLOWED BY PRODUCER/DIRECTOR, WHERE KNOWN,
DATES APPROXIMATE EITHER FOR RECORDING OR TRANSMISSION,
OR FOR COMMENCEMENT OF EITHER.

1946

December   Don Armado in *Love's Labour's Lost* by William Shakespeare.

1948

January   Giacomo in *The Bronze Horse*, by James Forsyth, Michel
Saint-Denis.

1949

April   Alexander in *Adventure Story* by Terence Rattigan.
August   Tamburlaine in *Tamburlaine the Great* by Christopher
Marlowe, Frank Hauser.

1951

February   Role unknown in *The Cross and the Arrow*, Peter Walts.
May   Axel in *Axel* by de Lisle Adam.
June   *The Nameless One of Europe*, by James Forsyth, Rayond Raikes.
July   *The Hawk and the Handsaw*, by Michael Innes.

1952

March Ralph Tolchett in *Portrait of a Lady*, ten episodes, by Henry James.

1953

May *Gryll Grange.*

May Lazarus in *Lazare*, Stephen King-Bull.

1954

May Ferdinand in *The Duchess of Malfi* by John Webster, Donald McWhinnie.

October *A Christmas Commission.*

1955

January King Edward in *Edward II* by Christopher Marlowe.

May Trigorin in *The Seagull* by Anton Chekhov, Archie Campbell.

December *The Hawk and the Handsaw* by Michael Innes, new production.

1956

August Siegfried in *Siegfried*, Stephen King-Bull.

November The cardinal in *The Prisoner* by Bridget Boland, Archie Campbell.

1957

January *The Diary of a Madman* by Nikolai Gogol, H.B. Fortain.

December Pericles in *Pericles, Prince of Tyre* by William Shakespeare, R.D. Smith.

1958

August *Welcome to London*, Ronnie Ronald.

October Rosmer in *Rosmersholm* by Henrik Ibsen, Mary Hope Allen.

1959

February Henry IV in *Henry IV* by Pirandello.

April *The Renegade*, H. B. Fortuin.

October   Tonya in *Dr. Zhivago* by Boris Pasternak, H.B. Fortain.

1964

October   Nijinsky in *The Diary of Nijinsky*, H. B. Fortuin.

November   Savrola in *Savrola* by Winston Churchill adapted Tydeman, Audrey Cameron.

1966

March   Macbeth in *Macbeth* by William Shakespeare, John Tydeman.

(1967 THIRD PROGRAMME BECOMES RADIO 3; HOME SERVICE, RADIO 4; INCLUDING SOME NON-BBC PRODUCTIONS)

1972

August   Othello in *Othello* by William Shakespeare, John Tydema, R3.

September   Oluwale in *Oluwale*, adapted Jeremy Sandford, Keith Slade, R3.

1973

May   Reading, *Death in Venice* by Thomas Mann, John Tydeman, R3.

1974

October   In *The Monday Play*, Ian Cotterell, R4.

1975

September   Eliot in *Private Lives* by Noël Coward. Ian Cotterell, R4.

November   Reading *The Wreck of the Deuschland* by Gerard Manley Hopkins, Shaun MacLoughlin, R3.

November   In *The Restless Heart*, readings from St. Augustine, Peter de Rosa, R4.

December   In *A College in Purer Air*, John Scotney, R3.

1976

January   Reading, *The Book of Job*, Ian Cotterell, R3.

May   Dimetos in *Dimetos* by Athol Fugard, Jenny Colvan, R4.

June Thomas More in *A Man for All Seasons* by Robert Bolt, Bernard Kindelsea, R4.

August Monologue *A Song of Summer* by Richard Jeffries, Keith Slade, R3.

October In *Restoria*, Martin Esslin, R3.

November Various roles, *Vivat Rex*, twenty-part history, Shakespeare & Jacobeans. Martin Jenkins, Gerry Jones, R4.

September Vergil in *Vergil Dying* by Gabriel Gosipivici, Guy Vaesen, R3.

November In *Robben Island*, Curtis Venning, R4.

1979

February In *A Voice From the Chorus*, Howard Tennyson, R3.

March Narrator in *Under the Volcano* by Malcolm Lowry, John Tydeman, R4.

March In *Just Before Midnight*, R4

April In *The Human Predicament*, Jane Morgan, R3.

June In *The Local Authority*, Gordon House, R4.

July Macready in *Mac and Mrs. Faust*, Ian Cotterell, R3.

1980

June Vershinin in *The Three Sisters* by Anton Chekhov, John Tydeman, R3.

1981

June *The Story of My Heart*, Keith Slade, R3.

December Salieri in *Amadeus* by Anthony Shaffer, David Spenser, R4.

1982

June Salieri in *Mozart and Salieri*, by Alexander Pushkin, Pieus Plowright, R3.

November Oberon in *A Midsummer Night's Dream* by William Shakespeare, R4.

1983

April Worms in *Worms* by Peter Barnes, Ian Cotterell, R3.

July   Captain Josiah Bennett in *A Voyage to the Indies* by John Harrison, Kay Patrick, R4.

1984
July   Reading, *A Changeable Report*, J. Theocharis, R4.

1987
September   Priam in *King Priam* by Andrew Rissick, Jeremy Mortimer, R4.

1990
February   In *The Cosmic Clock* by Jerzy Peterkiewicz, J. Theocharis, R3.

February   Merlin in *Arthur The King* by Graeme Fife, John Powell, R4.

November   Rubek in *When We Dead Awaken* by Henrik Ibsen, Ned Chaillet, R3.

1991
January   Quixote in *Don Quixote* adapted by Jane Morgan from the novel by Cervantes, Don Taylor, R3.

1992
December   Leo in *Rediscovering Leo* by John Harrison, Kay Patrick, R4.

1993
February   *Something Understood*, Katriona Wade, R4.

1998
May   Hermes in Trilogy, *Priam and his Sons*, Andrew Rissick, Jeremy Mortimer, R3.

1999
June   Old Chap in *The Summer of a Doormouse* by John Mortimer, Marilyn Imrie, R4.

— Reading, *Four Quartets* by T. S. Eliot, Keith Slade, R4.

December   Captain Vere in *Billy Budd* adapted by John Harrison from the novel by Hermann Melville, John Tydeman, R4.

2000

April Reading, *Wystan*, Auden, Gordon McDougall.

November Reading, *Diaries of Kurosawa*, d. Adam Lowe.

May Ibsen in *Dr. Ibsen's Ghosts* by Robert Ferguson, Ned Chaillet, R4.

2001

January *On the Train to Chemnitz* by Peter Tinniswood, Enyd
   Williams. R4.

— Reading, Joseph K, in *The Trial* by Franz Kafka, Keith Slade.

— Narrator in *The Magic Mountain* by Thomas Mann, Alison
Hindell.

— Reading, many Dickens novels: "am approaching the final three"
   PS.

September King Lear in *King Lear* by William Shakespeare, John
   Tydeman.

Acknowledgments

My thanks and gratitude are due to all who have helped in the preparation and production of this book. Listed below in the notes are those who generously gave of their time to be interviewed, supplied material, or helped in other ways. To them I owe my thanks and also to the editors, staff of newspapers and librarians who helped me in my research. My special thanks must go to: Christopher Sinclair-Stevenson; to the publishing staff at Macmillan; to Ian Chapman, who commissioned the book; to Gordon Wise, its publisher; to Ingrid Connell; to Linda Mitchell, who typed it; to Victoria, my wife, and to my children for help and support in innumerable ways; to Fred O'Connor for undertaking a specific piece of research; to Irving Wardle, John Tydeman, John Harrison, who read the typescript; to Ion Trewin, for permission to draw on J. C. Trewin's chronology for Scofield's early career. Above all I record my thanks to Paul and Joy Scofield for their hospitality and warmth towards the whole enterprise, and for their loan of photographs; to Paul again for his unstinting diligence in answering my letters, and for his reading and comments on my typescript. I must make it clear that he is not to be held responsible for any comments or opinions expressed in this book except where he is directly quoted, as he may well not agree with some of what I say or have included, so any strictures should fall on me not on him.

Source Notes

Specific copyright photographic acknowledgments

ABBREVIATIONS USED IN THE NOTES:
PAUL SCOFIELD = PS   GARRY O'CONNOR = GOC

1   YOU WOULD PLUCK THE HEART OUT OF MY MYSTERY?

p. 11	*I was not a good . . .*	PS to GOC, 9 Jan. 2000.
—	*They did one of his plays . . .*	*Daily Mail,* 21 Jan. 1975.
p. 12	*"Brilliant," Anouilh's English . . .*	Christopher Fry to GOC, 20 Feb. 2000.
p. 13	*"He sometimes seems like . . .*	John Barber, *Daily Telegraph,* 17 17 Feb. 1975.
—	*"We have a closeness . . .*	PS to GOC, 9 Jan. 2000.
—	*"the most difficult . . .*	*The Times,* 19 Jan. 1992.
—	*"You can only get so far . . .*	Frith Banbury interview with GOC, 30 Oct. 1999.

2   OBLIGATION TO THE FEW

p. 14	*"He has all the virtues . . .*	Hunter Davies, *Sunday Times,* 14 Aug. 1967.
p. 16	*"When you telephone his home . . .*	Sally Beauman, *Sunday Telegraph,* 8 Mar. 1970.
—	*"in his family" but "too. . .*	John Harrison to GOC, 3 Mar. 2000.
p. 17	*"I had a cook that did . . .*	Michael Winner interview with GOC, Feb. 2000.
p. 18	*What is the worst sensation . . .*	GOC, *Alec Guinness, Master of Disguise,* London, 1994, p. 280.
—	*It is not that one is nervous . . .*	PS to GOC, 29 Nov. 1999.

3   SUNSHINE AND SUMMER

p. 19	*"How can I play when . . .*	Anna Calder-Marshall interview with GOC, Dec. 1999. The director was Anthony Page.
p. 20	*"I always called my father Sir . . .*	*You Magazine,* 19 Feb. 1994.

p. 21 "uncontrollably" so, writes the . . . J. C. Trewin, *Paul Scofield*, Theatre World Monograph, 6, London, 1956, p. 17.

— "He seems like a changeling . . . Simon Callow interview with GOC, Dec. 2000.

— I wore blue in the first act . . . *You Magazine*, 19 Feb. 1994.

p. 22 He recalls his father . . . Donald Sinden interview with GOC, 8 Jan. 2000.

p. 23 Through his mellow, and . . . Channel 4, 29 Dec. 1987.

p. 24 "I have it, and soundly . . . Donald Sinden interview with GOC, 8 Jan. 2000.

4 VIRTUE AND FALLIBILITY

p. 25 He brings the skies and seas . . . John Barber, *Daily Telegraph*, 17 Feb. 1975.

— "The remarkable thing — . . . Christopher Fry to GOC, 20 Feb. 2000.

p. 27 Paul Scofield gave us yet . . . *Bideford Weekly Gazette*, 28 Jan. 1941.

p. 28 He was my first love . . . Sybil Mitchell to GOC, 6 Mar. 2000.

p. 29 "a most satisfying John Worthing . . . Candidus, *Bideford Weekly Gazette*, 10 Jan. 1941.

— I enjoy the loss of myself . . . PS to GOC, 9 Jan. 2000.

p. 31 Earlier turning points must . . . Diana Devlin, A Speaking Part, *Lewis Casson and the Theatre of His Time*, London, 1982, p. 183.

— I think his name was . . . Diana Devlin, *Lewis and Sybil*, London, 1972, pp. 12-13; Devlin to GOC, 12 Feb. 2000. ("Not true, I'm afraid." PS comment on GOC's typescript, 10 Aug. 2000.)

p. 32 "He came in a car down . . . Sybil Mitchell to GOC, 6 Mar. 2000.

— "After which, seriously out of . . . PS to GOC, 2 Feb. 2000.

p. 34 "Too much respectability . . . *Independent Magazine*, 5 Nov. 1994.

5 INTERLUDE: SCOFIELD'S TEAR

p. 36 "letting his face run through. . . *Theatre Quarterly*, 18, 1975.

6 JOY

p. 38 "of gentle, bewildered pathos . . . J. C. Trewin, p. 20; John Harrison interview with GOC, 1 Nov. 2000.

p. 39 *Joy and I simply decided to* . . . PS to GOC, 9 Jan. 2000.

p. 40 *"Wartime? Remember how* . . . PS to GOC, 9 Jan. 2000.

— *Munition Hostels were* . . . PS to GOC, 1 Mar. 2000.

7 INTERLUDE: BADDIE NUMBER ONE

p. 42 *"The fundamental thing which* . . . *Theatre Quarterly*, 18, 1975.

8 THE TEMPLE

p. 43 *"Finding one another so young* . . . John Harrison interview with GOC, 3 Mar. 2000.

— *"To me he was the first* . . . Peter Hall interview with GOC, 9 Jan. 2000.

p. 44 *"The nearest the British have* . . . Donald Sinden, *A Touch of the Memoirs*, London, 1982, p. 72.

— *"The great city with suspicion* . . . Peter Brook, *Threads of Time*, London, 2000, p. 31.

— *"The man was a wimp* . . . John Harrison to GOC, 1 Nov. 1999.

p. 45 *"To encounter a wall* . . . Eileen Beldon interview with GOC, quoted in GOC, *Ralph Richardson: An Actor's Life*, London, 1982, p. 53.

— *He recalls walking in* . . . John Harrison interview with GOC, 1 Nov. 1999.

p. 46 *"A terrifying warning signal* . . . PS letter to GOC, c. 1980.

— *"I remember every single blessed* . . . John Harrison, "Autobiography" ms, chapter 3, p. 7.

— *"from Warwickshire's rural heart* . . . J. C. Trewin, p. 30.

— *"temporized entertainingly.* . . *Birmingham Post*, 22 Nov. 1945.

p. 47 *"How to sustain intensity* . . . *Independent*, 5 Apr. 1991.

— *I have worked with Peter* . . . PS to GOC, 31 Mar. 2000.

9 PETER AND PAUL

p. 48 *"A pall of gloom* . . . John Harrison, "Autobiography" ms, chapter 3, p. 10.

— *"is a small sausage-shaped* . . . GOC, *The Mahabharata*, London, 1991, p. 32.

p. 49 *"In that small office* . . . Peter Brook, *Threads of Time*, London, 2000, p. 31.

p. 49 *"You just knew* . . . Harrison, "Autobiography" ms, chapter 3, p. 11.

p. 50   *Paul Scofield's John Tanner* . . .   *Birmingham Post*, 15 Aug. 1945.

—   *"I've always found it simple* . . .   John Harrison interview with GOC, 3 Mar. 2000.

p. 51   *The voice we heard* . . .   J. C. Trewin, p. 12.

—   *Joy was now much involved* . . .   "Chronologically not quite right," PS on typescript.

—   *"We walked on the Clent* . . .   Harrison, "Autobiography" ms, chapter 3, p. 12.

—   *"he tacitly proffers.* . .   *Birmingham Mail, Post*, 21 Nov. 1945.

p. 52   *"his truculent crusader* . . .   *Birmingham Post*, 19 Dec. 1946.

p. 53   *"For a brief spell it became* . . .   Harrison ms, ch. 4, p. 4.

10   THEATRICAL LORDLINGS

p. 54   *"To begin with," he said* . . .   Peter Brook, *Threads of Time*, London, 2000, p. 38.

p. 56   *"We lordlings," wrote Harrison* . . .   Harrison ms, ch. 3, p. 8.

—   *"faintly reminiscent of an* . . .   *Manchester Guardian*, 10 May 1946.

p. 57   *"curiously, meditatively* . . .   J. C. Trewin, p. 38.

—   *Most recently it is mentioned* . . .   Charles Duff, *The Lost Summer: Heyday of the West End Theatre*, London, 1995, xxx.

—   *"a crazy old man who ran* . . .   Peter Hall interview with GOC, 9 Jan. 2000.

—   *"The audience may be* . . .   Donald Sinden interview with GOC, 8 Jan. 2000.

11   WHAT IS AMISS?

p. 60   *We fell under her spell* . . .   PS to GOC, 31 Mar. 2000.

—   *We suddenly heard shouts* . . .   Donald Sinden, *A Touch of the Memoirs*, London, 1982, pp. 82-3.

p. 61   *In the summer of 1946* . . .   Tony Richardson, *Long Distance Runner*, London, Faber, 1993, p. 42.

12   STIR FRY

p. 62   *"has brought back to the English* . . .   *Crowell's Handbook of Contemporary Drama*, New York, 1971, pp. 165-70.

—   *"highly intelligent, amusing* . . .   PS to GOC, 13 Dec. 1999.

p. 63   *"I remember feeling how very* . . .   Christopher Fry to GOC, 20 Feb. 2000.

—	*seeming to know eternity* . . .	J. C. Trewin, p. 46.
p. 64	*"May I correct an error* . . .	PS to Val Gielgud, 29 Oct. 1946.
p. 65	*"Hot, violent, unromantic* . . .	Peter Brook, *Threads of Time*, London, 2000, p. 38.
—	*Harrison records that the* . . .	John Harrison to GOC, 3 Mar. 2000.
—	*"not the noisy bragger who* . . .	Trewin, pp. 45-6.
p. 66	Richard II *was followed by* . . .	Donald Sinden, *A Touch of the Memoirs*, London, 1982, p. 93.

13   THAT EARTH THAT KEPT THE WORLD IN AWE

p. 68	*"After a few years* . . .	Peter Brook, *Threads of Time*, London, 2000, p. 38.
—	*"Major Anthony Quayle,* . . .	John Harrison to GOC, 3 Mar. 2000.
—	*"Tony and I were not* . . .	PS to GOC, 1 Mar. 2000.
p. 69	*I do recognize that* . . .	*You Magazine*, 19 Feb. 1994.
p. 70	*He blinked a lot* . . .	PS to GOC, 1 Mar. 2000.
p. 71	*"I have not met a performance.* . .	J. C. Trewin, *Five and Eighty Hamlets*, London, 1988, p. 68.
—	*"It's absolutely personal* . . .	Peter Brook, *The Empty Space*, London, 1968, 90.
p. 73	*Ronald Harwood significantly* . . .	Ronald Harwood interview with GOC, Jan., 2000.

14   I HAVE THAT WITHIN

p. 74	*As he proved seven years ago* . . .	Kenneth Tynan, *Curtains*, New York, 1961, pp. 69-71
p. 75	*"I was always ill at ease* . . .	Claire Bloom, *Leaving a Doll's House*, London, 1995, p. 43.
p. 76	*"Sixteen years old I think* . . .	PS to GOC, 1 Mar. 2000.
—	*Even to that drop ten* . . .	*King John*, Act Sc.

15   AT LARGE IN ASIA

p. 78	*"all blue and silver* . . .	Harrison, "Autobiography" ms, chapter 5, p. 12.
p. 79	*"the language of the poet* . . .	B. A. Young, *The Rattigan Version*, London, 1986, pp. 82-9.
p. 80	*"What he lacked in technical* . . .	*Daily Mail*, 18 Mar. 1949.
—	*"All this fine actor's performances* . . .	*Sunday Times*, 20 Mar. 1949.

—	*"I didn't care for it at all . . .*	Peter Bull to John Harrison, undated 1949.
p. 81	*When I saw it on the first night . . .*	Peter Brook to John Harrison, undated 1949.
—	*"I went backstage to see him . . .*	Harrison ms, ch. 8, p. 4.

16   BINKIE-LAND

p. 82	*"The war has been the making . . .*	Richard Huggett, *Binkie Beaumont, Eminence Grise of the West End Theatre 1933-1973*, London, 1989, p. 323.
p. 83	*He knew his world and he . . .*	Peter Brook, *Threads of Time*, London, 2000, p. 42.
—	*When an actress, writer . . .*	*Ibid.*, 43.
—	*"Respect for actors, was . . .*	PS to GOC, 1 Mar. 2000.
p. 84	*Binkie would work on seven . . .*	Peter Brook, *Threads of Time*, p. 43

17   WARM-UPS? WHATEVER FOR?

p. 86	*My first long run and still . . .*	PS to GOC, 1 Mar. 2000.
—	*"It sounds delicious . . .*	PS letter, BBC archives, 3 Sept. 1950.
p. 87	*All our friends were . . .*	Harrison, "Autobiography" ms, chapter 8, p. 9.
p. 88	*"I am well aware . . .*	PS letter, BBC archives, 23 Aug. 1952.

18   INTERLUDE: THE RIVALS (BADDIE NUMBER TWO)

p. 89	*There is one resistance . . .*	Sören Kirkegaard, *Crisis in the Life of an Actress*, London, 1920, p. 30.
p. 90	*Sir Laurence Olivier (sorry . . .*	PS to GOC, 9 Jan. 2000.
—	*The night I faced him about . . .*	Kathleen Tynan's report to GOC of interview. See also Kenneth Tynan archive, British Library, "Interesting and quite new to me" — PS on type script. Add comment end R.L.'s book on LO

19   GIELGUD OBSERVED

p. 93	*"But when Marlon Brando's . . .*	John Gielgud, *An Actor and His Time*, New York, 1997, p. 127.
—	*This is not quite true . . .*	PS to GOC, 9 Mar. 2000.

p. 94	*"Hardness of heart," he . . .*	Charles Morgan, *The River Line*, London, 1952, Introduction p. xiv.
p. 95	*It has almost no . . .*	*Sunday Times*, 24 Aug. 1952.
—	*("If Morgan were only less . . .*	*Observer*, 24 Aug. 1952.
—	*I had been intending for . . .*	PS to Charles Morgan, 11 Jan. 1953.
—	*"Mr. Paul Scofield . . .*	*The Times*, 3 Sept. 1952.
p. 96	*"Scofield, strained and intense . . .*	Trewin, 65.
—	*Glamour is a trap if . . .*	*Daily Mail*, 10 July 1952.
—	*"Ours is a trophy which . . .*	Lord Byron, *Childe Harolde*, Canto IV.
p. 97	*After Stratford I worked with . . .*	John Gielgud, *An Actor and His Time*, New York, 1997, p. 116.
—	*As the King listens . . .*	*The Times*, 30 Dec. 1952.
p. 98	*"This old theatre was isolated . . .*	PS to GOC, 3 Mar. 2000.
p. 99	*In fact, the nicest theatrical . . .*	Kenneth Tynan to Cecil Beaton, 1 Jan. 1953 in Kathleen Tynan (ed.) *Kenneth Tynan Letters*, London, 1994, p. 190.
—	*When my wife and I . . .*	Charles Morgan to PS, 8 Jan. 1953.
p. 100	*"pitched somewhere between . . .*	Kenneth Tynan, *Curtains*, New York, 1961, p. 38.
—	*His wit, often unconscious. . .*	PS to GOC, 23 Dec. 1999.
p. 101	*("the fastest speaker on . . .*	Michael Powell, *Million Dollar Movie*, London, 1992, p. 367.
—	*Similarly Paul's more . . .*	PS to GOC, 29 Nov. 1999.
—	*I said, "Where does that . . .*	Powell, *Million Dollar Movie*, p. 370.
p. 102	*I explained that Paul . . .*	*Ibid.*, p. 65.
p. 103	*"Jennifer Jones did . . .*	PS to GOC, 17 Mar. 2000.
—	*"I've always wanted to . . .*	*Million Dollar Movie*, p. 65
—	*A very remarkable and . . .*	PS to GOC, 17 Mar. 2000.
p. 104	*"In* The Way of the World *. . .*	John Gielgud, *An Actor and his Time*, p. 107.
p. 105	*Rationalizing their grudges . . .*	Kenneth Tynan, *Curtains*, p. 51.
—	*I can recreate scene . . .*	Trewin, 68.

20 RING ARTIST DIRECT

p. 108	*"Burton . . . was almost an . . .*	*The Times*, 22 Apr. 1977. "Did I say this?" PS comment on typescript.
p. 109	*What we might see at . . .*	Laurence Olivier, *Confessions of an Actor*, 1982, p. 340.

—   *"There are too many . . .*   *Observer*, 10 Sept. 1989.

p. 110 *"An honour without the . . .*   Bernard Levin, *Daily Mail*, 19 Apr. 1963.

p. 112 *In Act one we see . . .*   Charles Duff, *The Lost Summer: Heyday of the West End Theatre*, London, 1995, p. 83.

p. 113 *What have you in . . .*   Wynyard Browne, *A Question of Fact*, Act III.

—   *"I cannot see you . . .*   Duff, *The Lost Summer*, p. 86.

p. 114 *"Mr. Scofield treats the hero's . . .*   *The Times*, Dec. 1955.

—   *"Few can look backwards . . .*   Trewin, 73.

p. 115 *"He might never have . . .*   *The Observer*, Dec. 1955.

p. 116 *"like eroded marble . . .*   Paul Dehn, quoted in Trewin, p. 75.

p. 117 *Brook said of Anouilh . . .*   GOC, *French Theatre Today*, London, 1977, pp. 75-7.

21   THE ACTOR AS WRITER

p. 120 *"We were supposedly . . .*   *The Times*, 22 Apr. 1977. "Isn't this thought to be dated earlier than 1977?" PS on typescript.

—   *As Ophelia she was . . .*   Tony Richardson, *Long Distance Runner*, London, 1993, p. 93.

p. 121 *"a poor reward . . .*   *Daily Mail*, 2 Nov. 1955.

p. 122 *Arriving at Moscow . . .*   PS to GOC, 16 Mar. 2000.

p. 123 *The city reminded him . . .*   Kathleen Tynan, *The Life of Kenneth Tynan*, New York, 1987, p. 170.

p. 124 *The audience reactions . . .*   Kenneth Tynan, *Curtains*, New York, 1961, pp. 426-7.

—   *"I have now discovered . . .*   *Daily Telegraph*, 24 Nov. 1955.

p. 125 *"They were very hospitable . . .*   *Manchester Guardian*, 7 Mar. 1956.

p. 126 *"This was truly exhausting . . .*   PS to GOC, 16 Mar. 2000.

p. 127 *Diana Wynyards's Gertrude . . .*   PS to GOC, 16 Mar. 2000.

22   PAUL IN GRIMLAND

p. 130 *For a moment we . . .*   Adapted from Peter Brook, *Threads of Time*, London, 2000, pp. 33-4.

p. 131 *I had cut off all . . .*   PS to GOC, 14 Mar. 2000.

—   *The diffused structure . . .*   PS. Source unknown, probably *Guardian*.

—   *"The evilly catalystic peasant . . .*   Laurence Olivier, *Confessions of an Actor*, London, 1982, pp. 261-2.

p. 132 *"I think it was the best . . .*   Roger Lewis, *The Real Life of Laurence Olivier*, New York, 1998, pp. 84-5.

—   *"trying to be humble . . .*   *Ibid.*, p. 86.

—   *"You know . . . Larry, I liked . . .*   Alec Guinness interview with GOC, 1989.

p. 133 *Mr. Eliot can always . . .*   Kenneth Tynan, *Curtains.*

23 MURDER AND ADULTERY

p. 135 *Mr. Paul Scofield, who put . . .*   *The Times*, 18 Jan. 1955.

—   *"A deep quavering . . .*   *Manchester Guardian*, 21 Oct. 1959.

—   *"An extraordinary play . . .*   PS to GOC, 14 Mar. 2000.

p. 136 *"Every time he said how . . .*   Charles Duff, *The Lost Summer*, p. 157.

p. 138 *The development of . . .*   *Sunday Times*, 2 June 1957.

p. 139 *"imaginative strength and . . .*   *Daily Telegraph*, 8 Dec. 1991.

—   *"It took me only one . . .*   *The Star*, 18 Jan. 1957.

—   *word had come from . . .*   Sheridan Morley, *Robert My Father*, London, 1997.

p. 140 *"Here is exposed the . . .*   *Sunday Times*, 12 June 1957.

p. 141 *"Light-hearted, delightful . . .*   PS to GOC, 27 Mar. 2000.

p. 143 *"calm and sweet and . . .*   PS to GOC, 3 Mar. 2000.

—   *"Very soundly theatrical . . .*   PS to GOC, 17 Mar. 2000.

24 INTERLUDE: ENCOUNTER WITH MERLIN

p. 145 *"If someone did ask me . . .*   *Sunday Times*, 14 Aug. 1967.

—   *"A sort of Billy . . .*   PS to GOC, 26 May 2000.

25 A BAD PLAY?

p. 147 *I am faintly shocked . . .*   Richard Eyre interview with GOC, 9 Jan. 2000.

p. 148 *"also thought his wife . . .*   Stephen Fay, *Power Play*, London, 1995, p. 114.

p. 149 *"A director might ask . . .*   Tom Conti interview with GOC, May 2000.

—   *"Martin, my son, was . . .*   PS to GOC, 9 Mar. 2000.

—   *"A strange letter . . .*   Fay, *Power Play*, pp. 114-5.

—   *"It nearly stopped . . .*   Peter Hall to GOC, 9 Jan. 2000.

p. 150 *"There would have been . . .*   PS to GOC, 27 Mar. 2000.
p. 151 *I do* not *want it to be . . .*   *Robert Bolt*, London, pp. 110-11.
p. 152 *He was not a man who . . .*   *The Times*, 26 June 1960.
—   *It's the voice, because . . .*   *Ibid.*, 11 Feb. 1971.
p. 153 *When I first read the . . .*   PS to GOC, Robert Bolt, p. 164.
p. 155 *"Scofield looks as if . . .*   *Sunday Times*, 6 July 1960.
—   *I think I was . . .*   PS quoted in *Robert Bolt*, p. 169.
p. 156 *"A phenomenon which . . .*   *Robert Bolt*, p. 175.
p. 157 *The success of the play . . .*   PS to GOC, 27 Mar. 2000.
—   *"You're taken over . . .*   Tom Conti interview with GOC, 8
        Mar. 2000.
—   *"Such charismatic talent . . .*   Richard Eyre interview with GOC, 9
        Jan. 2000.
p. 158 *"While this episode . . .*   PS to GOC, 27 Mar. 2000.

26   THE BIG ONE

p. 159 *"Paul will deliver what . . .*   Peter Hall interview with GOC, 9 Jan.
        2000. See also Peter Hall, *Making an
        Exhibition of Myself*, London, 1993, p.
        164.
p. 160 *"The disagreement . . .*   Ronald Harwood, *Sir Donald Wolfit*,
        London, 1971, p. 265.
—   *"horribly formidable . . .*   *Power Play*, London, 1995, p. 35.
—   *I am so slow and . . .*   *Ibid.*, pp. 135-6.
p. 163 *"implied, unsaid, and . . .*   Peter Brook, *Threads of Time*, London,
        2000, p. 34.
—   *Brook's "No-man . . ."*   Alec McCowen interview with GOC,
        31 Mar. 2000.
p. 164 *"He did a Svengali . . .*   Diana Rigg interview with GOC, 7 Apr.
        2000.
p. 165 *Brook added that the . . .*   Brook, *Threads of Time*, p. 34.
p. 166 *"this was a first . . .*   PS to GOC, 31 Mar. 2000.

27   INTERLUDE: MADNESS VS. METHOD

p. 168 *It's a grim play and . . .*   PS to GOC, 31 Mar. 2000.

28   PUBLIC AND PRIVATE EARS

p. 169 *The element of . . .*   PS to GOC, 29 Nov. 1999.

p. 170	*"a director is often . . .*	PS to GOC, 9 Jan. 2000.
p. 171	*McCowen ultimately . . .*	Alec McCowen interview with GOC, 31 Mar. 2000.
—	*"The voice always . . .*	Diana Rigg interview with GOC, 7 Apr. 2000.
p. 172	*for the first time in . . .*	And further. "Lay him to rest, the royal Lear, with whom generations of stage actors have made us reverentially familiar. You will never see such another."
—	*"appealed greatly . . .*	PS to GOC, 31 Mar. 2000
p. 173	*An unsuitably wide . . .*	*Ibid.*

29 INTERLUDE: MR. LEAR (AND THE RETURN OF BADDIE NUMBER TWO)

p. 175	*"I don't think he . . .*	*Life Magazine,* 1 May 1964.
—	*"Larry's article . . .*	Peter Brook to Kenneth Tynan, 2 May 1964.
—	*"like an immovable . . .*	Kenneth Tynan undated notebook, Tynan archive, British Library.
p. 176	*"Finally, the panel . . .*	*Oxford Today,* Spring 2000.
—	*"I don't think either . . .*	PS to GOC, 31 Mar. 2000.
—	*Lear is a character . . .*	Undated, believed to be a *Guardian* article of 1974.

30   DIPPED IN THE SAME DISH

p. 179	*"It seems to me . . .*	PS to Kenneth Tynan, 30 Mar. 1968.

31   INTERLUDE: GENERAL FILTH AND GREEN VIRGINITY

p. 181	*"took any kind of . . .*	PS to GOC, June 2000.
—	*"It would seem that . . .*	*The Times,* 11 Jan. 1966.
—	*Let me look back . . .*	*Timon of Athens,* IV, i, 1-32.
p. 182	*The need for equality . . .*	PS to GOC, 29 Nov. 1999.
p. 183	*"Not since the famous . . .*	Bernard Levin, *Daily Mail,* 2 July 1965.
—	*"powerful philosophical . . .*	Clive Swift interview with GOC, 31 Mar. 2000.

32   MORE TRIVIAL PURSUITS

p. 185	*"It is something . . .*	PS, BBC letter, 15 Dec. 1966.

—   *The best thing about . . .*   Angela Huth was the interviewer, ca. 1966

33   SELF-DECEPTION — CONTINUED

p. 188   *"Every voice he has . . .*   *The Times,* 21 Jan. 1966.

p. 189   *"very effervescent . . .*   PS to GOC, 26 Apr. 2000.

p. 190   *A voice that now grates . . .*   *Illustrated London News,* date unknown.

34   SAINT, HOMOSEXUAL, AND REGICIDE

p. 191   *"a handshake was no . . .*   Fred Zinnemann, *Autobiography,* London, 1991, p. 300.

p. 192   *"I was surprised and . . .*   *Robert Bolt,* p. 258.

p. 193   *"Basically," said Box . . .*   Zinnemann, *Autobiography,* p. 302.

p. 195   *"We needed an actress . . .*   *Ibid.,* p. 207.

—   MORE: *What would you . . .*   Robert Bolt, *Three Plays,* London, 1978, p. 147.

p. 197   *Shaw's agent commented . . .*   John French, *Robert Shaw: The Price of Success,* London, 1993, p. 102.

p. 198   *Fred Zinnemann was . . .*   PS to GOC, 5 Jan. 2000.

—   *Perhaps you remember . . .*   *Guardian,* exact date unknown, 1971.

p. 200   *"Zinnemann has done . . .*   *The New York Times,* 11 Dec. 1966.

—   *"I suppose a lot . . .*   Peter Greig interview, *Daily Express,* 1973.

p. 201   *Legend has it . . .*   Sheridan Morley interview with GOC, 8 June 2000.

—   *Once I wanted . . .*   *Daily Mail,* 25 Oct. 1964.

p. 202   *Paul and she . . .*   GOC, *The Secret Woman, A Life of Peggy Ashcroft,* 1997, p. 189.

35   UNDER MURDERER'S REPORT

p. 203   *"The difficulty of . . .*   Peter Hall interview with GOC, 9 Jan. 2000.

—   *"the actor starts from . . .*   Richard Eyre interview with GOC, 9 Jan. 2000.

p. 204   *"I've studied Macbeth . . .*   *Sunday Times,* 20 Aug. 1967.

—   *Vivien Merchant . . .*   Ian Hogg interview with GOC, 21 May 1999.

p. 210   *The stage is hidden . . .*   *Sunday Times,* 20 Aug. 1967.

p. 211   *The line seems to be . . .*   *The Times,* 7 Aug. 1967.

p. 212   *"short of a new . . .*   *Daily Mail,* 17 Aug. 1967.

—   *"Impeccable teamwork . . .*   *Sunday Times,* 10 Dec. 1967.

—   *"Original terrifying . . .*   *Sunday Telegraph,* 7 Jan. 1968.

—   *To play Macbeth . . .*   *Observer,* 7 Jan. 1968.

p. 213   *For the core of . . .*   *The Spectator,* 12 Jan. 1968.

p. 215   *"I'm very glad that . . .*   PS to GOC, 26 Apr. 2000.

36   FOUR SCORE AND DOWNWARDS

p. 216   *We filmed in . . .*   PS to GOC, 31 Mar. 2000.

p. 218   *An extraordinary . . .*   *Ibid.*

p. 219   *He once wrote to John . . .*   John Harrison to GOC, 1 Nov. 2000.

—   *The Danes could not . . .*   Ian Hogg interview with GOC, 21 May 1999.

38   RUST ON THE LEAF

p. 214   *It was a matinée . . .*   Sally Beauman, *Telegraph Magazine,* 6 Mar. 1970.

—   *"Anyway, you could . . .*   Robert Stephens, *Knight Errant,* p. 160.

p. 226   *"I met that friend . . .*   David Burke interview with GOC, 7 Apr. 2000.

—   *"People always ask . . .*   *Daily Telegraph,* 6 Mar. 1970.

p. 229   *Paul had been Anna's . . .*   Anna Calder-Marshall interview with GOC, Dec. 1999.

p. 230   *Scofield read the . . .*   *Guardian,* 22 July 1971.

39   GREAT RICHES

p. 233   *("You almost have . . .*   Roger Lewis, *The Real Life of Laurence Olivier,* New York, 1998, pp. 235-7.

—   *"Paul went to see . . .*   Peter Hall interview with GOC, 9 Jan. 2000.

p. 234   *"that if it was . . .*   *The Times,* 30 Sept. 1970.

p. 235   *"took the man . . .*   Simon Callow interview with GOC, 2000.

—   *"from vagrant . . .*   *The Times,* 10 Mar. 1971.

p. 236   *At once he seems . . .*   *Observer,* 14 Mar. 1971.

p. 237   *It wasn't so much . . .*   *The Times,* 11 Feb. 1971.

—   *This is also reported . . .*   John Harrison, Tom Conti interviews with GOC, Mar. 2000.

40   INTERLUDE: PRINCE OF THE BORGIAS

p. 238 *"Paul once said to me . . .*   Angela Fox, *Slightly Foxed,* London,
                                                    1986, p. 196.

p. 239 *"We were shunted . . .*   Angela Fox interview with GOC, 1998.

—   *"I don't want to commit . . .*   PS to Angela Fox, 4 Oct. 1975.

p. 240 *"I told him [Bob . . .*   PS undated letter to Angela Fox.

41   MONSTERS OF THE PIT

p. 243 *The first [Anthony] Hopkins . . .*   John Dexter, *The Honourable Beast,*
                                                    London, 1993, pp. 35-6.

p. 244 *"I think I have said . . .*   Tynan archive, British Library.

—   *"The new Peter . . .*   Dexter, *The Honourable Beast,* p. 30.

p. 245 *"Paul's not a first . . .*   Christopher Hampton interview with
                                                    GOC, Dec. 2000.

p. 247 *"He was sort of . . .*   *Ibid.*

—   *Hampton's* Savages . . .   Dexter, *The Honourable Beast.* p. 50.

42   NATURE AND BRUTALITY

p. 250 *"I've been living . . .*   Michael Winner interview with GOC,
                                                    2000.

p. 253 *I found the play . . .*   Tony Richardson, *Long Distance Runner,*
                                                    London, 1993, pp. 236-9.

—   *"This was a witty . . .*   PS to GOC, 5 Nov. 2000.

p. 254 *"ebullient and . . .*   *Daily Telegraph,* 17 Feb. 1975.

p. 255 *In one interview . . .*   *Daily Mail,* 26 Sept. 1974.

p. 256 *This Prospero is . . .*   *Sunday Telegraph,* 20 Jan. 1975.

—   *The longest recorded . . .*   Harrison, "Autobiography" ms, chapter
                                                    13, p. 8.

p. 257 *"They simply didn't . . .*   *Sun,* 6 Sept. 1977.

—   *"It is his [Paul's] . . .*   Jack Tinker, *Daily Mail,* 3 Mar. 1975.

p. 258 *It's not quite . . .*   *Evening Standard,* 21 May 1978.

—   *"A bearded Scofield . . .*   John Barber, *Daily Telegraph,* 25 May
                                                    1976.

p. 60   *"Live all you can . . .*   Quoted in Anthony Storr, *Solitude and
                                                    Genius,* London, 1994, p. 181.

p. 261 *"In the great seduction . . .*   *Guardian,* 27 Apr. 1971.

43   INTERLUDE: A FAMILY

p. 262 *"The reality of family . . .*   *Evening Standard,* 30 June 1978.

p. 263 *He arouses, for . . .*   *The Times*, 18 May 1978.

—   *"If you are offered . . .*   *Daily Mail*, 12 May 1978.

44 BRICKED UP IN FAME

p. 264 *"Mr. Caution strikes . . .*   *Peter Hall, Diaries*, 1983, p. 295.

p. 265 *"Last night of . . .*   *Ibid.*, p. 334.

—   *"the longest sleeve . . .*   Stephen Fay, *Power Play*, London, 1995, p. 254.

p. 266 *The centre of . . .*   Hall, p. 30.

—   *"I think Dexter . . .*   John Dexter, *The Honourable Beast*, London, 1993, p. 220.

p. 267 *"Dinner, Shaffer . . .*   *Ibid.*, p. 42.

p. 268 *"It's all about money . . .*   *Ibid.*, p. 214.

p. 270 *"It celebrates . . .*   Hall, p. 448.

—   *As all great actors . . .*   *Ibid.*, p. 110.

p. 273 *"No more lines, please . . .*   Simon Callow interview with GOC, 2000.

p. 275 *"The line of contact . . .*   Felicity Kendall interview with GOC, Apr. 2000.

p. 276 *"The audience becomes . . .*   *Guardian*, undated.

45 COMPLETING THE QUARTET

p. 277 *I didn't want to do . . .*   PS to GOC, xxx xxx 2000.

p. 278 *"the awful loading . . .*   *Life Magazine*, 1 May 1964.

—   *I don't think an actor . . .*   *Radio Times*, 11 Nov. 1972.

p. 279 *"There is so little . . .*   *Guardian*, 20 Aug. 1972.

p. 280 *I recorded Edgar . . .*   Robert Stephens, *Knight Errant*, p. 160.

p. 282 *"Thought he did . . .*   *Ibid.*, p. 160.

—   *"is a reduction of . . .*   *The Times*, 21 Mar. 1980.

p. 283 *"I have never before . . .*   *Evening Standard*, 21 Mar. 1980.

p. 284 *"Even if I know . . .*   *Sunday Telegraph*, 27 Oct. 1985.

—   *"Somebody who has a . . .*   *Observer*, 8 Oct. 1981.

46 RETURN TO CENTRAL PARK

p. 288 *"It is becoming more . . .*   *The Times*, 30 Nov. 1985.

p. 291 *Paul Scofield's Don . . .*   *Ibid.*, 24 June 1982.

p. 292 *Martin Esslin . . .*   *Plays and Players*, Aug. 1982.

—   *The line suggests . . .*   *The Times*, 24 June 1982.

—	"I also talk more . . .	*International Herald Tribune*, 21 July 1986.
p. 293	*King concluded . . .*	*Sunday Telegraph*, 6 July 1986.
—	"Not for many years . . .	*Daily Mail*, 4 July 1986.

47   FLEET STREET NAPOLEON — OTHER WORLDS ELSEWHERE

p. 294	*"rumoured to be based . . .*	*Ibid.*, 14 Jan. 1989.
p. 295	*There is a ruthlessness . . .*	*Ibid.*, 14 Sept. 1989.
—	*"I wanted to do . . .*	Bernard Crick, *Jeffrey Archer*, London, 1999, pp. 328-31.
p. 297	*McCowen told him . . .*	Alec McCowen interview with GOC, 30 Mar. 2000.
—	*"By the end of the . . .*	*The Times* etc., 9 Dec. 1989.
p. 298	*It was a very odd . . .*	*Evening Standard*, 9 Aug. 1991.
p. 300	*"He aspires to the soul . . .*	Helen Mirren interview with GOC, 8 May 2000.

48   IF YOU WANT A TITLE, WHAT'S WRONG WITH MR.?

| p. 301 | *Name another actor . . .* | *The Times*, 9 Dec. 1994. |
| p. 303 | *Paul's tortured face . . .* | Imogen Stubbs interview with GOC, 8 Apr. 2000. |

49   WHO IS THE HERO? WHO IS THE VILLAIN?

p. 306	*"And he started . . .*	Kevin Brownlow, *David Lean*, London, 1995.
—	*I knew none of this . . .*	PS to GOC.
p. 307	MONYGHAM: *You should . . .*	Christopher Hampton, *The Secret Agent*, London, 1996, pp. 193-4.

50   YOU WILL NEVER FIND AN ENGLISHMAN IN THE WRONG

p. 310	*"marvelling at . . .*	Trevor Nunn interview with GOC, 16 July 2000.
—	*I have asked him . . .*	*Sunday Times*, 12 Apr. 1992.
—	*"This is an ensemble . . .*	*Ibid.*, 12 Apr. 1992.
p. 311	*Emrys Jones wrote . . .*	*Times Literary Supplement*, 10 Apr. 1992.
p. 312	*"Actors and actresses . . .*	PS to GOC, 5 Jan. 2000.
p. 313	*"It was a true Shaw . . .*	Imogen Stubbs, 20 Apr. 2000.

—	"*Critics agree . . .*	*Sunday Times*, 22 Mar. 1992.
p. 314	"*innocent, flustered . . .*	*Sunday Telegraph*, 22 Mar. 1992. xxx. 1998), 249.
p. 315	"*more densely . . .*	David Lodge interview with GOC, 15 Dec. 1999.
p. 316	"*Everyone ogled. . .*	Philip Franks interview with GOC, Jan. 2000.

51   AND THE OTHER GIANT

p. 318	"*It is hardly his . . .*	*Daily Telegraph*, July 1996.
—	"*I'm taking a hard . . .*	Robert Redford interview with GOC, 27 Feb. 2000.
p. 319	"*a happy experience . . .*	PS to GOC, 5 Jan. 2000.
—	"*incredibly sympathetic . . .*	*You Magazine*, 19 Feb. 1994.
—	"*He has a very . . .*	Richard Eyre, 9 Jan. 2000.
p. 320	"*It smacks of . . .*	*The Times*, 20 July 1996.
p. 321	"*likes a dialectic . . .*	Richard Eyre, 9 Jan. 2000. But this is not true of PS's feelings for Richardson, which were warm and affectionate.
p. 322	*The revelation of . . .*	PS to GOC, 18 May 2000.
—	"*Every time I heard . . .*	Richard Eyre, 9 Jan. 2000.
—	"*His acting is of . . .*	Eileen Atkins interview with GOC, 13 Apr. 2000.

52   L'OREILLE EST LE CHEMIN DU COEUR

p. 325	"*It is a snare and . . .*	*Sunday Times*, 20 June 1982.
p. 326	*The physical sensation . . .*	*The Times*, 11 Jan. 1966.
—	"*by becoming a sort . . .*	*Financial Times*, review by Simon Callow of GOC's *Alec Guinness*, 29 Oct. 1994.
p. 327	"*he can only be . . .*	*The Times*, 17 Jan. 1966.
p. 327	*It is vitally . . .*	Source unknown, believed *Guardian* c. 1986.
p. 328	"*Ibsen's wife's . . .*	PS to GOC, 10 Dec. 2000.
p. 329	*profoundest work . . .*	PS to GOC, 18 May 2000. Olivier played the role in a stagey and remote manner on TV in 1958.

Index

PICTURE ACKNOWLEDGMENTS

P.1 All photographs from Paul Scofield's private collection.

P.2 As Donald and as Alexander © Angus McBean. Joy's illustration from Paul Scofield's private collection.

P.3 As Alex Morden © John Vickers. As Jack Tanner and as Stephen Undershaft by Lisel Haas, from Paul Scofield's private collection.

P.4 As Philip Sturgess and as Richard II © Angus McBean. As Tegeus-Chromis © John Vickers.

P.5 As Hamlet © Angus McBean. Drawing of Paul as Hamlet from Dame Diana Rigg's private collection.

P.6 *Expresso Bongo* from Paul Scofield's private collection. A priest in *The Power and The Glory* © Snowdon.

P.7 All photographs from Paul Scofield's private collection. Reproduced by permission of Columbia Pictures.

P.8 Lear (top) from Paul Scofield's private collection, and (centre) © Dr. Jaromir Svoboda. From Paul Scofield's private collection. Lear (bottom), photographed by Gordon Goode. From Alec McCowen's private collection.

P.9 Timon of Athens both © Dr. Jaromir Svoboda. From Paul Scofield's private collection.

P.10 All photographs from Paul Scofield's private collection. Reproduced courtesy of the Royal National Theatre.

P.11 Photograph from Paul Scofield's private collection. Reproduced courtesy of the Royal National Theatre.

P.12 As Laurie, photo by Zoe Dominic. All photographs from Paul Scofield's private collection.

P.13 As Prospero, photo by Zoe Dominic. As Volpone, photograph by Reg Wilson, and as Othello reproduced courtesy of The Royal National Theatre. All photos from Paul Scofield's private collection.

P.14 As Colonel von Valdheim, from Paul Scofield's private collection reproduced courtesy of MGM. As Verner Conklin photographed by Vincent Russell, © BBC Picture Archives. As Zharkov reproduced by permission of Michael Winner.

P.15 As Salieri, photo by Nobby Clark, from Paul Scofield's private collection. As Nat from Paul Scofield's private collection. Reproduced courtesy of the Royal National Theatre.

P.16 In the garden at Balcombe © *Mail on Sunday*. From author's private collection. As Captain Shotover, photo by Michael Ward © *Sunday Times*.